AMONG
WARRIORS
IN IRAQ

BOOKS BY MIKE TUCKER

Poetry:

Unreported

Non-fiction:

The Long Patrol: with Karen Guerrillas in Burma

Hell is Over: Voices of the Kurds after Saddam

AMONG WARRIORS IN IRAQ

*True Grit, Special Ops, and Raiding
in Mosul and Fallujah*

MIKE TUCKER

THE LYONS PRESS
Guilford, Connecticut
An imprint of The Globe Pequot Press

This book is dedicated in memory of all Coalition Forces,
Kurdish *peshmerga*, and Iraqi allies who have died in the Iraq War,
and for our comrades who remain at war in Iraq.

And in memory of Ernest Hemingway.

● ● ●

The Lyons Press is an imprint of The Globe Pequot Press.

10 9 8 7 6 5 4 3 2 1

Printed in the United States of America

Library of Congress Cataloging-in-Publication Data

Tucker, Mike, correspondent.
    Among warriors in Iraq : true grit, special ops, and raiding in Mosul and Fallujah /
Mike Tucker.
        p. cm.
    Includes bibliographical references.
    ISBN 1-59228-732-8 (trade paper)
    1. Iraq War, 2003—Campaigns. 2. Iraq War, 2003—Personal narratives, American.
3. United States. Army—History—21st century. I. Title.
DS79.764.U6.T83 2005
    956.7044'342—dc22

                                                                    2005001893

CONTENTS

ACKNOWLEDGMENTS

● ● ●

Gratitude to all those listed below. Many thanks to the countless people who cannot be named without compromising their operational security. Their aid and counsel were essential to keeping me alive in Iraq to complete both this book and *Hell Is Over*.

Long life and a good death.

Lieutenant J. Robert Kerrey, U.S. Navy SEALS (retired) and President, New School University, New York. Thank you for your letters of introduction to the Kurdish leadership in northern Iraq, without which I never would've been able to write either this book or *Hell Is Over*. God bless you.

Kurdish Democratic Party Military Intelligence and KDP Al Shaiyish counter-terrorist commandos. You were my eyes and ears up north, after I returned from Fallujah. You kept me alive. May the Kurds live free forever. Thank you for the smokes, the tea, the wise counsel, and the bodyguards.

KDP *Peshmerga* and General Babakher Zebari. Thank you for introducing me to U.S. Army Special Forces and the 101st, up north.

The United States Army. My gratitude and thanks for the honor and privilege of joining your warriors in Iraq.

Mr. Gregory B. Craig, Esquire. Many thanks for your kind counsel in Washington, D.C., June 2003.

Senior Publicist Jane Reilly, The Lyons Press. Thank you for your extraordinary help.

Senior Editor Tom McCarthy, The Lyons Press. Many thanks for giving my work a chance.

Mr. Patrick J. Clancy, Esquire. Great Chieftain, may the good saints protect 'ye, and the devil neglect 'ye. Long live the Great Chieftain!

Mr. Edward Hume, artist. Long life and blue skies over Newport Beach for you and your family, Cool Papa Ed! Long live Jackson Pollock.

Master Sergeant Henry Campbell, U.S. Army (retired). Long live the Big Red One! Many thanks for your advice on raiding. Your comrades in North Africa, Sicily, Italy, and Europe in WWII were not forgotten in Iraq, brother.

General Antony Zinni, U.S. Marine Corps infantry (retired). Thank you for leading our raid training in Okinawa in June 1988. *Semper Fi.*

*"Things could always be worse, and I could've been
dead a long time ago."*

—Coalition Special Operations commando, Mosul, northern Iraq,
to the author, March 27, 2004

◉ ◉ ◉

*"Hemingway's dead-solid right about war—it's a street fight.
War is a street fight, simply on another level. And the same rule applies:
put the other guy down so that he stays down. If we lose the street
fight in Iraq, all the glad-handing and politicking and money we've
spent here won't amount to dust in the wind. We've gotta' fight the street
fight. All the way. Win the street fight, and you win this war."*

—Specialist Sylas Carter. U.S. Army combat infantryman, twenty-one years old.
Hometown: Marion, Indiana. Mortars Platoon, 3rd Battalion-502nd
Infantry Regiment, 101st Airborne (Air Assault).
Mosul, northern Iraq, November 8, 2003

◉ ◉ ◉

". . . and with you I shall endure what has to be."

—Clearchus the Spartan, to Greek light infantry.
Southwest Asia, 401 B.C.

PROLOGUE:
THESE BRAVE MEN

⊙ ⊙ ⊙

WAR IS A JOURNEY INTO THE UNKNOWN, with death on your back and a woman on your mind. At war in Iraq on January 9, 2004, we rode to raid on Xenophon's trail, deep in southwest Asia. It was dawn and gray and cold in the western Iraqi desert just east of the Euphrates River. We were lead gun truck, on point for a ten-truck raiding party, a hawk's flight from the sands where Xenophon's Greek light infantrymen prevailed over Persian cavalry four centuries before Christ walked the earth.

I was with hard-core light infantry, 10th Mountain warriors with the spirit and heart and wit of the Karen guerrilla fighters I'd patrolled with behind Burmese Army lines in July 2002. I'd fought with the Karen on December 13, 1992, when we'd together raided a Burmese Army slave labor party near Shotoh Mountain, across the Salween River from northwestern Thailand. Ten years later, after five years of living in Thailand and an MA degree on the GI Bill, I was fortunate to link up with Karen National Liberation Army guerrilla fighters behind Burmese Army lines and patrol on long-range reconnaissance in Karen highlands. Like the Karen, the men of 10th Mountain Division in Fallujah were combat veterans, eyes hardened by sun and wind and rain and war. Xenophon the Athenian likely commanded a few like 10th Mountain in these sands.

We fire rifles and the Greeks threw spears, but victory still goes to the commander with the most guts and guile and the fighter with the most heart. These are men who have sharpened the tip of the spear and held point and, therefore, know a wee bit about winning a street fight, once they're in it. One such man was Sergeant Shawn Hall of Buffalo, New York.

Hall, a fire team leader from 1st Platoon, Attack Company 1-32, had talked at length about the guerrilla war in Iraq the night before with his comrades of 10th Mountain in a concrete bungalow crammed with olive-green cots and flickering lights and clips loaded with live rounds. Guitars screamed from Specialist Peter "Wildman" Marston's small portable stereo, rifles and machine guns hanging off the walls. Wildman hailed from the forests and fields shadowed by stone cliffs deep in New Hampshire.

The next morning, Wildman stood tall on the Ma Deuce, a .50-caliber machine gun mounted on a thick steel pole, gripping its triggers. Fallujah was far to our three o'clock as we rolled on desert trails, minarets and clusters of date palms and mud huts some three thousand meters northwest, easy. There were donkeys and sheep on the southern horizon, moving slowly in the brightening dawn. Wildman was at our twelve o'clock, to my immediate right. Hall sat on my left, the stock of his M.203 assault rifle/grenade launcher jammed in his right shoulder. He asked me to scan the desert from our nine to twelve. I raised my scopes.

After nineteen weeks of raids, patrols, and desert reconnaissance in Iraq, I flew in the darkness north for Mosul on Valentine's Day 2004. I prayed a Hail Mary as we took off in Sinatra's wee dark hours of the morning from Baghdad, all tactical lights off, a blacked-out plane on a black moonless night, and unstrapped my Kukri knife. I carried a Kukri in Fallujah. A Kukri is the fighting knife for the Ghurka light infantry of the British Army, a heavy-bladed knife; mine was a gift from an American warrior in Mosul. On four occasions in Iraq, I was handed a 9mm Beretta sidearm and told, "Do not hesitate to use it." I knew what would be the consequence of capture by the insurgents: beheading. No one ever gave me combatant status in Iraq, but no one ever told me not to carry my Kukri fighting knife, either. On several occasions, the Kukri proved crucial, in truth. Every combat commander I had the good fortune to see action with told me, "Stay close to my men, move when they move, never get in front of my men, and always tell us when you see enemy." I wanted to see the insurgency killed, not negotiated with, and I listened closely to the men I saw action with accordingly.

In the mid-morning of Valentine's Day, I thanked the lovely U.S. Army nurses at the Mosul airfield for their delicious coffee, linked up with Kurdish translators, and made my way back to Dahuk, an ancient Kurdish mountain town.

Dahuk was my base when I traveled throughout Iraqi Kurdistan, interviewing Kurds from all walks of life, from July 18 to September 25, 2003, before linking up with U.S. Army snipers, scouts, light infantrymen, paratroopers, and U.S. Army Special Forces commandos in Mosul and Fallujah. I am a former Marine infantryman, and despite my prior service on active duty in a special operations capable unit and my work as an author and war correspondent, 1st Marine Division Public Affairs Office had denied me embedded journalist status in November 2002 and again in March 2003. From Bangkok in April 2003, with my combat narrative *The Long Patrol* behind me, I reckoned that Bob Kerrey, former U.S. Senator and a Congressional Medal of Honor recipient for his actions as a U.S. Navy SEAL in Vietnam, might be able to help me get into Iraq. He knew well of my long-range reconnaissance behind Burmese Army lines for *The Long Patrol*. I reckoned that he'd find me qualified for Iraq. Fortunately, I was right: Bob wrote me letters of introduction to the Kurdish leadership in late June 2003.

I had no quarrel with President Bush's decision to lead America and the Coalition to war. America, along with other Western powers, was responsible for keeping Saddam's regime in power for decades. I believed we were, therefore, entirely responsible for taking it down. Like Captain Mark Zawachewsky of 1st Battalion-505th Parachute Infantry Regiment, 82nd Airborne Division, an Afghan and Iraq veteran, I felt that America, more than other Western nations, "had a moral responsibility to end Saddam's regime."

As Zawachewsky said in Fallujah on February 4, 2004, "We supported this regime, we armed it, and we didn't end it in ninety-one. When you kill a cobra, chop off its head. This is unfinished business. We make a huge mistake, backing dictatorships for short-term geopolitical strategy, without reflecting on the long-term consequences. We had a moral responsibility to end Saddam's regime. I didn't see a need for the

United States to go hunting for reasons to take down Saddam. There is never a wrong reason to end a dictatorship, particularly one as brutal as Saddam's was. And Uday and Qusay will not take power."

A few weeks earlier, a brother U.S. Army officer, Captain Terrence Caliguire, echoed his comrade when he told me in Fallujah on January 16, "There's an old saying in the army: never choose the easy wrong over the hard right. It was the right call to make and it was a very tough call. But President Bush did the right thing. We are in a just and noble cause here, and we must end it right. We must not cut and run. We ended a brutal and vile dictatorship. And at least three hundred thousand mass graves in the deserts of Iraq cry for justice."

I entered northern Iraq on July 18, 2003. Among Kurdish guerrilla fighters and farmers and artists, I documented previously unreported war crimes, such as the Gizi massacre. When I linked up with the Screaming Eagles in northern Iraq, through the Kurds, I handed war crimes reports of the Gizi massacre and Soriya massacre to 101st Division headquarters on September 27, 2003, as well as to the unit I was attached to as an embedded writer, 3rd Battalion-502nd Infantry Regiment.

From Mosul, I rallied to the 82nd Airborne, 10th Mountain, and Big Red One in Fallujah. In Dahuk, on Valentine's Day 2004, I reunited with Kurdish military intelligence and *peshmerga* commanders, laid down my Kukri knife and war gear, and dusted off my books. The Kurds embraced me, slapping me on the back and offering tea and cigarettes all afternoon, and asked loads of questions about Mosul and the Saddam loyalist Sheikh Gazi Al Bowisa, the terrorist Zarqawi, and Al Quaeda in Fallujah. We ate hot, fresh bread and beef kebab and drank steaming, dark, sweet Ceylon tea. Dinner over, more smokes were passed around and more tea was served.

After farewells were made and the stars rose high in the western sky, I walked up a mountain trail in the clear cold night and watched Dahuk erupt in a sea of lights bordering the high rocky mountains to the north.

On the southern reaches of Dahuk, the ruins of the Kurdish village of Nazarkhay lie south of a former Ba'athist prison, stones piled and scattered amidst high wild grass in a wide valley. Nazarkhay was destroyed by Ba'athist secret police and Iraqi Army troops in the reign of terror Saddam unleashed against the Kurds in 1987 and 1988, *Al Anfal*. The ruins lay east of my quarters on the KDP peshmerga base. Training for reconnaissance, raids, and patrols with Coalition forces in the late sum-mer of 2003, farmers and shepherds would wave to me and shout Kur-dish greetings, and I'd wave back and run on past the mounds of stones in the yellow-green grasses and golden fields of wheat.

Hall scoped the desert south of Fallujah, dust boiling up behind us as our raiding party slowed over massive ruts in the hard-packed sand, and spoke in a hard, low-toned voice, never losing his fields of fire, eyes on the desert south of us.

"Guerrilla warriors win guerrilla wars. And we are guerrilla warriors, Mr. Tucker, we damn sure are. But to *win* this war, we've gotta' *fight* as guerrilla warriors. The more we raid and patrol and seize the initiative, the closer we'll come to winning this war. Closer to Fallujah, keep your scopes up. Scope the mosques. Heads-up on mosques for snipers."

"Roger that," I said, and Hall nodded, shouldering his M.203. The truck jolted, breaking left slightly. Wildman, a distinguished scholar of hard rock like many of his comrades in 1st Platoon, Attack Company, shifted the barrel southwest as he gazed out over the far rock-strewn sands and scattered date palms.

We were deep in desert that had seen Persian lances answered by Greek spears and swords in that long ago, east of the wide brown waters of the Euphrates and west of the Tigris River's dark blue-green currents winding through the heart of ancient Mesopotamia. It was a bright, cold winter morning, and we rode on rutted and bumpy desert jeep trails, seagulls and ospreys and starlings swooping over us and gliding west to-ward the Euphrates.

The sun was behind us. The wind lashed at the American raiders in the back of the truck who were clad in desert camouflage fatigues, Kevlar helmets latched on their heads, flak jackets wrapped around their torsos.

Wildman, a big, barrel-chested man, swung the machine gun back to twelve o'clock, bending his knees as the truck lurched and rocked over the desert trail west. "Goddamn it's cold!" he yelled, and we laughed, grinning, dust drifting up behind us. High above us, flocks of seagulls headed for the Euphrates.

As he scanned the sandy, rolling slopes south of us, Hall kept his eyes on his fields of fire. A shepherd waved to us from perhaps two hundred meters south. I waved back as we rolled on. And Wildman leaned back and lifted his head and hollered, "Judas Priest! AC/DC! Metallica! Old School Warriors *rock*!"

Sergeant First Class Steve Huber from Hawaii, a career soldier, laughed and said in his gravelly, exuberant voice, "Old school heavy metal, Mr. Tucker, ancient warrior style, climb to glory! This is 10th Mountain. You're riding with Attack Company, 1st Platoon. Lieutenant Chesty and the Old School Warriors. Slay the fuckin' dragon, baby! Eighteen summers in the army, I've got now. My nineteenth will be in Iraq. Fuckin'-a guerrilla fighters!"

There were brave men at war in Iraq, brave and witty and kind and generous, and I was blessed to be among them. If I had ten thousand words, I could not do justice to their honor, commitment, and courage. Crossing the desert on that bitter cold January dawn near Fallujah were Marston and Huber and Hall. They kept eyes on the sands and far palm-shaded fields, clips jacked in, weapons locked and loaded. And they cursed the wind and the cold and Al Quaeda as they scanned the desert that stretched west to the Euphrates.

Dust clouded the trucks behind us. Hall winced, the cold winter wind burning his face. Huber, the tough, big-hearted platoon sergeant from Hawaii, shouted, "Beware the devil, because that bastard is in Fallujah. Death to Al Quaeda!"

And the Wildman laughed and hollered into the brightening Iraqi skies, "Goddamn Al Quaeda to hell, and all Bin Laden's motherfuckers!" In turn Hall screamed, "Hell yes Wildman!" and we hailed the Wildman's exhortations. Our truck rocked on over the rugged trail. Huber shouldered his rifle, eyeing the desert.

Wildman stood fast on the Ma Deuce, steady, .50-caliber linked bullets falling from the machine gun into an ammo can in the bed of the truck, the linked live rounds swaying as we rode to raid, wind ripping down cold on us from out of the north.

Minarets of distant mosques in Fallujah loomed up on the western horizon like lighthouses on a far shore. I scoped the minarets for snipers and saw birds circling the tan stone towers. Hall nodded and kept his eyes on the desert south of us.

I left Fallujah on February 6, 2004, swooped to Coalition Provisional Authority in Baghdad, and a few days later, had the good fortune to interview Lieutenant General Ricardo Sanchez, commanding general of the Coalition Joint Task Force-7.

A cheerful, down-to-earth Texan, Sanchez has thick black hair, piercing coal-black eyes, and is built solid like a middleweight prize-fighter. When he listens to you, he leans forward slightly, giving you his full attention. An amiable, good-hearted gentleman, I'd first met him on a January 21, 2004, raid in Fallujah led by First Lieutenant Chad Jenkins of Dublin, Ohio, and Sergeant First Class Vernon Pollard of Hobbs, New Mexico, and our comrades in 10th Mountain. I nicknamed the general "Sun Tzu," after the legendary Chinese general, poet, and author of *Art of War*. Like Sun Tzu, Sanchez never hesitated to unleash lightning raids on his enemies.

We were now ten months beyond President Bush's May 1, 2003, declaration that "major combat" had ended in Iraq. Having seen combat throughout Iraq, knowing that there is no such thing as a small firefight, and knowing that Al Quaeda had succeeded in linking up with Iraqi insurgents in western Iraq, I knew that our men and women were still very much at war in Iraq.

All combat is major. Kurdish Democratic Party Military Intelligence had warned me, before I left Dahuk in late September 2003, that their intelligence network throughout Iraq was reporting greatly increased contacts between former Ba'athist intelligence, military, and political leaders in Iraq—contacts to Al Quaeda in western Iraq and to Iraqi insurgents in western and northern Iraq. Western Iraq, of course, was never cleared, held, and secured in the initial March to April 2003 actions of the Iraq War.

One ancient law of war is you must never relinquish the initiative, once seized. Yet President Bush had violated that ancient law of war in Iraq, refusing to order the Coalition to strike and kill all former elements of the Iraqi Army and Saddam's regime. Still, I remember thinking as I waited to talk with Sanchez, the men I'd seen action with in Iraq were damned glad to have ended Saddam's regime.

Sanchez greeted me in Baghdad on Lincoln's birthday, February 12, 2004, and we shook hands. I set my coffee down and fished out my notebook from a bellows pocket. He leaned back on a black leather couch, a black leather shoulder holster rigged over his desert fatigues, M-9 Beretta 9mm sidearm holstered, clip jacked in, and four clips set in leather pouches on his rig.

"Lieutenant General Sanchez," I said, "Private First Class Steve Newport from Idaho, a combat infantryman from the 101st, said the following on November 1, 2003, in Mosul: 'When my grandchildren ask me what I did in the great war to defeat Saddam, I'll tell them that I was there, with my brothers, on the front lines. And we slept in bomb factories. And we fought in the sand and wind and rain. And we freed Iraq from a brutal dictatorship. When we talk to Iraqis on the street, on patrol—really, Americans have no idea how vicious Saddam was, how brutal he was. I know why I'm here. I know why we came. And we will see it through, to the end. We must win this war.'

"Sir, I heard similar remarks from many of our warriors in Iraq. What are your own thoughts, on PFC Newport's reflections on the war in Iraq?"

"I'm proud to lead men like PFC Newport," he said without hesitation, sitting bolt upright now, his face hard. "To know that our soldiers are inspired to carry on, to fight the fight, and believe in our cause here. Saddam was a very brutal dictator, as PFC Newport says. And Saddam is not coming back. Ba'athism is not coming back. The message I've been giving the troops is that this war has been a noble endeavor. Truly, a magnificent endeavor. The fact that a dictatorship in Iraq is gone is a great thing. We broke the chains. We liberated Iraq. Saddam's Ba'athist dictatorship had suppressed Iraqis for thirty-five years. Horrifying oppression. Saddam used weapons of mass destruction against his own people," he said, squinting.

"And it's an honor to lead young warriors like PFC Newport," Sanchez continued, speaking very softly now, eyes blazing. "Everything he said is right on the mark—our soldiers and all our servicemen and women have sacrificed greatly in this war. They slugged it out, just as he says, 'in the sand and wind and rain.' Valiant, determined warriors. They are the future of our nation's army, and they are the backbone of our country."

"Roger that," I said, and he nodded. I sipped from my coffee and he drank from a liter bottle of water. He set the bottle down and leaned back, spreading one arm over the back of the couch.

"General, Captain Caliguire—"

"Didn't he get a nickname?" Sanchez broke in, grinning merrily now, his black eyebrows raised.

"Hell yes! Vegas, sir. You must never sit down at a card table with Vegas. His favorite saying is, 'If I were a gambling man, and I *am*!' A great combat commander from Task Force 1Panther in Fallujah. Captain

Caliguire said the toughest thing he has had to do in Iraq is talk to his men about carrying on after the loss of Staff Sergeant Paul J. Johnson, a very-well-respected paratrooper and solid NCO. Staff Sergeant Johnson was from Calumet, Michigan, sir. Captain Caliguire talked about the burden of command. One thing the captain said that has stayed with me is, 'Staff Sergeant Johnson would've wanted us to carry on and crush the insurgents.' You've had to deal with that same reality of war, of losing good men and women in Iraq," and Sanchez looked down, squinting some more. After a spell he glanced up quickly.

"When all the parades are over, it is inevitable that you'll lose a soldier," he said softly, and his voice was deeper now. He shook his head slowly, wincing. There was no weariness about him, just the gritty toughness of a soldier who has spent his life serving America in war and peace and has seen his comrades fall. A reflective look came over him, his eyes bright. I was reminded of General Douglas MacArthur's warrior creed: "Duty. Honor. Country." The general sat back in Baghdad and folded his arms.

"War is a rough trade, and it's hard to carry on sometimes," he said softly. "Our fighting men and women, who are putting it on the line night and day, both here and in Afghanistan and in so many other battlefields right now, must know that if they die in this war, it is because of a struggle that was worthy, not because of a failure of leadership. The question I ask myself as a commander, as a leader, is 'Am I leading men and women into battle because of a struggle that is worthy?' If we as leaders cannot answer that question, then we have a tremendous burden to bear. We must be able to answer that question with a just answer, we must go into combat for a struggle that is worthy. I have no doubt our cause is just here and this struggle is a worthy one," Sanchez said, eyes intense. "Did you see *Saving Private Ryan*?" he asked quickly.

I told the general that I'd seen that movie, directed by Steven Spielberg—perhaps the best film on men and war, and certainly one of the most moving. Mr. Spielberg's father had fought in Burma in WWII, and there is a strong, deep spirit of homage in the film for American warriors of his father's generation.

"And you recall the scene in the church?" Sanchez asked.

"The Ranger captain talks about losing his men and dealing with their deaths. Tom Hanks played the captain," I said, and he nodded, lines deep in his forehead.

"Exactly. Speilberg really got it right, there. Speilberg saw right to the heart of it. It's a powerful scene and it is very real, strikes a chord with anyone who has ever led men in combat. Spielberg really gets to the heart of the burden of command. It never leaves you. It's something you live with, something you wrestle with, something you accept. That scene is far more eloquent than anything I could say—really. It's very moving, profoundly moving. This is a worthy endeavor in Iraq and no matter what price we pay, it is worth the price to defeat tyranny and terrorism in Iraq. Every single soldier I've met in Iraq—I've never heard a complaint about fighting this war. Every soldier I've met who has been wounded, the first thing they say to me is 'Sir, how do I get back to my buddies?' That is a testament to their fighting spirit and their faith in their comrades," he said, leaning forward slightly.

"America has kind of lost touch with our military, due to the all-volunteer army, navy, and air force. The Marines, of course, have always been an all-volunteer force, with the exception of a few years during the Vietnam War. There's a gap there, between our military and our society. What the American people must know is that American sons and daughters are making a huge difference in Iraq. They are making history, and I am proud to have the privilege of commanding them. It is an extraordinary honor."

It is November 23, 2004, as I write from Malaysia, and many 10th Mountain infantrymen I was privileged to call comrade just recently returned to America. Grunts like Huber and Hall and Marston were deep in sands south of Al Iskandiriyah, dodging RPGs and raiding Al Quaeda and the *feydayeen* at every opportunity. With their comrades, they completed nearly thirteen months in-country in Iraq, which strangely was my own time in-country: thirteen months and thirteen days. As their paratrooper comrade, Private First Class Joshua Gordon of Seattle, Washington, and the 82nd Airborne, said in Fallujah, "They will never have a park named after them or a war memorial or a school or a boulevard. But our grunts are the real heroes in this war, raiding night and day, taking down Ba'athist generals and Al Quaeda."

When I was Gordon's age, I witnessed Spanish counter-terrorists liberate 180 hostages in Barcelona, Spain, at the Siege of the Banco Central, on May 24, 1981. We came under fire from fascist terrorists seeking a return to Franco's dictatorship. I watched those brave men, bearded counter-terrorists carrying HK MP-5 submachine guns, 9mm sidearms, and long-barreled sniper rifles, never take one step backwards. They moved hard and fast up the wide cobbled avenue that is Las Ramblas in Barcelona, kiosk to storefront, sun in their faces, and the eyes of all Spain upon them. That was the first time in my life that I knew for a fact that courage is a living thing. I have been fortunate to realize that truth on more than one occasion since Barcelona in 1981. Among warriors in Iraq, I saw it every day. It was an honor and a privilege to be with you, comrades. To the commanders and U.S. Army public affairs officers who granted me that honor and privilege, may the good saints protect 'ye and the devil neglect 'ye.

Long life and blue skies,

Mike Tucker
Tiluk Bahang, Malaysia
November 23, 2004

MOSUL

"Honor the men who bleed with you."

Specialist Joseph Thoman, U.S. Army combat infantryman
Mosul, northern Iraq, September 28, 2003
(Specialist Thoman was promoted to Sergeant on November 1, 2003.)

◉ ◉ ◉

"JONAH MISSES THE SEA, WE GOT RAIN," Specialist Joe Thoman said softly, as he gripped a .50-caliber Browning machine gun in chill black zero five A.M. in Mosul, northern Iraq. Rain fell steady in the darkness. Jonah's tomb lay on a hilltop east, within the massive marble and stone walls of the Nabi Younis mosque. The Tigris River was a hundred meters west of us, and across its wide dark waters were the grassy banks of Arab Mosul, where water buffalo roamed in the late morning and midday. In Jonah's time, Mosul was known as Ninevah. A screeching-loud first-prayer call had just sounded from a mosque perhaps five hundred meters east of us, and you could still feel it echoing on the streets. I remember thinking that I'd lived near a mosque in Al Ain, United Arab Emirates, ten klicks from the Omani border, for eighteen months and never heard a bone-rattling, ear-deafening prayer call like that one.

It was a cold, wet, black dawn in Mosul, October 3, 2003, my seventh day with Screaming Eagles' snipers and scouts of Scout Platoon, 3rd Battalion-502nd Infantry Regiment, 101st Airborne Division (Air Assault). Thoman was a quick-witted man from Kentucky, and he was twenty-six. I called him "Kentucky Rifle."

1

There were three teams of Scouts riding to patrol and raid in the black pouring rain in Mosul: Alpha Team, led by Sergeant Brett Lotto, the "Zen Master," from Wisconsin; Bravo Team, led by Staff Sergeant Chapman, from Utah; and Charlie Team, led by Sergeant Ariel Morales, from Miami, Florida. Each team had five scouts, including the team leader.

The scouts carried fighting knives, sidearms, sniper rifles, assault rifles, machine guns, and assault rucks packed with ammunition and grenades and their hopes and fears and dreams; photos of their wives and children and girlfriends and families pasted inside their helmets, the photos often double-wrapped in plastic and waterproof tape.

Kentucky Rifle, like all his brothers riding in the rain on that black dawn in Mosul, had crossed the berm at Kuwait in March and fought north to Baghdad before swooping on a Blackhawk to Mosul on April 22, 2003. He stood at our twelve o'clock, lead gunner on the lead truck, on point for the dawn patrol. He squinted as the rain poured, wincing. He opened the feed tray of his Ma Deuce and laid in a long link of .50-caliber brass-jacketed live rounds, the bullets streaming down to a green ammo box at his feet.

All told, he had twelve hundred live rounds of .50-caliber ammo on board; "Every patrol is a combat patrol," he'd said on my first mission with the Scouts, a night patrol on September 28, 2003.

Leaning against the left front corner of the bed of the truck was an M-4 5.56 assault rifle, a clip jacked in. At his feet, between the base of the machine gun mount and the front of the truck's green steel bed, was a light machine gun, caliber 5.56. Brass-jacketed bullets snaked down from the feed tray of his light machine gun to a small camouflaged loam-and-green bag jacked in under the action. There were two hundred live rounds in the small bag.

Thoman's light machine gun is a preferred machine gun of the British Army Special Air Service commandos, the SAS, who call it the "Minimi"—made in Belgium and called the SAW (squad automatic weapon) by Americans. His version in Mosul had a very short barrel and no stock, with a thick black nylon strap attached, so it could be carried over the shoulder and held at the hip on assault.

He pointed to his M-4 as the truck slowed, nearing the gate. "Full clip. We go out the wire, lock and load. If we're attacked, throw down. Cover our nine o'clock, all right, Mr. Tucker?"

"Roger that," I said. He nodded and rain poured off his poncho hood.

"Good. We're attacked and we halt, grab my M-4, unass the truck, and put rounds downrange. Kill the bastards. I'll stay on the Ma Deuce. Thirteen clips in my assault ruck, and Gordy's got all kinds of ammo."

I nodded to Thoman and he gave me a thumbs-up. I remember thinking—thirteen magazines, thirty rounds per clip is 390 rounds right there plus one clip jacked in, 420 live rounds, plus Gordy's ammo. The normal combat load for grunts in Iraq is seven clips, or 210 live rounds, for anyone carrying an M-4 or M.203. This is what I'd been told up north by U.S. Army Special Forces commandos, before attaching as an embedded author to the Screaming Eagles.

I realized everyone on that truck had at least double combat load. The Scouts had heavy guns on point and trail, additionally, rolling with two .50-caliber machine guns.

A poncho-clad sergeant carrying an M.203, his flak jacket sagging with 40mm grenades for the .203, waved toward us as we approached the gate on the eastern banks of the Tigris River. The eastern banks of the Tigris River in Mosul are strongly Kurdish, with sizeable Arab, Turkoman, and Assyrian neighborhoods threaded throughout Kurdish Mosul's maze of alleys, streets, and markets. The western banks are nearly all Arab.

Ba'athist sympathies run deep in Arab Mosul, as it was the northern "second capital" for Saddam's regime; many of Saddam's high-ranking political and military commanders had vast residences in Mosul.

Iraqi Arabs in Arab Mosul, as throughout Iraq, did not resist Ba'athist rule. Saddam's tribe, the Tikriti tribe, was given richly furnished villas throughout Arab Mosul, further cementing the iron grip the Tikriti tribe had on Ba'athist rule in Iraq. I was warned by a veteran CIA clandestine operations officer on June 13, 2003, over coffee at Los Angeles International Airport, not to enter Arab Mosul "without Kurdish bodyguards. The Kurds know Arab Mosul like a marlin knows blue water, they know the Ba'athists in Mosul, their names and faces, where they sit and where they eat, they know the river, they know the streets, they know the shoreline and they know the skyline. Major Ba'athists are operating with the insurgency in Mosul, and Arab Mosul is their safe house." Saddam's regime maintained the vast share of its armories and the main airfield he used to drop chemical bombs on Iraqi Kurdistan in Arab Mosul.

In my experience, Kurdish Mosul was the only place south of Iraqi Kurdistan where Iraqis of all ages warmly welcomed Americans. No surprise there, really; every Kurdish family in Mosul has at least one relative murdered by the Iraqi Army or the *Mukhabarat*, the Ba'athist secret police. Kurds in Mosul, as throughout all northern Iraq, fiercely resisted Ba'athist rule. Many Kurds in Mosul fought against Saddam's regime. The argument I heard from Iraqi Arabs and occasionally from U.S. soldiers and officers in Iraq concerning Ba'athism was that Iraqis had no choice but to join the Ba'athist Party, and that membership ensured privilege and status. But this cut no ice with Iraqi Kurds in Mosul or anywhere else in northern Iraq. For they, too, had lived in Iraq under Ba'athist rule, and the vast majority of Kurds had not only denounced Saddam's regime, they took up arms against the Mukhabarat and Iraqi Army. So they fought and so they suffered, and now in the fall of 2003 in Kurdish Mosul, they smiled as we passed them on patrol on the very streets where they'd run their own counter-intelligence operations against Saddam's regime, from 1961 to 1991.

In ancient times, both banks of the Tigris in present-day Mosul were Kurdish. Kurdish Mosul was not without its dangers in autumn 2003; there were Ba'athist loyalists spread throughout all Mosul, and there still are, for that matter. One of Saddam's laws, enforced under penalty of death, was to evict Kurdish families in Kurdish Mosul from their homes, homes that for many of them predated Ottoman rule in Iraq, going back some eight centuries. These ancient stone homes in Kurdish Mosul were then handed to Arab families and new titles and deeds written for the property and homes. The largest Kurdish villas in Mosul uniformly were handed to prominent Ba'athists.

Throughout northern Iraq, Saddam doggedly pursued this policy of Arabization of Kurdish lands, evicting entire Kurdish villages and also evicting whole Kurdish neighborhoods from cities such as Kirkuk and Hawlerr. (*Hawlerr* is the original Kurdish name for the Iraqi Kurdish city, mistakenly referred to in Arabic as *Irbil*.) North of Mosul, in the village of Dormeez, U.S. soldiers like Thoman and Morales were ordered by Major General David Petraeus to evict Kurdish families in the late spring of 2003 and return those houses to Ba'athists. After U.S. Army 10th Group Special Forces and Kurdish had liberated Dormeez in early April 2003, the Kurds had taken their houses back. Under Major General

Petraeus' orders, American soldiers evicted Kurdish war widows and their families, at gunpoint, and Ba'athists returned to inhabit Dormeez, just as they had under Saddam's regime. Why Major General Petraeus elected to give Ba'athists houses they'd stolen from the Kurds, was unfathomable to me and also, to many of the Screaming Eagles under Petraeus' command. Kurdish protests, from Kurds of all ranks, fell on deaf American ears.

Dormeez was a retirement village for Kurdish widows of prominent Kurdish *peshmerga* who'd fought all their lives against Saddam's regime. As the Kurdish General Babakher Zebari informed me in late February 2004, in Dahuk, "Dormeez was always a Kurdish village; in the revolution, we built those houses for the widows of our bravest fighters, men you would call Medal of Honor winners. We felt the widows could help each other, they know each other's sorrows. There are few currents that run as deep together as those in a river of common suffering. When you grieve together, you can also rebuild together. Saddam had captured Dormeez, evicted all our widows and their families, and turned it into a spy nest and operations center for Ba'athists. The Green Line, drawn up by the UN and agreed upon with Saddam's regime, conveniently included Dormeez within it. This protected the Ba'athists there from 1991 to 2003 and allowed Saddam to maintain Dormeez as an intel/ops center for the Mukhabarat. In the March-April 2003 actions, U.S. Army Special Forces liberated Dormeez, along with our peshmerga, of course. Many of the Ba'athists who fled Dormeez in the March-April actions were military and intelligence officers for Saddam. Among these Ba'athists were those who'd planned and executed chemical attacks and massacres of Kurds. These were the Ba'athists who tortured Kurds to death at the prison you run by, near Nazarkhay. The Ba'athists in Dormeez are very well connected to Ba'athists in Arab Mosul."

All Mosul was liberated when CIA paramilitary commandos, U.S. Army 10th Group Special Forces, and Kurdish peshmerga led by the legendary Kurdish General Jamil Besefky raided across the Tigris River at midnight of April 9, 2003. By April 12, Kurdish peshmerga had seized all crossroads, strategic points on the Tigris, and the airfield and cleared all major supply routes. A Marine expeditionary unit swooped in and took command of the Mosul Airfield, linking up with U.S. Army 10th Group Special Forces. The Marines were in Mosul for approximately a week before Petraeus led the Screaming Eagles (U.S. Army 101st Airborne Division [Air Assault]) on the longest air assault in history, from Baghdad to Mosul, and relieved the Marines in place on April 22, 2003. From late April 2003 to January 31, 2004, the 101st had the northern area of operations in Iraq, a vast stretch of desert, mountain, and valley that borders Syria, Turkey, and Iran.

The mountains of Iraqi Kurdistan, leading east to Iran, were shrouded by mist and rain as Kentucky Rifle nodded to the sergeant at the gate. We slowed to a stop, sheets of rain beating down in the darkness. A sandbagged machine gun position held the roof of a concrete bungalow to our right. A specialist inside the gray sandbagged walls nodded down at us, a heavy machine gun in his hands, barrel pointed east toward the shell of a Ba'athist building, eight stories reduced to jagged concrete slabs and rusting steel rebars bombed by the U.S. Air Force in April 2003.

Private First Class Tyler Gordy, the "Eureka Kid," a native of northern California, was in back of me. He leaned forward slightly, covering our three o'clock. He nodded back to the guard tower gunner and flicked the rain off his neck, unsmiling.

The Eureka Kid was nineteen. He carried an M-4 5.56-caliber assault rifle with a forward grip, like the forward grips on Thompson submachine guns in WWII, and thirteen thirty-round clips in magazine pouches on his flak jacket. At his feet, in a loam-and-green camouflaged assault ruck, lay some six hundred more 5.56-caliber live rounds.

He was quiet. Maybe it was the rain or the war or both. Likely, it was the patrol. There is a saying in the infantry: Payback is a motherfucker. Today was payback.

I remembered Patton, rolling out the gate: "We must be eager to kill, to inflict on the enemy—the hated enemy—wounds, death, and destruction." Now, I thought as we began the dawn patrol in Mosul, now I understand him. The rain drenched us and the scouts glared in the black pouring rain, and Iraqi men in long gray and black robes, their heads covered in black-and-white-checked *kaffiyeh* scarves, walked slowly up an alley away from a mosque, rubbing beads in their right hands, glancing down and walking slowly in the rain in Mosul. The ivory white cross of an Assyrian Catholic temple perhaps three hundred meters northwest of us showed briefly through the mist and rain, veiled and unveiled in the darkness. The Nabi Younis mosque was lost to the north in the darkness, where Jonah's bones lay on a hilltop above teeming markets and narrow streets packed with donkeys and horse-drawn carts and vendors calling out their wares in rapid-fire Arabic.

Near Nabi Younis, Gordy, Morales, Thoman, and all of Charlie Team and Bravo Team, Scout Platoon, had been ambushed in Mosul on September 13, 2003. At about eight in the evening, Iraqi insurgents had tossed grenades wrapped with C-4, ball bearings, metallic shards, and det cord and nearly killed their comrade, Specialist Derick Hurt.

Hurt now lay in a hospital bed at Walter Reed Army Medical Hospital in Washington, D.C., his right leg gone below the knee and his left leg shredded from shrapnel. And on a chill dark October dawn in Mosul, rain sluicing off our green ponchos, we rode to raid the Iraqi insurgents who'd ambushed the Scouts.

We were some thirty klicks west of Xenophon's trail, where the Greek mercenary's light infantry had marched north up the Tigris River from Cunaxa—near present-day Fallujah in western Iraq—on its retreat from Mesopotamia in September 401 B.C. On his long march north, Xenophon had fought near Nimrud, on the eastern banks of the Tigris. Nimrud was a day's ride on horseback south from Mosul in his time.

Far south of Mosul and west of Baghdad, Xenophon the Athenian had seized battlefield command on the eastern banks of the Euphrates River, near where Fallujah is now. With Cyrus (Prince of Persia), his general, killed by Persians under command of the King of Persia and half of the Greek officer corps killed or captured, Xenophon rallied the Greek light infantrymen and won the day. The Greeks then ended their expedition with a grueling retreat known as "The March of the Ten Thousand," an epic journey that took nearly a year. Fighting as they marched, they crossed the Tigris and patrolled north, bypassing the settlements that grew into present-day Baghdad and Mosul.

Skirting Kurdish attacks, Xenophon led his men over the green rolling hills and wheat fields west of the Zagros mountains toward the valleys and highlands of Turkey, marching west of what is now the jewel of northern Iraqi Kurdistan, the beautiful mountain town of Dahuk. North of Dahuk, Xenophon's light infantrymen carried their swords and shields and pain and pride across the Harburr river through a mountain pass where, today, a bridge spans the dark waters between the towns of Harburr, Turkey, and Zhakho, Iraqi Kurdistan.

He then led his men through the Kurdish highlands of southeastern Turkey and on across Armenia to the Black Sea, where his men famously, joyously proclaimed "the sea, the sea" after months of long march and close-quarter combat and little food and less water, nearly a year since they'd last seen the Mediterranean's bewitching blue-green waters.

First Lieutenant Joe Thomas, the "Guerrilla Fighter"—Scout Platoon leader in Mosul and a Mogadishu veteran of Task Force Ranger—had planned a regular counter-IED foot patrol at dawn on October 3 through Iraqi Arab neighborhoods bordering Whiskey India sector, the neighborhood in central Mosul where the Nabi Younis mosque stands.

IEDs are improvised explosive devices, roadside bombs command detonated or, more often, remote-control detonated by insurgents. IEDs are often found on main supply routes and are aimed at Coalition supply convoys. The Scouts had main supply routes running right through the heart of their sector, in all compass points. We'd walk along like human mine detectors on the counter-IED patrols in Mosul, eyeing every gold-and-green palm-oil can for wires sticking out of it; the wires could be tied to grenades or plastic explosives or TNT within the cans. On foot patrol, you'd scan heaps of plastic bags and market refuse and empty plastic jugs, scoping especially for loose scattered dirt, which would indicate a freshly dug hole and, bloody likely, Iraqi Army artillery rounds daisy-chained together with baling wire—as grunts in Iraq said, for maximum blast, to kill or maim us.

Our foot patrols that cold, wet, black dawn of October 3 in Mosul were also a deception. We were hunting IEDs, par for the course; we were also setting the raid in motion. The Guerrilla Fighter and Captain Daniel Morgan, Headquarters company commander who employed Scouts and Mortar Platoon in Mosul as a special operations element on raids and reconnaissance, knew there were insurgent lookouts throughout neighborhoods near Nabi Younis. They used the insurgent lookouts to our advantage in the raiding plan.

One more reason, I reflected that dawn, to call Morgan the "Commando." The Commando had served in U.S. Navy Special Warfare in the late 1980s. Like Thomas, Morgan knew Arab Bedouin culture, and he showed it well in his operational savvy on October 3.

The insurgents were Arab Bedouin, and Arab Bedouin gossip at the drop of a hat. I reckoned that the gossip that morning among their lookouts would be that the Americans are staying true to form. *And the Commando and the Guerrilla Fighter understand that*, I remember thinking as the rain poured down in the cold black dawn, the Scouts drinking coffee and cupping their smokes from the rain and checking gear and weapons and flak jackets for body armor plates, final pre-combat inspection, before getting up on the trucks.

"Excellent battle plan, brother," I said to Morales, acting Charlie Team leader, as he grabbed my hand and pulled me up on the truck. He grinned, a poncho draped over him like a cape.

We would roll back toward the compound after the counter-IED foot patrols, normal patrolling pattern, and then circle around Whiskey India and swoop down tight, narrow streets to raid the insurgents. Morgan felt the Scouts could kill or capture the insurgents: the ground intelligence was worked, the time was right, and the op order was succinct and clever.

"We'll roll off the foot patrol and make the raid," Thomas told me that dawn, eyes the color of the sea, looking like he'd go kill Saddam all by his lonesome. He was carrying an M-4 and an M-9 9mm Beretta sidearm on his right hip. In the street fight in Mogadishu on October 3 and 4, 1993, he'd carried a light machine gun and was led by First Lieutenant Tom DiTomasso in that two-day siege in Somalia. At that time, the Guerrilla Fighter was Specialist Thomas, U.S. Army Ranger.

I'd nodded, reflecting that Thomas would likely get the *feydayeen* lookouts to report to their cell leaders that the Americans were making regular foot patrols, and get them to drop their guard. And if the feydayeen thought we were headed back inside the 3rd-502nd riverside compound, as they bloody likely would, all the better. Deception is the mother of stealth. And stealth is key to victorious raiding—indeed, to victory in war.

Raising his M.203 in the pouring rain, the sergeant at the gate waved to a specialist. The specialist, carrying an M-4, grabbed the gates and flung them open, the creaking steel dripping with rain. Flocks of seagulls rushed up over the high sand-colored stone minaret towers east of us. There was a collective, metallic "crack," like a heavy steel-gauge door slamming in a deserted alley, as the men locked and loaded their rifles and machine guns and sidearms, bolts locking forward in the cold dark rain.

We rolled out and swung left. The raw sewage stench of Mosul drifted on the wind, Gordy grimacing as we rolled north into the rain. The wind gusted and howled and torrents of rain soaked us bone-deep, Gordy shivering a bit but steady on his weapon. Black storm clouds blanketed the northern horizon, distant whitewashed minarets poling the black dawn. I prayed a Hail Mary under my breath and made the sign of the cross; there were three trucks behind us and we were rolling hard past bomb-cratered buildings. Iraqi Arab kids waved to us from behind bullet-scarred concrete, taking shelter in the ruins of Ba'athist buildings.

In the last truck, on tail-end Charlie for the patrol, was another Ma Deuce, manned by Private First Class Justin Rush, from Indiana. Rush was about six foot three, lean as a sapling, and, on patrol, solid as Mount McKinley. You always felt better with Rush on the Ma Deuce. He was always looking out for his comrades, always hard-core warrior serious outside the wire. On missions, he never took his hands off a .50 caliber.

Rush was twenty-two. He'd manned a machine gun in the actions north from Kuwait in the spring of 2003, and he stood there on that cold wet autumn morning in Mosul, glaring, his face hard. Rush rarely talked, but his eyes always seemed to say, "I'll make it through this war and I'll kill any sonofabitch I have to, to make it through." We rolled in four trucks, packed with sandbags on their wooden sides. Heavy guns on point and trail, and our middle two were mounted with light machine guns. The Scouts of 3rd-502nd, like their battalion, were on point for the 101st throughout much of the action in March and April 2003 in the Iraqi War.

Thoman and Rush and their comrades had been in Mosul since late April 2003, putting down riots and patrolling for IEDs and killing insurgents in counter-ambushes.

They had been told directly by their commanding general, Major General David Petraeus, on May 1, 2003, that they would be home on Labor Day 2003. It was now early October and "home is Mosul," as Rush, a quiet, self-contained man and scholar of techno-rave music, put it to me on my first night with them, September 27, 2003.

Dawn was a dim gray line far to the east as we rolled in the pouring rain on October 3, spires of Muslim minarets and ancient Assyrian

Christian domed temples and bombed-out Ba'athist buildings stark on
the eastern horizon, rain bringing no joy to the Scouts.

Morales, who'd immigrated from Havana to Miami at seventeen, sat
to my left, M.203 shouldered, eleven 40mm high explosive grenades
snug in camouflaged vest pouches on his flak jacket. I called him "El
Tigre de Havana," Havana Tiger. Morales was twenty-four and vigilant
on patrols and raids, and had a street fighter's spirit and a keen mind. He
was solid like a young welterweight, raven-haired, and he was acting
leader of Charlie Team on October 3. His team leader, Staff Sergeant
Charlie Everhart from Mississippi, the "Deerhunter," was on a short R
& R on the island of Qatar.

The Havana Tiger missed his girlfriend in New York City, "*la rosa
de Nueva York, que bella.*" You could always tell when he was thinking
about her, he'd cast his eyes away and look down, a musing glance come
over him. But that was only when we'd get back through the wire. He
was quick off the trucks, a superb raider, calm on missions, and Charlie
Team listened well to him and the Deerhunter.

And he said that morning in the rain, stench rising from streams of
raw sewage and refuse scattered in the streets of Mosul, "Stay sharp,
Charlie Team, you know I hate the rain just like all of you, stay sharp.
You O.K., Mr. Tucker, *tranquilo?*"

I nodded to him and said, "*Tranquilo, Tigre de Havana,*" Spanish for
"all's well, Havana Tiger," and he grinned, shouldering his M.203. Thoman, live wire of the Scouts and possessed of a madcap wit, shouted without looking back, "No Spanish, Mr. Tucker, this is a Spanish-free zone!"

"Hey Thoman, you just stay on the Ma Deuce, *cabron*," replied
Morales, smiling broadly. The men laughed as they scanned their sectors,
looking for RPG gunners rushing out of an alley or around a street corner, scoping the minarets of mosques for snipers, scanning the streets
and rooftops for snipers, their eyes busy—eyes always busy—and
weapons on safe.

Specialist Morrone from Green Bay, Wisconsin, the "Big Hungry,"
who could chow down two steaks for appetizers, revved up as we rode
north toward a traffic circle, passing donkeys laden with plastic-covered
packs, Iraqi Arab men tugging at loose fraying rope halters tied over the
donkeys' heads and mouths. A month later, Morrone, promoted to sergeant, picked up his chevrons. He was an avid hunter and fisherman

raised on the Great Lakes, and on that day in Mosul he was our wheel-man. He was twenty-two.

"Here we go," he said, his M-4 on his right side.

"Don't get us lost," Morales said.

Morrone grinned. "Green Bay has better driver's ed than Havana, sergeant, don't sweat it! We're in Mosul and I am Big Hungry! Have no fear, Big Hungry will not fail you, brother!"

He was the sergeant's assistant team leader and good friend. "Hey, let me tell you Mr. Tucker, Morrone is the Big Hungry, he's a big old crazy Wisconsin *hombre*. Before we go to chow, he wants to eat something any-way. He stands there with his mouth full of three granola bars and he says to me, 'Sergeant Morales, I'm hungry. You want to go to chow?'"

Kentucky Rifle swung the .50 caliber, his hands on the triggers, keeping the Ma Deuce under control as the truck rolled into the turn. There were people out on the sidewalks now, Iraqi Arab women with their heads covered in black scarves and wearing the long billowing black dress called the *abaya*; children tagging along with their mothers, heading to school in the early morning with clear plastic sheets draped poncholike over them; and Kurds, men in peshmerga-style baggy trousers with cummerbunds at the waist and women in silk and cotton dresses in all the colors of the rainbow, their hair falling down their backs. They walked by vendor's stalls stacked high with apples and or-anges and heaps of onions, small yellow bulbs flickering from jury-rigged wires in the ramshackle vendor shacks near Nabi Younis, donkeys and horses meandering along the sides of the cracked concrete sidewalks of Mosul.

Next to Havana Tiger, sitting on a wooden box covered with a long thin cushion and a dark-green tarpaulin, the Guerrilla Fighter scanned the road falling behind us as Kentucky Rifle watched the road ahead. The rain fell stronger, soaking us as we passed wide-open fields to the west, fires smoldering from burning tires and heaps of burning garbage in the open fields. Mosul was a dark haze of cinder-block walls and pot-holed streets and concrete rubble, great slabs of gray concrete jutting out in all directions from bomb craters. Wild dogs loped along in the rain, and streetlights glowed a faint yellowish-white in the darkness.

Kentucky Rifle cursed the rain and held steady on the Ma Deuce. The Eureka Kid grinned, hearing Thoman. He eyed the scope on his

M-4 and said, "What, didn't you like Elvis singing 'Cold Kentucky rain,' Thoman? 'In the cold Kentucky rain, hell yes, cold Iraqi rain!'"

Havana Tiger laughed, tapping the clip jacked in his M.203, and Big Hungry shouted, "You tell 'em, Gordy!" Thoman snorted, and we shot down a long narrow street east of the Tigris River, three-story cinder-block and brick houses crowding both sides of the one-jeep-wide pot-holed street, Arabic scrawled on the walls in black and red paint, the stench of raw sewage thick now. Kids leaped up from balconies and shouted, "*Amerikee, Amerikee*," smiling and screeching at us, their paja-mas soaked as they grinned, waving madly as we rolled down the streets past piles of garbage scattered everywhere.

Morales raised his .203 toward the rooftops and balconies, squint-ing, his dark eyes hard, and said in a low voice, "Keep eyes on down-range for us. Alley corners and rooftops. Balconies. Mosques. I want to see my girlfriend in New York. She's a beautiful girl, *que mujer hermosa, encantisima*. I miss her, brother."

"Roger that," I replied, and Morales smiled, eyeing the street. There were eleven curved magazines (curved mags are called clips, or banana clips), each holding thirty live rounds, jammed in magazine pouches on his flak jacket and along with his eleven high explosive grenades (HE grenades), he carried three white-star parachute flares for his .203, to boot. In the small, green camouflaged assault ruck at his feet, he had about two hundred more 5.56-caliber rounds for his rifle.

Kentucky Rifle flexed on the .50 caliber, lifting the barrel slightly as he swung it toward the rooftops and balconies overhanging the narrow street where the streams of raw sewage and rubbish flowed along the low curbs. I could see minarets and beautiful white domes of old mosques stark on the skyline west, gulls and ravens swooping in the rain over the stone and cinder-block rooftops of Mosul.

We turned right and swung hard onto a main drag, Morrone brak-ing to avoid a taxi, rain still heavy in the breaking day. Kentucky Rifle eased the barrel down slightly. "Thoman, you gotta' fuckin' love the cold Iraqi rain, cold Kentucky rain!" the Eureka Kid shouted, grinning, as we rolled through the rain and cold, sidewalks bare but for a few men in ragged clothes lying on cardboard and with small gray blankets and red-and-white-checked kaffiyehs draped over them as they slept under rusted awnings.

"You're still my son, Gordy, don't piss off the old man! I taught you everything you know about soldiering," Thoman said, grinning back. "By God, I'm Dean of the College of Ma Deuce, President of the University of Sniper Rifles, and my Ph.D. is in kicking ass and taking names! You're still working on your bachelor's degree in drill and ceremonies, Gordy. You'd still be in the playpen, without me!" he hollered, scanning rooftops and balconies, and we all busted up, men steady on their fields of fire in the cold rain in the streets near Nabi Younis. "Elvis . . . mercy. What the hell did he know about Kentucky? He was from Memphis! He could've sung about Tennessee rain, but no, he must've lost a Louisville baby doll to one of my Kentucky brothers. O yeah, broken-hearted Elvis, in the cold Kentucky rain!"

"Eyes on, we're on patrol. Steady now," the lieutenant said as his scouts scanned the rubble and the mosques and the alleys and the rooftops. The sky lightened as we headed for Whiskey India sector, and I could see fog on the western banks of the Tigris River misting up over saw grass, minarets of distant mosques barely visible. Seagulls glided over the river and flocks of starlings and sparrows rushed in black waves toward the minarets and concrete rooftops.

Morrone hung a hard right and drove on, heading for the ancient stone gates of Ninevah, Iraqis packing the sidewalks now. Black funeral banners, announcing deaths of Iraqis in Mosul, shrouded street corners. Yellow and white painted Arabic broadcast the obituaries throughout our sector. Some Iraqis slowed down as they walked along the potholed avenues to read the black flags.

Horse-drawn carts jammed us and the Big Hungry eased down, letting them make their turn; the last cart, pulled by a white-and-gray-dappled horse with a bad left-rear hoof, carried green-and-yellow-striped tins of palm oil. You could see the ribs of the horse. Its eyes were black like midnight, and they glowed slightly in the mist and rain.

The dappled-gray horse's mane was loose and long, gray streaked with white, and raindrops shook off it as the horse limped along, gamely trying to negotiate the hard asphalt roads of Mosul. There were bells and trinkets and fine embroidered cloths hanging from the horse. The man on the cart, sitting forward slightly, tugged gently at its reins as we passed, and the horse slowed, easing off its lame hoof.

A line of cars behind the cart began beeping their horns. The man on the cart held a whip but he didn't raise it. He turned his head and shouted something in Arabic at the cars, fierce and brief, and then turned back toward his horse, shrugging his shoulders. The horse trotted on, limping slightly, palm-oil cans rattling on the cart.

Likely palm oil, I remember thinking, but every palm-oil tin is a potential roadside bomb. Sergeant Brett Lotto, the Zen Master and a great raider, had informed me of the palm-oil cans being used to pack C-4 and metal shavings and all manner of explosives the day before.

On a dawn counter-IED patrol, he'd pointed to one beat-up, rusted palm-oil can—which Iraqis tend to toss anywhere—and said softly, "Go easy." We'd walked up to it as his team behind him—Sergeant Shaun Smith, Private First Class Justin Rush, Specialist Patrick Texeira, and Private First Class Kevin Houchek—scanned alleys and rooftops at dawn near a mosque. We had no sappers and no mine detectors.

IEDs are sometimes command detonated, meaning the person trying to kill you actually sees you near the IED. The Zen Master's team was looking for anyone watching us, scoping for any opened windows or drawn curtains or kids peeping around corners to alert lookouts. The streets near us were quiet and there were no apparent signs of insurgents.

Lotto checked around the palm-oil can for wires, found none, and looked closely at the dirt around the can. The dirt was unmoved and showed no signs of digging. Insurgents could've placed a pressure-sensitive mine under the palm-oil can, of course. Finally, he lifted the rusted tin can with a stick. It was empty.

We'd continued on the foot patrol, walking slowly, ever watchful for roadside bombs. Each dawn, either Scouts or Mortars would roll out the gate, headed out on counter-IED patrols in four heavily armed trucks for the dusty rubble-strewn and sewage-ripe streets of Mosul—glared at by some Iraqis, cheered by others, and ignored by the rest. Our counter-IED patrol on October 3 was likewise greeted with equal shares of hate, love, and indifference.

Our presence, no doubt, made some difference; many of the men agreed with Sergeant Brian Finucan of Mortars Platoon, 3rd-502nd, who strongly argued that the foot patrols built rapport with the locals and gained us good, real-time ground intelligence—invaluable in a street fight. The sergeant's combat-earned opinion, shared by many of his comrades, was backed up by many months of night-and-day foot patrols throughout Mosul.

I brooked no disagreement with Sergeant Finucan on the positive impact of foot patrols vis-à-vis ground intelligence. Ground intelligence, as Bob Kerrey has said, "is absolutely vital to victory in war, especially guerrilla war. Nothing can ever replace eyes on the ground. That's how you get ground truth." Another SEAL leader, Commander Tom Dietz, reinforced his comrade Kerrey when he said, reflecting on ground intelligence operations carried out by the SEALS in the Persian Gulf War, "obtaining ground truth is having a real person in an area who can come back and debrief the exact intelligence that's there." The grunts I was with in Mosul, like the grunts I would later meet in Fallujah, were adamant about having *eyes on the ground* at all times.

As Finucan said in Mosul, "A satellite can give you a picture, but eyes on, a real person on the objective, can give you insight. In war, nothing beats ground intelligence."

I knew that if I wanted to stay alive in Mosul, I could only do so by listening to men like him who had captured and killed insurgents— American fighting men who knew the color of dawn on the Tigris River and the line of sight on alley rooftops on patrol in Mosul.

We could've been more aggressive and creative in how we were combating IEDs in Mosul; my own view was to strike the insurgents first. I also never understood why we didn't kill the IED bankers in Mosul, the Iraqi insurgent leaders who paid Iraqis to kill us.

Listening to First Sergeant Nathan Fulks, a brilliant and tough Texan who ran laps around the Widowmakers compound in body armor ("flak jacket PT," we called it in the Marines), I thought he really spoke wisdom on IEDs. Fulks spoke genius on guerrilla war, period, so I nicknamed him the "Einstein of Special Operations."

Einstein of Special Ops was a Ranger, before he was with Special Forces and later, a Delta Force sniper. He fought at Panama. He was with Special Forces deep in Kurdish highlands for quite some time in 1991. He was a CAG sniper at Mogadishu in 1993 (U.S. Army Special Forces Operational Detatchment-Delta, Combat Applications Group, popularly known as Delta Force [SFOD-D, CAG]).

The two CAG snipers, Sergeant First Class Randall D. Shugart from Lincoln, Nebraska, and Master Sergeant Gary I. Gordon from Lincoln, Maine, who received posthumous Congressional Medals of Honor for their brave and selfless actions to rescue a downed U.S. Army Blackhawk pilot, Chief Warrant Officer Michael Durant in the Battle of Mogadishu, Somalia, October 3 and 4, 1993, were his comrades.

Fulks is a straight-talking, easygoing man with hard eyes and a good sense of humor. Like the 3rd Battalion-502nd Infantry Regiment sergeant major in Mosul, Sergeant Major Boykins ("Samson"), he is an avid reader, a dedicated weightlifter, and a son of Beaumont, Texas. Samson would lift the heavy metal and listen to Creed's hard rock and trade stories with Einstein of Special Ops on the eastern banks of the Tigris River in the late afternoons in Mosul, sun burning through the camouflaged netting above them. They were warriors all their lives, they were far from their families, and their combat wisdom was vast and deep. Sergeant First Class Thomas McNair, "Super Scout," the Scouts Platoon sergeant, a re-served, self-contained man who was kind and soft-spoken, would often lift weights with them. When he did, the volume on the Creed would rise. It was good music.

Fulks called our counter-IED patrols "Hope it ain't me" patrols. He compared our counter-IED foot patrols in Mosul to the patrols he'd made deep in the mountains of northern Iraq in 1991, in the Persian Gulf War, when he'd patrolled in Kurdish highlands mined by Saddam Hussein.

He rubbed a hand against his shaved head, grinned slightly, and said, "Well, we'd say, up in those Kurdish hills, 'Hope it ain't me,' because your greatest fear is stepping on a mine. Same thing here; your greatest fear is coming across an IED. And our supply convoys have it the worst, all over this country. Any stretch of highway or road can be an IED kill zone. We have twenty-four-hour satellite surveillance but we're not using it in Mosul. We could set up one satellite with eyes on, round the clock, strictly for IEDs in Mosul. Do the same thing throughout Iraq, for that matter. Coordinate the real-time intel with IED hunter-killer teams: Snipers, Scouts, Special Ops, line infantry with M-14 scoped out sniper rifles, and a few gun trucks for heavy weapons fire support. All right then. Get your hunter-killer teams roving, patrolling, able to make hasty raids at the drop of a hat. Then, when you get real-time intel, you actually see the insurgents digging to set in IEDs, you roll and strike. Give them the surprise of their life. Kill them where they stand. But we're not doing that. Why we're not doing that in Mosul, I don't know. That's above my pay grade. But I know how I'd end it. I can tell you for a fact how I would go after the IED cells. And you have to kill the IED financiers—that's the main thing. You have to kill the IED bankers. Chop off the head of the cobra. The way we're doing it, it's more like we're striking at the cobra's tail."

The sidewalks and narrow streets grew crowded by mid-morning on our counter-IED patrol on October 3, donkeys and horses tied to black-painted steel poles near the markets. A light drizzle fell now all along the waterfront of the Tigris where Alexander and his Greek warriors had patrolled ages past, 331 B.C., seventy years after Xenophon had skirted Mosul on his long march north out of Mesopotamia. We rode east from the Tigris now in the chill northern Iraq drizzle, Thoman and Gordy trading gibes, Morrone steady at the wheel.

We halted near the Nabi Younis mosque, in the shadow of Jonah's bones, and patrolled for IEDs on foot. The lieutenant and his translator, a Kurdish gentleman, jumped off the back of the truck and moved up the northern side of the four-lane boulevard; the boulevard cut right down the middle with a fairly wide median, bushes lining both outer edges of the median.

Morales, Gordy, and I crossed to the southern side of the Nabi Younis mosque, a finely crafted stone temple set on a high mound. On that hill, in Xenophon's time, stood an Assyrian palace. Eureka Kid veered north slightly, solo, right up the middle of the median, his M-4 at the ready. *Tabla* drums and guitarlike strains from *ouds* and *bouzoukis* rocked out of taxi stereos as the orange-and-white-bodied taxis passed us in the rain, children smiling and staring goggle-eyed at us from the taxis.

We looked for oddly placed palm-oil cans and loosely dug-up dirt, and especially any wires or detonation cords snaking out from cans, bags, scrap metal, dirt, rubble, or rubbish; any wires or det cord laying askance along curbs and from piles of rubbish.

Iraqis hurried along the sidewalks and I greeted the men with "*As-saalam Ah Laekum.*" Some smiled slightly and responded, "*Wahh Laekum Ah Salaam.*" There was a fair number of Kurds near Nabi Younis, donned in the baggy trousers and fatigue blouses common to Kurdish peshmerga and wearing the small Kurdish turbans. I spoke to them in Kurdish, "*Chaowanee*," and they smiled broadly, enthusiastically returning my greetings with "*Boschaa*," and "*Zor Boschaa*," the Kurdish for "I'm good," and "I'm very good."

Arabs walked in the rain, men wearing leather jackets and suit coats over loose, long robes, their heads shrouded in white-and-red-checked scarves, the Arab *kaffiyeh*. A few Arabs carried umbrellas. Some of their women were with them, striding along and covered from head to toe in long, wet, black robes. There were also Kurdish women in long dresses, their heads uncovered, dark hair falling long down their backs. Children carrying small plastic and nylon backpacks over their shoulders scrambled along with older brothers and sisters, all running for beat-up, rusted school buses in the rain.

And there were also homeless men and their sons who slept on the ground between bushes in the medians of the wide roads that converge on Nabi Younis. Green and blue plastic sheets covered them as they slept.

On patrol, I could see Thomas fifty meters north of us. The Guerrilla Fighter was patrolling along a hill north of us on the opposite side of the boulevard, his M-4 shouldered, left hand on his forward grip, clip jacked in, scanning the ground for IEDs. He moved quickly, eyeing the ground, stepping out. To the west, on the far outskirts of Mosul, I could see patches of blue breaking through gray waves of rain clouds, the tiles on the minarets shining in the distance. The lieutenant's translator, a survivor of seven years of brutal Ba'athist torture as a political prisoner under Saddam, stayed in step with him on the barren hill that ran west and bordered the tightly packed neighborhood of concrete and stone houses southwest of the Nabi Younis mosque. I nicknamed the lieutenant's translator, "Hero of the Kurds." Following Coalition guidelines set up to protect translators, his real name remains anonymous. He was my age, forty-four, and he loved Vienna and mountains and Beethoven's music, and more than anything else, he deeply loved and adored his wife.

In the distance, Havana Tiger gestured toward Hero of the Kurds and Guerrilla Fighter. The rain had soaked us both, drenched us now. Hero of the Kurds waved to us, smiling, as Iraqi Arabs walked slowly by him, glancing curiously at him, their eyebrows raised.

I drank some brandy from my steel canteen. It was right on time, smoky-sweet and warm in the cold drizzling rain.

"I'll tell you what, Mr. Tucker, Lieutenant Thomas was Special Forces for a long time, *hombre*. Hard-core guerrilla fighter. High-speed Johnny Bravo, hard and smart. A good man. He really knows his shit. He knows more about guerrilla war than I could ever learn in ten lifetimes," Morales said as he scanned heaps of garbage on the side of the road for IEDs, mist drifting over the green and tan minarets south of us.

"Earned his guerrilla war theories in combat."

"Hell yes," he replied, and waved to the Eureka Kid in the median. Havana Tiger pointed to the sidewalk we were on and motioned for Eureka Kid to cross and patrol up the sidewalk.

Eureka Kid nodded, checked the traffic, and hustled across, rifle at his hip in the slow falling rain. As he crossed, we jogged to the median and Morales looked up at me, grinning slightly.

"You're not in bad shape for Geritol generation, Mr. Tucker."

I laughed as he grinned like a pirate now, Hero of the Kurds looking back at us and Morales giving him a thumbs-up.

"*Vitaminas, amigo*, vitamins and whiskey. Just call me *Senor Geritol, companero*."

"OK brother, *Senor Geritol! Que magnifico, Senor Geritol*. You see this ground here?" he said, pointing to hard-packed dirt between two long, chest-high rows of bushes in the median. I nodded to him as we patrolled on.

"This is where we shot *dos pendejos*. That's the night I call "Night of the Ass Rapists." We shot the motherfuckers. Shot two *hijos de la chingana*," he said, the Spanish curse for "sons of the great whore." We walked on slowly. I asked him what had happened.

"Well, we had a sweet little sniper overwatch. That's back when we'd actually go out and set up sniper hides. Real scout missions. Real sniper missions. Can't do that anymore. Division said it's too dangerous. Fuck dangerous, we're at war. Anyway, that's back a while ago. So, we see these *pendejos* popping up and down in the median here. About nine at night. Weird shit, brother. Strange. *De veras en si. Pues, es la pura verdad,*" he said, meaning, "It's the purest truth." He shrugged his shoulders.

"But this is Iraq, you know? You see some strange shit in this country. And we think, IEDs, the motherfuckers are digging in and setting up IEDs. Perfect place for IEDs, right in the middle of an MSR [main supply route, used by Coalition supply convoys]. *Hombre*, that's why we'd set up the sniper overwatch—we'd *anticipated* IEDs being dug in here. We were on that roof," he said, pointing back to the rooftop of a three-story, gray, cinder-block building at our seven o'clock, some one hundred meters southeast of us.

Gordy glanced at us as he patrolled slowly up the sidewalk and Morales gave him the sign for *it's all good*. Gordy nodded his head and scanned rooftops west and kept patrolling up the pebbled-stone sidewalk in the rain.

I scoped rooftops and alleys to the south and west of us on the southern side of the wide avenue. No signs of snipers; I had yet to see any snipers in-country. A lone seagull flew over the rooftops, heading west for the Tigris in the rain. Morales glanced at me, grinning.

"You and Big Hungry, hell yes, always looking out for snipers. That's good brother, that's real good. Eyes on. *Magnifico.*" Morales turned his head slightly, looking behind us for the Zen Master, Sergeant Lotto. Zen Master led his team up the long sidewalk. I called him the "Zen Master" because he'd once said about raiding, "A raid is a raid. The danger never changes. The uncertainty is always the same. A raid is a raid." Pure Zen to the core—direct and exact, with a touch of mystery.

Lotto's men were some one hundred meters behind us and evenly spaced, roughly ten meters between each scout. Lotto was a big cat, like the great Chicago Bears middle linebacker Dick Butkus, and he loped along like a panther, stalking the cold wet ground for IEDs. Texeira, who loved punk rock and was a good friend of DJ Rush, covered Lotto's six o'clock.

Tex and Zen Master carried M-4s. Up the median, covering their three o'clock, patrolled Sergeant Shaun Smith, whom I'd nicknamed "Sergeant York" after the legendary WWI warrior from Tennessee.

Like Sergeant York, Smith was an excellent sniper, and he possessed a wealth of wisdom on small arms. Sergeant York was stocky and solid, about six foot even, and carried an M.203.

All U.S. Army infantry platoons, I came to discover, have at least one master gunner—one warrior who is passionate about small arms.

Sergeant York was that man for the Scouts. He was a reserved, no-nonsense raider who missed his wife and sons dearly. When he talked of his family in Tennessee, his eyes would brighten and he'd smile. The Zen Master's team reflected the Zen Master—they were quiet, professional raiders who came to fight and came to win.

West of us some one hundred meters, the Guerrilla Fighter was standing just behind one of our trucks, talking into his I-Com, a small handheld communications device that enabled him to talk with his team leaders at any time. Hero of the Kurds was up in the truck ripping open an MRE package and gazing around in the steady light drizzle.

We were all still in the street, patrolling in the rain. Morales had a musing look about him.

"We check out plastic bags, right?" I said to Morales as I kicked at a large plastic bag, making sure it was empty and had no explosives or grenades in it.

"Roger that," he said, glancing quickly at the plastic bag. His eyes skated north and he raised his .203 slightly, squinting in the rain. "I tell you what, IED motherfuckers. So, we went to check it out that night. Night of the Ass Rapists. I kid you not, brother, craziest fuckin' thing I saw in this war yet. *Pendejos* bouncing up and down like pogo sticks. Got closer. Strange noises. Real dark, there. *Loco, hombre.* We got up close and the motherfuckers ran! Grabbing at their long robes."

"Their *dishtashas?*"

"*Pendejos* were naked! *En verdad! Dos locos!* That nightgown thing they wear was down around their ankles."

"Dishtasha."

"Right. Ass-rapist motherfuckers! This poor kid, he was on his knees in the dirt. Crying. They'd been ass-raping him! Our guys shot the two *hijos de la chingana. Dos pendejos locos!* Shot one of them in the ass. We shot an ass rapist in the ass!"

"Did you kill them?"

"We should've killed them, *no? Dos pendejos!*"

"You've gotta' be cops and warriors at the same time. That ain't easy. A lot of lawyers here now, what you all have been saying inside the wire. Is that right?" I asked him, remembering conversations with the Scouts inside the barbed wire on the 3rd-502nd compound in Kurdish Mosul.

"Our rules of engagement aren't the same as back in March, *hombre.* We have to positively ID that the enemy is enemy. And too many fuckin' lawyers in the war now. Rules of engagement come from where? From lawyers. And staff officers. *Pogues.* But if the motherfuckers are running away from ass-raping a kid, what the fuck? Sure, kill the motherfuckers. But I tell you what, I *guarantee* if we'd *killed* the motherfuckers, Night of the Ass Rapists, we would've been investigated. There it is. You're at war but people above you, who have never seen action, who don't *know* war, tell you you're no longer at war. And they'll send you to Leavenworth in a heartbeat. What kind of bullshit is that! The Iraqis have AK-47s right in their houses! AK-47 is a weapon of war, Mr. Tucker. AK-47 is the *preferred* weapon of the Iraqi insurgency. Remember, the Iraqi Army never surrendered. They just changed uniforms and hid their weapons. *Pendejos!* I'll tell you what, you see some weird shit in this country. Night of the Ass Rapists. This is a strange fuckin' country sometimes, *hombre.*"

"Looks like we're rolling," I said, looking up the street at Morrone raising his M-4, by the side of our truck. "Big Hungry's ready."

Morrone gestured to the trucks and we crossed the street, Gordy checking everything to our backs, covering our six as we jogged across the boulevard, flak jackets heavy with the rain.

Thomas grabbed my hand and pulled me up on the truck. Thoman was already up on the Ma Deuce and Gordy jumped up on the truck. Rain dripped off his chinstrap onto his flak jacket. He reached into his assault ruck and pulled out a small, green towel and wiped the rain off his face. He tossed the towel on the bed of the truck and shouldered his rifle. "Thoman, I hate the fuckin' rain," he said in a low tone, shaking his head. Kentucky Rifle grinned.

"Gordy my son, the rain is good for farmers. Trust me. Your father is wise. And accurate with the Ma Deuce. In the halls of Valhalla, the ancient ones gather round and praise my warrior's ways. Yes, my son, you must learn to love the rain. Be at one with the rain. The rain is a friend of cab drivers and umbrella salesmen. Mr. Tucker, I heard you caught a little rain in Burma."

I laughed. "Well, a few monsoons made my acquaintance."

He grinned. "But the Burmese Army didn't greet you."

"They sent two battalions with warm regards. But I was with good men in that rain. Guerrilla fighters. Kind of like now. Can't say I miss the monkey meat though. Chow's much better in Iraq."

Gordy frowned and tapped me on my shoulder.

"Monkey meat? You really ate monkey meat? My God!"

"Monkey meat is an acquired taste, gents, and I didn't exactly acquire it. But the grilled squirrel was tasty. *C'est la vie.*"

Morales grinned. "*Que va*, I'll take grilled steak in New York with my baby, *en verdad*, any day of the week. *Magnifico!*"

Thoman approved, cracking a wide grin, and he gave Sergeant Morales a big thumbs-up. "Now you're talking!"

"Troopstrap up," Morales said to Morrone as Thomas secured the troopstrap, clamping it solid.

"Roger that," Big Hungry said and he swung out left, leading us back toward Widowmakers compound on the eastern banks of the Tigris River, DJ Rush and the Zen Master's raiders checking our six. Hero of the Kurds looked west toward the Tigris, one arm resting on the plastic roof of the truck. He turned back and looked at Eureka Kid and gave him a thumbs-up.

Gordy nodded, his face serious, scanning his sector, his M-4 on safe. I could hear Thoman in my mind, six days earlier in a small candlelit room, the electricity on the blink, remembering Specialist Hurt nearly bleeding to death in a dark, tight, narrow street in the shadow of Jonah's bones.

"The street was just wide enough for our truck. It was eight, maybe a little after eight. Real dark that night. Like being on the Ohio River when the moon is down. Streetlights were shot out. That neighborhood is all fucked up, Whiskey Hotel. You saw it tonight."

Kentucky Rifle paused and sipped from his orange electrolyte drink, from an MRE package. It was 'round midnight on September 28, 2003. We'd just come off a night patrol in Whiskey Hotel and Whiskey India sectors, four hours of riding down sewage-thick roads and past cheering children, who'd smiled and waved in front of their stone-walled houses, the men smiling back and always at quick action, rifles shouldered, scoping rooftops and balconies and alleys.

Kentucky Rifle leaned back in his chair, candlelight dim behind him. A small lamp came on to his left. "Ah, the electricity ghost is smiling. That was a rough night. Rough, dark night. September 13th." He set his glass down and folded his arms.

"Hurt was driving the trail truck. Staff Sergeant Chapman, Gordy, Sergeant Turcotte, and Hurt were all riding trail. I was in the lead truck. I was on the SAW [light machine gun]. Big Hungry was driving lead. Sergeant Everhart, Morrone, Sergeant Morales, and me. All lead truck. We came around a corner. There were blasts behind us, multiple explosions.

Smoke everywhere. Staff Sergeant Everhart got on his I-Com, 'Drive through, drive through!' Morrone got ahead. I got off the truck and got along the wall. Staff Sergeant Everhart asked, 'Do you have casualties?' There was no answer from our trail truck. It was all covered in smoke. There was smoke everywhere and sparks shooting out from the truck. Sergeant Morales was already up alongside the truck, trying to help Hurt. Staff Sergeant Everhart was trying to get us help.

"Fifty meters up the road on the right side I could see an entrance to a courtyard. I could see Gordy near it. He'd jumped off the trail truck. I ran up to Gordy. He said, 'Thoman, I can still fight. I can still fight!' He was bleeding. I could see blood on his face.

"Gordy yells, 'Those fuckin' cocksuckers hit me!'

"I kept seeing a guy about a hundred meters down the road. On a rooftop. We didn't know what had hit us. He kept popping up. I shot him. All this was happening very, very fast. This car kept coming, right after I put down that guy. Coming hard and fast, right for us. He wouldn't stop. We lit his car up. He reversed.

"People kept coming out. We had no idea who'd hit us, but there had been multiple explosions. Gordy had the courtyard secured and I was near him. A guy came running at us from out of nowhere. I fired a warning shot. He kept running toward me. I shot over his head. He didn't stop. I put him down.

"I ran up to Hurt. Sergeant Morales was really upset. Half of Hurt's right foot was blown off, his lower right leg was mangled. It was shredded. He lay there, moaning. Sergeant Morales already had the wire tourniquet on Hurt's right leg. Sergeant First Class Rodriguez, our great medic, treated Hurt later and told us, 'Morales saved Hurt's life.' I tried to get Hurt to focus. 'You gotta' help me Thoman, I'm hurt real bad,' he said to me. I tried to keep Hurt from going into shock.

"You gotta' know this: Hurt was really tight with McClure, Morrone, and Sergeant Morales. Back in March and April, McClure and Hurt were one sniper team. McClure was Hurt's spotter. Everybody loved Hurt, he had that personality, real laid-back, super polite. A good sniper and an excellent soldier. Really respected, by all the men. He would call his girlfriend, all the time. Real tight with his family, too. We miss him. Staff Sergeant Chapman was wounded, too, but he was still in the fight, like Gordy. Me and Staff Sergeant Chapman grabbed Hurt.

Adrenaline was wearing off. He was so fuckin' heavy. We got him on the truck. Intersection of Nabi Younis market, the Blackhawk set down. I wish I could give that chopper pilot a medal. Morrone had called the medevac earlier but medevac was refused. I never understood that. Only thing we could do was get him to a fuckin' medevac. He's our fuckin' buddy and he was all fucked up. But that Blackhawk mama came in the nick of time. Hell yes.

"I mean, she just swooped down from out of the night. Rocked our world. Badass Blackhawk mama. We'll never forget her. Blackhawk was Eye in the Sky. 101st keeps a Blackhawk up twenty-four hours, for emergencies, reconnaissance, you name it. Eye in the Sky. Freak luck she was right there. Gutsy lady, let me tell you. Brought that fuckin' Blackhawk down on a dime in that tight intersection. When she got him to the airfield, his blood pressure was at ninety-five.

"Sergeant Morales saved Hurt's life. I'm sure Hurt would've bled out, right there on the street.

"And I'll tell you, Gordy was something else. I was really impressed with Gordy that night. He kept going. He showed real courage. He is a warrior.

"Anybody tells you they're not scared in an ambush, they're full of shit. We were all scared. But we all did well, we reacted well, and we fought back and killed the bastards. The sons of bitches that did this to Hurt, we will find them. We will track them down. We will hunt them. We will get these motherfuckers.

"They had no regard for their neighbors, either. There was a bunch of screaming coming from a house, after we'd cleared the courtyard. Gordy and I checked it out. An Iraqi's chest was all full of shrapnel. One of the IEDs had hit him. He was on his way. Just blew his chest out. The insurgents know that, Hawk. [Author's note: Hawk is my nickname, and men up north and out west often called me by my nickname.] They know there are Iraqi civilians around and they will not hesitate to kill Iraqi civilians, if it means they can get at us. If it means they can kill us. You're dealing with an enemy that has no regard whatsoever for the Geneva Convention. The enemy here is fighting under a black flag.

"We had to go back for the truck. When we got there it was stripped clean. IED had blown the whole floor out. We had two vehicles that night; you know, we'd just stopped Iraqis from ripping off other Iraqis,

with black market propane sales. Hearts and minds. Right in that neighborhood. About an hour before the ambush. We never roll in less than
four vehicles, now. Heavy guns, two trucks. Ma Deuce and MK 19s.

"You know that sign on our compound, 'What have you done
today to win Iraqi hearts and minds?' We *despise* that sign. We fuckin'
despise it. For Chrissakes, we lost that war. Why are we resurrecting a
worthless slogan from a war we lost? I could give a rat's ass about Iraqi
hearts and minds. How are you going to really change Iraqi minds, at
least the Arabs? The Kurds love us. We don't *need* to change their
minds. We really did wrong with the Kurds up here. We stabbed the
Kurds in the back.

"The Kurds bled with us. They died in this war, for our cause. They
are our comrades. They know this city. They know Mosul. Good God,
they know all northern Iraq. Our CG [Author's note: Commanding
General, Major General David L. Petraeus] ordered us to disarm them.
And he booted them. Where the fuck did he learn that? Is that what
comes with a Ph.D. from Princeton?

"No common sense at all, and no honor. No warrior's code. I guess
once you make general, you've forgotten what it means to honor warriors. Honor the men who bleed with you. If you don't, it will come
back to haunt you. We should've honored the peshmerga. They bled
with 10th Group. We should've rewarded the Kurds."

The light went out. The candle cast a glow on the room and he
chuckled. "Electricity ghost. He does frown, occasionally."

He shook his head. I'd heard similar complaints from U.S. Special
Forces I'd met in northern Iraq, who'd aired strong grievances concerning Major General David Petraeus's disarming of the Kurds in Mosul
and the wrong message it sent to all Iraqi insurgents. I gestured to him
and he looked directly at me.

"A Karen guerrilla fighter told me there is an old saying among warriors. Told me a year ago, behind Burmese Army lines."

"What is it?" Kentucky Rifle asked, his voice low in the darkness.

"Where there is no honor, there is only shame."

Kentucky Rifle grimaced, nodding, and drank down his orange electrolyte drink. He folded his arms and looked down, leaning forward
slightly. Then he glanced out at the black night and spoke slowly in a
low, hard tone.

"Up north, in Dormeez, I had to tell Kurdish families they could not move back into houses Saddam had stolen from them. Saddam's Arabization. Saddam stole Kurdish houses. Saddam gave them to Ba'athists. Ba'athist secret police, Ba'athist officers.

"And I had to tell the families, families of Kurds who'd been fighting against the Ba'athist dictatorship since before I was born, that they could not move back into their houses.

"We rewarded Ba'athism and we punished the Kurds. We rewarded Arabization. And whose idea was Arabization? Saddam Hussein's idea. You tell me what the hell kind of sense that makes. For shame! I was ashamed. I was ashamed to be representing the U.S. government on that day. Why did we reward the Ba'athists? Why? The Ba'athists murdered Kurds at Halapja. And the killing fields at Hatra. Look, the Arabs hate us but we're told to win their hearts and minds. You can't get inside someone's mind, someone's heart. Only they can do that, for themselves. How in hell am I supposed to understand Iraqi Arabs? You've got to know the steps if you're going to dance the hearts-and-minds fandango.

"I don't understand Iraqis at all. Their attitude is, 'I lived in fear and poverty all my life under the Ba'athists, and Oh, I love Saddam!' That's madness! I don't understand the fanatical devotion to Saddam, not at all. It's insane. What did Saddam ever do for Iraqis? He made them live in horrifying poverty."

"You don't think money is ammunition, then, as Major General Petraeus likes to say?"

He laughed, shaking his head, and rubbed a hand through his short-cropped red hair.

"The money comes back at us as 7.62 rounds and RPGs and IEDs. Oh, money is ammunition, all right. We spend it, and the Iraqis smile real pretty, take the money, and buy ammunition with it. Strange, come to think of it. Feydayeen never attack the Kurds. Well, look at the ambush. Look at that night. We go out on patrol. We find corruption. Black market sales of propane. We root it out. We keep Iraqis from getting ripped off. We keep Iraqis from getting separated from their money. Hearts and minds. So, we do the good-cop thing, we help people keep money in their pockets. We roll through an Iraqi Arab neighborhood and do all that and our thanks is we're nearly killed. They don't care about the money. They love the dictator, some of them. The Ba'athists. They truly love Saddam.

"You can't buy the allegiance of Ba'athists. You've gotta' kill them. Because they will come right for you, to kill you, to maim you. With IEDs, with RPGs, with AK-47s, with mortar rounds, with rockets, with machine guns.

"They love IEDs because it's the cowards' way of fighting, and they were bullies, all these years, the Ba'athists. The Ba'athists are still bullies. They'll never change. All dictators are bullies. All bullies, at heart, are cowards. And they're cowards, how they fight. But make no mistake, they are fighting a war against us. We're in a war, here. We need to kill the Ba'athists."

"We are now entering Whiskey Grenade sector. Passengers, prepare to defend yourselves. Mr. Tucker, fire my M-4 if we're engaged."

Thoman nodded to me. It was nine thirty-one in the morning of October 3 and we rode to raid in Mosul. Gordy tapped a magazine on its side, the clip full, and set it back in a pouch on his flak jacket, two other full clips beside it.

Thoman flexed on the Ma Deuce, skies gray above us. Morrone drove fast down narrow streets, splashing through puddles and rocking out over potholes and curbs. Hero of the Kurds hung on to the wooden rails of the truck and leaned into the wind. Arabic music thumped from taxis and cars we passed, some of the passengers waving and giving us thumbs-up in the gray mid-morning, concrete slabs jutting up from bomb craters in Mosul like wrecked bows of clipper ships on a bouldered shore.

Pajama-clad children waved at us and smiled and shouted from the sidewalks, "*Merhaba, Merhaba,*" a greeting both Arabs and Kurds share in Iraq. Hero of the Kurds waved back at them and grinned as I shouted the return greeting in Arabic, "*Merhaba tain,*" meaning, "Welcome, and good wishes to you."

Iraqi Arab women in long black gowns and black headwraps and scarves looked at the children and laughed. The women emptied buckets of dirty water and refuse into streams of raw sewage. The stench was awful, like elephant dung in Burma.

Trash fires burned in blackened and rusted oil drums along the sidewalks. Small crowds of men, in two-piece suits and collared shirts, kaffiyehs wrapped about their necks, hung back from the sidewalks along the stone and concrete walls, warming their hands over the fires, breath misting in the Mosul chill.

The raiders scanned the sidewalks as we rolled hard, Thomas up front in the TC seat (passenger's seat of a gun truck) with his rifle outboard, next to Morrone, minarets stark on all horizon lines.

We were checking rooftops and alley corners and balconies, scoping for insurgents, hoping and praying that no RPG gunner or any other insurgent would rise up swiftly and squeeze off a lucky shot. The sun was a dim ember of fire far to the southeast, glowing faintly behind broken gray clouds. Morrone drove like a man possessed.

The Guerrilla Fighter laid the barrel of his M-4 over the open window of his door and pressed his back against the hard plastic seat cushion, shifting slightly, getting a better firing position. He glanced back and nodded and cast his eyes back on the streets. Poker-faced, but his eyes were on fire. Eureka Kid held three o'clock, M-4 shouldered, squinting hard, a fierce look on his face. Morales checked our six, his M.203 shouldered, on safe, one finger just above the trigger.

Behind us, Staff Sergeant Chapman, "who'd been with the Scouts since he was born," according to Morales, waved at us and pointed ahead, pumping a fist. Chapman had hunted and trekked many ridgelines of Utah in his youth. I called him "Jeremiah Johnson," after the legendary mountain man of the West.

Purple clouds flooded low hills to the east. To the west, high blue cloudless horizons stretched toward Syria; to the north and south, shafts of sunlight shot through gray and violet clouds, cathedral light.

Iraqi Arab men glared at us and I smiled at them and shouted, "*Mala Mustafa Barzani!*" They scowled, hearing the name of the legendary Kurdish guerrilla commander whose guerrilla warriors had fought Saddam Hussein "with nothing but their *Kalashnikovs* and their balls," as one U.S. Army 10th Group Special Forces commando said in Dahuk in the spring of 2004.

Mala Mustafa Barzani died of cancer in America in 1979, but his bold spirit of dignity and defiance was with us as we raided on streets liberated by the sons of his warriors, Kurdish peshmerga who'd freed Mosul in three days in April 2003.

⊚ ⊚ ⊚

Kurdish and Arab children danced and shouted at us, "Amerikee, Amerikee!" smiling, gleefully waving and giving us thumbs-ups and raising both arms and making the V for victory sign with both hands, in the way of Churchill and Roosevelt, as we dodged horse-drawn carts and donkeys and slow-moving white-and-orange taxis, Gordy scoping minarets near the Tigris, checking for snipers. We slammed to a stop near the massive concrete and stone fortress of a house, two stories, raiders leaping off all four trucks, machine gunners standing fast, Gordy saying "Go go go, goddamn, let's go!" Morales took point.

I could see a man on a rooftop opposite the massive house, just west. Morales saw him and scoped him with his rifle and the man dropped behind a low wall.

"There's a guy on the roof, he bounced!" yelled Morales as we hustled on for the main target house, Thomas saying in a firm, hard voice, not shouting, "Keep moving, keep moving." Morales rushed forward, turning his rifle back toward the massive castle of a compound.

From behind us, Chapman shouted, "Stocker, grab the SAW!" Private First Class Nicholas Stocker hollered from Bravo Team's truck, "I've got it, Sergeant!" and he unlatched the light machine gun from its steel mount and hefted it easily, carrying it from the hip and leaping off the back of the truck, two hundred linked 5.56 rounds in a small camouflaged loam-and-green pouch attached to the light machine gun and six hundred more rounds in an assault ruck thrown over his shoulders.

Stocker was built like a fullback and deceptively quick, a good man on a raid. He had a laid-back way about him and was very observant. The men called him "Hootch," because he'd said once on the field radio, in response to Widowmakers command inquiring about the Scouts whereabouts, "Rolling back to the *hootch*, over," a fairly casual radio transmission and one the Scouts never let him forget. Like DJ Rush, Hootch had been a machine gunner in the March and April actions during the war in Iraq.

Sergeant First Class McNair, Super Scout, came up behind Hootch as he moved toward Chapman and together they rushed toward the main target house. Sergeant Jason Turcotte from Boston, an ace sniper and Jeremiah Johnson's assistant team leader, ran from the opposite side of Bravo Team's truck and dashed over to Jeremiah Johnson and said something quickly to him, glancing west and pointing. I called Turcotte the "Pathfinder." He was twenty-five and knew Cape Cod well. The Pathfinder loved the Red Sox, smoked Cuban cigars, and often talked fondly about his woman in New England, when inside the wire.

Jeremiah Johnson nodded to the Pathfinder and pointed to an alley corner near the T-intersection some twenty meters west of us. Turcotte sprinted to it and kneeled, holding the corner, his M.203 shouldered, facing north, his right knee down, black plastic kneepad flush against the cold wet concrete.

I could hear the pounding of boots on the wet potholed asphalt street and Morales said, "Watch the balconies, watch the rooftops," and I turned and saw Iraqis coming out on balconies from the tightly packed houses on all sides of the T-intersection.

Zen Master hustled up with Alpha Team and secured the alleys and corners near the fortress of a house, on the southern side of the T-intersection, as Morales got up to the gate, leading Charlie Team on main raiding element.

DJ Rush stayed back on the Ma Deuce for Zen Master, and a gun truck from Mortars checked our six: Specialist Daniel Watkins on an MK 19, Private First Class Chris Burris and Sergeant Juevon Green with him, the mortarmen securing the rear as we raided. They were solid, the mortarmen, and had joined the Scouts on many raids in Mosul between late April 2003 and that October 3.

I stayed with Charlie Team. I could hear dogs barking in the distance, howling, and looked up at the roof opposite us, where we'd just now spotted one man.

The roof was empty. South, just behind it, on an adjacent rooftop, a little girl stood smiling at us. She touched a hand to her face and smirked, a mischievous look come over her. She wore a purple blouse. Her black hair hung down all over her shoulders and she smiled at us from behind a cinder-block wall. Foul stench drifted on the wind, mixed with smoke from an oil-can fire in the Mosul backstreets.

The rooftop walls were all jury-rigged, built with cinder blocks by stone masons who'd worked without levels. The little girl draped both her arms over the gray, unpainted cinder block and kept smiling. A shrill high-pitched female Arab voice, perhaps her mother, caught her attention and she giggled and turned, looking down, shaking her head slightly. The little girl turned back toward us and draped her arms over the wall again. She raised a hand toward us and waved, giggling and smiling. I waved back. She had a beautiful smile.

Havana Tiger checked the gate for any wires or det cord and jabbed it open with the barrel of his M-4, Hero of the Kurds and Guerrilla Fighter and the Eureka Kid right behind him, Iraqi Arabs gathering on the sidewalks of houses just south of the compound.

Red stone, still damp and puddled in places, covered the ground inside the gate. Faded gray wool blankets and white sheets hung from the old metal-framed windows of the house. Rusted propane tanks stood inside the gate, up against a gray stone wall.

An Iraqi man in a white headdress with a small black rope and tassel wrapped about it, and a long gray dishtasha, his feet clad in orange plastic sandals, came out slowly and said softly to us, "Merhaba." Hero of the Kurds returned his greeting and spoke quickly to him, gesturing with his left hand as he spoke to him.

The man shrugged his shoulders and spoke in a low tone to him. Hero of the Kurds grinned slightly, and nodded to the man. He turned to the Guerrilla Fighter and told him the man had no problems with us searching his house and he'd be happy to answer any questions. Morales kept his eyes on the rooftops south of us, checking for movement.

Gordy and Thoman did likewise, to the north and east. I scanned the western rooftops. There was no movement, nothing but the wind buffeting a few starlings and sparrows perched on telephone lines and mazes of electrical wires. A pigeon fluttered down at our feet. The little girl in the purple dress was gone.

Thomas said, "Clear the house, separate the men from the women. I've got a feeling they're not here, though."

Morales nodded and led Charlie Team through the inner door to the courtyard, his M.203 shouldered, his head moving like a pinball wizard, scanning quickly, motioning to two teenage boys to get inside a room, the boys staring wide-eyed at him. Arabic music sounded low from within their room, tabla laying down a steady beat and a woman's voice singing plaintively over the tabla drum and violins and the oud.

The boys wore long, white dishtashas. They looked at a white-haired man who looked to be in his mid-sixties and of medium height. White stubbled beard covered his face. The old man nodded to them and followed them. Morales continued to search the house, Thoman and Gordy checking rooms carefully.

Children in various states of undress gazed goggled-eyed down at us from a walkway spanning the second deck, a small courtyard open to the sky before us.

Havana Tiger led us up a flight of concrete steps to the second deck, the Eureka Kid behind me and Kentucky Rifle, carrying an M-4, with him, scoping the empty rooms on the second deck.

I could hear the raiders on both decks shouting, "Clear, clear," as they rushed from room to room, opening closets and checking under beds and looking for anything on the roof that indicated flight-fresh footprints, wires disturbed or broken in flight, half-lit cigarettes, unfinished cups of tea or coffee—any signs of flight.

Eureka Kid and Kentucky Rifle spoke short, clear bursts of Arabic to the children, and the children giggled and went into one room. There was a strong, pleasant scent of burning kerosene from the room, and for once in Mosul I could not smell the raw sewage from the streets.

A woman came up from the ground floor. She was perhaps forty. She wore a dark-blue house robe with gold and red thread woven all through it. Streaks of gray ran from her temples through her thick black hair, and she wore a braided silver necklace. Her eyes were dark brown and she was without expression, coming toward me and Eureka Kid and Kentucky Rifle.

I greeted her in Arabic and she smiled slightly and returned my greeting. She entered the room and the children hailed her but did not address her as mother. There was a kerosene heater in the room. The woman lit three huge white candles. An old, faded black-and-white poster of Pele, the great Brazilian international football star, was pasted on one wall. Opposite Pele, a poster of the voluptuous blonde Columbian singer Shakira was plastered to the wall, the corners torn. The children sat cross-legged on gray wool blankets near the red-painted small kerosene heater, a steady blue flame burning from its core.

There were no signs of flight in any of the rooms. We were raiding to kill or capture both the insurgent who'd planned the ambush that had nearly killed Hurt and the actual grenade thrower—the insurgents were thought to be at the courtyard mansion. From the second deck, I could see the lieutenant and Hero of the Kurds listening to an Iraqi woman who was perhaps in her mid-thirties. She wore a black scarf over her head and her red-streaked brown hair fell to her shoulders. She was gesturing west with her left hand and tugging at her billowing black dress with her right. Her black eyes were bright and she spoke rapidly, her left hand making circles. Her words misted in the cold, damp autumn air in Mosul.

A gold necklace in the shape of the sun, with the sun's rays beaming out in small gold bands, hung from her neck. The man who'd opened the house to us, whom I presumed to be her husband, was off to one side, his arms folded, and he was frowning and looking down. I could see no movement on the rooftops west.

The Zen Master stepped in briefly and spoke with the Guerrilla Fighter. Lotto scanned the courtyard as Thomas talked to him. Smith came up and stood off to Lotto's left, his M.203 held at the hip.

Sergeant York carried thirteen high-explosive 40mm grenades on the front of his flak jacket for his M.203 and more in his combat assault ruck. Havana Tiger gave him a thumbs-up and Sergeant York grinned slightly, looking about the puddled courtyard. In the center of the courtyard, Hero of the Kurds tugged at the lieutenant's sleeve. Hero of the Kurds had coal-black eyes, and he was squinting as the mist cleared in the cold, wet courtyard. The faint scent of burning kerosene was drifting about us.

"She says the house across the street has one of their mothers. Across the street. The one who planned the ambush. His mother is across the street."

The Guerrilla Fighter looked hard at the woman and then glanced quickly up at Havana Tiger.

"Sergeant Morales, we're done here. Let's get across the street. Sergeant Lotto, let's go."

The sergeants nodded and rushed out, Eureka Kid saying to me as we ran down the stairs, "Careful, slick stairs, brother, be real careful," and I thanked him.

Kentucky Rifle was already out the gate, heading across the street, running with his M-4 held from the hip, as I got out. A faint mist rolled over the rooftops west, and I could feel the flak jacket heavy on me in the gray autumn morning chill.

Hootch secured the southern side, his loam-and-green ruck sagging off his shoulders. His light machine gun hung off a black nylon and cloth strap, padded on the shoulder, and he carried it like John Henry carried a sledgehammer—effortlessly. Stocker was like DJ Rush in that way, like all the Scouts; he inspired confidence when he was on a raid.

He mopped sweat off his brow and kept his eyes on the small crowds gathering on the broken sidewalks south of us, potbellied Iraqi Arab men in gray-and-black dishtashas scowling at us, talking out of the sides of their mouths to one another, their arms folded.

Barefoot Iraqi Arab kids in pajamas swarmed about them and waved as we crossed to the second target house. The raid became an improvised raid, the Guerrilla Fighter in full command. I remember thinking that Thomas has a trait vital to victory in war; he knows how to improvise in combat at the drop of a hat.

The kids' fathers scolded them, grabbing their arms and shouting at them. Their mothers huddled near partly opened steel gates behind them, shouting something in Arabic. Some of the children cried, hearing their scowling fathers berate them on the puddled, broken pavement.

The children looked down and pounded their fists against their shirts and blouses and beat feet back to their houses, some of them throwing one last wave at us before they dashed into the small, steel-gated compounds appearing south of us in the clearing mist, sunshine filtering a strange white light down the sewage-ripe streets.

There were clear blue skies now to the west as we entered the second house, Zen Master on point, Tex and Sergeant York moving in smartly behind Zen Master. Hootch was steady on his light machine gun, covering the southern approaches.

I gave Stocker a thumbs-up and scanned the streets south of him. Stocker saw us out of the corner of his eye and nodded to Gordy as we crossed.

Gordy nodded back, frowning slightly, his eyes intense, face flushed red. There were Arabic voices coming from within the second house, and I could hear Hero of the Kurds talking quickly in Arabic and a woman's voice answering him.

Charlie Team moved up behind Zen Master's raiders. There were concrete stairs straight ahead and I glanced up and saw blue skies and drifting gray and white clouds.

Gordy was right in front of me, rushing forward, rifle shouldered and leaning to his right slightly, saying to Havana Tiger, "Sergeant Morales, the stairs." Zen Master turned toward us and said, "Ground floor's clear, rooftop's clear."

Now we were all in and still rushing forward. Guerrilla Fighter, listening to Hero of the Kurds translate, nodded to us and motioned up with his rifle. Kentucky Rifle patted me on the back and I turned and he said quickly, "When we get to the roof, scope north, check our three o'clock." Havana Tiger led us, Eureka Kid swift up the steps, Kentucky Rifle behind me.

Morales raided left and swept the air with his M.203, his eyes alive in all directions, rushing over to the southern wall of the roof. The rooftop was cluttered with gray shards of cinder blocks and broken toys and scattered, shattered glass. A hip-high wall ran along the southern edge of the rooftop. East, our gun trucks commanded the T-intersection.

Rush looked up at us from behind his Ma Deuce on a gun truck, his hands on the triggers, and Thoman gave him a thumbs-up. DJ Rush grinned. I looked north and saw a huge field at our three o'clock, soccer goals at each end.

Streets east of the field were crowded with excited children. The boys and girls, some in pajamas and others in long nightgowns, smiled and shouted, "Amerikee!, Amerikee!" I waved to them and smiled back.

Charlie Team held the rooftop, checking closely for any signs of flight, looking for footprints and broken wires and warm cigarette butts. Southeast, skies were clearing, gray scudded clouds drifting south toward Iraqi Kurdish mountains far in the distance, toward Kirkuk and Suleiymaniyah and Halapja.

Roughly 120 meters northeast of us, a smiling young boy in black baggy trousers and a green jersey held a framed picture of Mala Mustafa Barzani high in both hands.

The Kurdish boy was perhaps six years old. By his side, a younger boy, in blue pajamas, carried the yellow and red *Partika Kurdistane Demokrati* flag of the Kurdistan Democratic Party. The flag was unfurled and a slight breeze caught it and opened it full, the flag Kurdish peshmerga had carried into battle for decades against Saddam's regime.

It was still a battle flag for Kurds in Mosul in the autumn of 2003 as we raided in northern Iraq. Saddam was still on the loose and the Kurds still believed in us, still believed that we were in Iraq to defeat and destroy Ba'athism.

For here—on these same streets we raided for the planners and perpetrators of the IED attack on the Scouts, the ambush that nearly killed Hurt—here the Kurds had seen their mothers and fathers and aunts and uncles, blood of all kin and kind, tossed into open-bed trucks by Mukhabarat and Iraqi Army soldiers and officers.

Mosul was a key center for Ba'athist leaders. The Kurds of Mosul knew that all too well. And the Kurdish children of Mosul, many who will never know their grandparents, remembered. The children remembered in the shadow of Jonah's bones.

Iraqi Army officers and the Mukhabarat, Ba'athists all, had driven Kurds from Mosul and all northern Iraq to an unmarked desert in Hatra and Hilla, locked and loaded AK-47 Kalashnikov assault rifles, and shot them, massacres discovered only scant months before this raid—massacres found by Coalition forces in the liberation of Iraq.

Here, indeed, on the streets of Mosul, the war-crimes perpetrator Iraqi Army First Lieutenant Abdul Kharim Jahayshee, a prominent Ba'athist in northern Iraq, still walked free as we struck to kill or capture the Iraqi insurgents who'd ambushed the Scouts. And the Kurds still loved us, watching us raid. The little boy grinned wildly and waved the flag at us, holding it in both hands, like a Kurdish peshmerga going into battle. Looking at him, I could tell that he and his mates would never forget this day. He truly dug us being on his turf, that kid did, as did his older brother.

Havana Tiger scoped south, sheets and trousers flapping on a clothes line, gusting winds strong from the west, cedar trees swaying south of us now. Below him, Hero of the Kurds and Guerrilla Fighter talked with a heavily built Iraqi Arab woman in a black house gown and purple head scarf on the courtyard deck of the second house as Zen Master's team walked slowly about the ground floor, weapons at the ready.

Zen Master's raiders spoke in hard sharp voices, no one yelling, raiders moving quickly around the courtyard from room to room. Tex kept his M-4 shouldered. His khaki-and-sand camouflaged helmet was sepia-toned now, soaked from the heavy dawn rain. I scanned rooftops north, remembering Thoman's commands.

Below us, the woman kept glancing down and looking away as Hero of the Kurds questioned her. The lieutenant shook his head and looked hard at her and turned his head slightly, toward Hero of the Kurds.

"She's lying," he said, his tanned face darker now. "Tell her I know she's lying. We know there was a man on the roof. Was it her son on the roof?"

Thomas took off his helmet and wiped his thick blond hair dry with a faded green bandana. The deep crow's-feet around his eyes spread as he looked at Hero of the Kurds talking with the woman, and he glanced directly at the woman, frowning slightly.

His M-4 was cradled in his left arm and he set his right hand over the black plastic grip of his M-9, 9mm Beretta sidearm strapped to his right leg. It was ten years before, on this day, that he had descended into the streets of Mogadishu with Task Force Ranger.

Some one hundred meters north, in a field of rocks, pebbles, and sand where we'd seen the neighborhood kids playing soccer two days earlier on a daylight patrol, Kurdish men walked, carrying small wooden toolkits and mason's canvas bags. The field was all puddled now and their black sandals were caked brown with mud. They were grinning to one another, like old friends.

The men wore the uniform of Kurdish peshmerga, khaki military-style blouse and baggy drawstring trousers, and they walked jauntily, gesturing to one another as they crossed the wet muddy field.

Dark-green and brown kaffiyehs were wrapped loosely around their necks. Some of the children cheering us called to them, and they turned and smiled and waved back. Below me, I could hear Hero of the Kurds.

"She is the mother. Her son is feydayeen. He was here last night and he left." The Guerrilla Fighter breathed in slowly, then breathed out, frowning.

"Who was the man on the roof?"

Hero of the Kurds translated, gesturing slightly with his left hand, but not raising it above his waist. I remembered my friend Mohammad Al Quaati, an Arab Bedouin, telling me in Al Ain, United Arab Emirates, in June 2002, that when you gesture chest-high in Arab culture, it's a sign you're not pleased. And when you gesture above the chest, extending the arm and wrist out, pointing your fingers and waving your hand directly at the person opposite you, leaning forward toward the person as you're jabbing your hand at him, it's the Arab way of saying, "You go to hell."

Hero of the Kurds set both hands on his hips as the woman spoke. He shook his head as she talked; she was looking down. I walked over to the southern ledge as Kentucky Rifle took over the three o'clock, his light machine gun at his hip. Gray clouds crept up from the west, covering Mosul's northern reaches. To the east, Kurdish mountains rose from the earth like a woman lying on her back.

"She says there was no man on the roof."

Havana Tiger walked over toward the stairwell and looked down into the courtyard.

"Sir, I saw a guy bounce. There was a guy on the roof. Hawk saw him, too."

"You saw him, too?" Guerrilla Fighter asked me, his face hard.

"He took cover behind this wall," I said, pointing to the rooftop wall that faced east.

Below us and south of us on the street, crowds of potbellied, corpulent Arab men in black, gray, and faded white dishtashas, scowling and jabbing their fingers at Chapman and his team on the T-intersection, surveyed the scene. Nearly all of them were smoking. Behind them, their children waved to Eureka Kid on the roof near me and he grinned at them. I glanced down over a ledge.

There were fresh muddy footprints on the adjoining rooftop. The footprints faced west. Dry dirt was up against the wall; disturbed, loose clumps of dry dirt scattered about. The dirt looked scuffed up, as when you dig your feet in before leaping.

I looked down and could see a house below, and one open door. The gate to the house was open. Hootch held his ground on the southern approaches to the T-intersection, light machine gun at his hip, facing south. He was just outside the gate to the house and he glanced west at it, narrowing his eyes. I gave him a thumbs-up and he grinned.

There was a street behind the house. I could hear Hero of the Kurds talking in the courtyard, in between bursts of Arabic from the mother. I could hear Thomas saying, "She can lie to me in jail, for all I care. Tell her we're taking her to jail. I know she's lying."

I motioned Gordy over and pointed to the footprints. He glared and called out to Havana Tiger, "Sergeant Morales, Hawk's got footprints, the guy must've bounced out here."

Morales gestured to Thomas and shouted, "Sir, we've got something up here."

Morales rushed over, his 40mm grenades jostling and bouncing slightly on his vest. We moved aside and Gordy pointed down at the footprints.

"Right there, Sergeant."

He glanced down quickly. Stocker was near the door of the house below us. He looked over at Chapman, near Bravo Team's truck.

"*Magnifico!* Good work, good! Yeah, those look fresh. Could've gone down into this house. *Pendejo* must've bolted out the back, no one saw him run from the front. *Cabron!* We'll check it for rear entrance. Thoman," he said, looking back at Kentucky Rifle.

"Sergeant?"

"Tell the lieutenant we need to clear this house, next to us. Guy must've bolted out the back. Check it for rear entrance. And we've got footprints. He headed west, jumped to the roof behind us."

Thoman nodded and rushed over toward the stairwell leading down to the courtyard, scanning rooftops north as he moved. He kept his eyes on rooftops and balconies north of us as he spoke hurriedly to Thomas.

"Sir, the guy bolted west. Rooftop behind us. We think he got down through the house and out the back. Search the house?"

The lieutenant nodded.

"Roger that, sir," said Thoman. Morales pointed to Chapman and shouted, "Lieutenant says search the house! Hootch is on it, check for rear entrance."

Chapman ran over, looking north and south as he sprinted, his team following him. Hootch glanced back at him and Chapman said quickly as he ran toward him, "Do it," and Hootch with his light machine gun rushed forward into the house. The rest of Bravo Team, Private First Class Nicholas Dalip from Connecticut and Private First Class Kevin Nguyen from California, carrying M-4s followed, Nguyen with a radio strapped to his back, a small black antennae jutting out of the loam-and-green camouflaged assault ruck.

Zen Master's team swooped south out of the courtyard house, filing out swiftly under muddled gray skies, and took over the southern security, spreading out about ten meters apart. I could hear the mother talking again, long bursts of Arabic punctuated by Hero of the Kurds' deeper, calmer Arabic. Eureka Kid glanced at Havana Tiger and said, "I hope we get the sonofabitch. You think it was him?"

Morales grinned at Gordy.

"*Que va*, why else bolt? *En verdad*, I think it was the *cabron*. Mr. Tucker, you seem comfortable," he said to me, chuckling. "I think you're the only one who really *wants* to be here," he added, and all Charlie Team laughed with him, as did I. He smiled merrily. I shook his hand and thanked him. He was right; I was damned glad to be in the fight.

Morales nodded and a reflective look came over him. He reached out his right fist, his left hand firm on the forward grip of his M-4, and I tapped his fist. Starlings rushed up west of us, near an alley about one hundred meters west of us. Arab men in dishtashas and kaffiyehs glanced west down the alley.

To the east, DJ Rush stood fast on his Ma Deuce, glaring in the way of DJ Rush, all eyes. Zen Master walked among his team, talking quickly to Texeira and Smith, glancing back at Specialist Houchek, the driver for Lotto's team and a tough, jovial warrior who was thick-skinned and always upbeat. Lotto gave a hand-and-arm signal to Houchek, gesturing to him with his left hand as he raised his M-4 slightly with his right, and Houchek moved east about ten meters, raising his M-4, scoping an alley that ran out west toward the southern approaches to our raid. I could hear Hero of the Kurds speaking English, his voice louder, more insistent now.

"She swears her son was not here. She keeps saying there was no one on the roof. She's lying, I tell you." His hands were on his hips.

The Guerrilla Fighter slapped the black nylon cover to his sidearm, shaking his head furiously. He looked hard, right at the woman. "Tell her she's going to jail. Now."

Hero of the Kurds translated and the woman stepped back slightly, grabbing at her hair with her right hand.

Her left arm jolted up, pointing west, and she shouted, "*Aiyeeee, Aiyeeee!*" and then spat out a long stream of Arabic, jabbing enthusiastically west with her left hand, her black nightdress rising and falling as she jerked about, wailing.

Hero of the Kurds smiled broadly, folding his arms.

"She says her son was on the roof! He fled. She knows exactly where he is. She will lead us to him, now."

"He was here," I told Morales. "She knows where her son's at." Havana Tiger came over quickly, scanning east and north as he stepped across the rooftop, Eureka Kid and Kentucky Rifle vigilant on their sectors. I could see the Kurdish kids still north of us, waving the KDP battle flag and holding framed photos of Mala Mustafa Barzani.

I waved to them and they shouted, smiling, "Amerikee, Amerikee!" Gulls soared over the kids, heading west for the Tigris River, dipping their gray and white wings as they glided west over Mosul.

Morales looked down. The mother was talking loudly, wildly, and Hero of the Kurds was motioning to her to slow down. Thomas glanced up and saw Morales and said, "We're moving out. Hasty raid. On foot."

"Roger that, sir," Havana Tiger said. He waved one fist in the air to Charlie Team and headed down the damp concrete steps to the ground floor of the courtyard, Thoman and Gordy following him. I came down last and nodded to Hero of the Kurds as I headed out the gate, Gordy rushing left, stench of raw sewage strong again in the air.

The trucks revved up as we dashed out the house, drivers talking into I-Coms and radios, Lotto's team peeling back from the southern perimeter, Iraqi Arab men staring at us, open-mouthed, as we moved out, rubbing beads in their hands, their heads cocked to one side. We ran hard, hell for leather across the field, heading west through the mud. I looked back and could see Hero of the Kurds helping the mother up into Big Hungry's truck. The Kurdish kids were whooping now, incredibly happy, and their parents came out and waved to us and smiled. I waved to them and ran on, trying to keep up with Eureka Kid and Kentucky Rifle, the Guerrilla Fighter passing me like I was going in slow motion, talking into his I-Com as he swooped forward, leading the hasty raid.

Iraqi Arabs on the western sidewalks, across the field, froze and stared at us like they were glued to the concrete. We passed them and headed into a neighborhood of two- and three-story concrete and stone houses, women in long house gowns hosing down sidewalks and forcing rubbish into curbside streams in the mid-morning. Seeing us they halted, hoses held out, water falling all over the hems of their house gowns, and stared at us as we ran past bullet-scarred stone walls.

Rifles shouldered and light machine guns at the hip, the raiders stopped at alley corners and checked both ways and hauled ass, Gordy shouting "Clear, clear, go goddammit go!" when he'd check and clear a corner, Thoman racing up behind him.

Thomas led the hasty raid down the streets and alleys of Mosul. He was out five meters ahead of Morales, speaking furiously into his I-Com as we ran, glancing back and checking our six, nodding to us and pumping a fist.

Making the hasty raid, the raiders covering each other, we hustled, sprinting, skies clearing now in all directions, going down alleys trashed with clumps of black electrical wire and broken glass and across busted-up concrete pavement. Coming down a long, fairly wide street, we slowed. Our trucks met us, Thomas talking into his I-Com, glancing back as he talked and nodding, looking forward again and halting near the opening left to an alley. He ran over to Houchek's truck and talked to Hero of the Kurds.

The Guerrilla Fighter ran back and pumped a fist and pointed down the alley. Houchek stopped the truck some twenty meters south of us, and I could see the mother and Hero of the Kurds getting off the back of the truck slowly, Morrone pulling up now to our north, the Texan Watkins on Charlie Team's Ma Deuce, steady on the .50 caliber.

Thomas scoped down the alley and said, "Clear," and he pulled his I-Com off his flak jacket and talked softly into it, still talking into his I-Com as Lotto hustled up and met him at the opening to the alley, both of them taking cover just inside the alley wall.

I turned and checked our six, scoping balconies and rooftop walls behind us. Iraqi Arab kids came out on the balconies and waved, and I waved back at them and they grinned and jumped up and down.

The Guerrilla Fighter wasn't even breathing hard. Neither was Zen Master. I got behind a low wall. I could see clearly to the north and south down the street, our trucks rolling slowly now toward us, traffic backing up behind our trucks. I waved to Big Hungry and he pumped a fist, grinning back at me.

I looked back and could see Kentucky Rifle talking to Havana Tiger on a southern corner, same side of the street, gesturing behind us at rooftops and balconies, Havana Tiger listening and nodding and pointing to an alley corner between me and them.

Thoman moved up to the alley and scoped down it, scanning the alley, and glanced toward me and said, "Good cover, Mr. Tucker." I gave him a thumbs-up and he grinned. "We're close, brother," he said. He glanced up at a balcony, sweat pouring down his face.

They are smart, tough, professional raiders, I remember thinking. The best we have. Hard and smart. Able to make a hasty raid at the drop of a hat. On foot. Excellent raiders: solid communication skills, covered each other instinctively, always looking out for one another, always there.

Hero of the Kurds approached with the mother in tow. She tried keeping her head down as Iraqi children stared from balconies, and she grabbed at her black house gown with her left hand, pulling it up as she neared the alley. Thoman nodded to me and gestured down the alley as Thomas came up quickly, Charlie Team and the Zen Master following him, Tex relieving Thoman, securing the eastern edge of the alley.

Thoman hustled down the alley, securing the western edge of our hasty raid, traffic loud from a wide street at the west end of the alley. The alley was two-carts wide, maybe; I thought two horses running side by side would make it easily.

The mother pointed to a blue steel door set in a high, wide concrete wall. The wall was the color of ivory. There was a steel latch on the door. There was no house number.

In truth, it looked more like the rear steel door of a bodega on the Lower East Side in New York City. Pigeons swooped down at the west end of the alley and pecked at seeds and breadcrumbs scattered on the pavement. The mother moved toward the door. She stopped in front of the door and slowly lifted the latch.

We all stood off to the side—Hero of the Kurds, Guerrilla Fighter, Zen Master, Havana Tiger, Tex, and Eureka Kid, all away from the door. Guerrilla Fighter nodded to Zen Master and glanced in the direction of the door. Zen Master nodded quickly, squinting hard.

The woman rapped on the door and it creaked open and I heard her say, "Merhaba, merhaba." There was a woman's voice from inside, saying the Arabic response, "Merhaba tain." With a bejeweled finger, the mother lifted the latch. She smiled and stepped inside, grabbing at the long, loose folds of her black dress, dipping her head slightly as she moved forward.

Lotto rushed in, M-4 shouldered at quick-action, shouting "Down, stay down," in Arabic, Tex on his six right with him, the rest of us coming on behind Tex.

Entering the house was like entering a candlelit cave, dim light everywhere and dark walls, maroon and dark blue painted walls, rear windows covered with old gray wool blankets, a kerosene heater burning brightly in a small room to the right of us.

Lotto had one hand on the shoulder of a slightly built Iraqi Arab man and was lifting him up from a black rug, like a lumberjack lifting an axe. The man wore a white dishtasha.

The man was perhaps in his early thirties and had a thick black mustache. His hair was black and unkempt. He had the five-day beard stubble common to Iraqi Arab men. He shuffled slightly on his feet.

Another Iraqi Arab man, of similar age, heavier-set, hung back against the wall, on his haunches. Both men shifted their eyes all around, never looking up.

There was bread and cheese on a small porcelain plate and half-empty glasses of tea on the rug. A young Iraqi Arab boy, perhaps six or seven, moved back against a wall, on his haunches, staring at us.

Hero of the Kurds looked straightaway at the mother's son and asked him if he'd planned the ambush on the Scouts on September 13, 2003.

Zen Master stared at the man, and Eureka Kid glanced over at him. The mother looked down. Guerrilla Fighter set his right hand on the butt of his sidearm, M-4 cradled in his left, scanning the room.

"*Naam*," the man replied, Arabic for "yes."

Hero of the Kurds smiled at me. The man looked down, still shuffling his feet. Gordy nodded, his face hard. Thomas stepped toward the man and spoke softly to Hero of the Kurds. I moved over toward the kitchen.

Tex was clearing the kitchen. He was checking through cabinets and closets, looking inside the stove and along the baseboards, sticking a long thin bamboo stick down into full rice bags, looking for ammunition and grenades and weapons. He glanced up at me and I said to him, "We got the rat bastard!"

Tex grinned, closing drawers, and raised his M-4 in one hand, like a guerrilla warrior raising a sword in triumph in Xenophon's time.

"That's so fuckin' punk! Fuck yeah we got the motherfucker. No IEDs here, no fuckin' weapons. Kitchen's clear, no worries."

I moved aside and he came past and patted Gordy on the shoulder. In the front room, a woman in a blue house gown was crying. She was perhaps fifty. She sat on a battered purple couch. The mother was sitting by her, saying "*Afwan, afwan,*" the Arabic for "I'm sorry." The crying woman kept on crying. She wailed as Hero of the Kurds talked to the insurgent, the insurgent saying "Naam, naam," to every question.

I heard Thomas say, "We got him, let's get him out, I want to talk to these people," and Lotto flex-cuffed the insurgent, tying his hands behind his back with plastic ziplock cuffs.

Lotto shouted back, "Tex," and pointed outside, and Tex rushed past us and out the blue steel door. The Eureka Kid, red-faced and sweating and a long way from northern California, watched over the women.

Zen Master took the insurgent outside and told Kentucky Rifle to keep watch on him. I followed Zen Master.

Eureka Kid came out and headed east up the alley, motioning to Big Hungry and Houchek, who'd kept the engines running, and they pumped their fists and the trucks crept forward, Watkins looking around, hands gripped on the triggers of the Ma Deuce. Behind me to the right of the blue steel door, Kentucky Rifle motioned to the insurgent to kneel on the ground, and the man nodded and slowly started to kneel. The insurgent was shaking his head from side to side as he kneeled. He wore a long grayish-white dishtasha. He raised his head up, looking west down the alley, and lowered his left heel, starting to plant his foot, like he was thinking of bolting.

"No," Thoman said, his voice hard, skies clearing now, shafts of sunlight beaming down in the alley.

Texeira glanced back at us from down the alley. Thoman said, "I've got it, Tex," and Tex nodded.

Thoman put the barrel of his light machine gun in the middle of the man's back and the man's feet went loose and he bent forward. I could hear the crying woman screaming now and she came halfway out of the blue steel door, and I stood between her and the insurgent, saying to her in Arabic, "*la, la,*" "no, no."

Thomas and Hero of the Kurds snapped their heads around and glanced back. They were already up the alley, headed east for the trucks. The lieutenant hustled back.

Thomas nodded at me and I stepped aside and she stood in the doorway screaming and wailing, tearing at her hair, spouting out Arabic like a dam burst by floodwaters. She was a veritable banshee, the insurgent's mother behind her, grabbing at her blue house dress, trying to pull her back inside.

Thomas stood right in front of her and raised his right hand off his sidearm. She stared at his hand, her whole body shaking violently, still tearing at her hair, screaming and wailing.

Her eyes followed his right hand as he raised it up like he was waving hello to her, and she began trembling. She wiped at her tears with both hands, trembling, her voice lessening a bit, her long, thick, black hair falling down her back.

The Guerrilla Fighter looked into her dark eyes like he was some kind of American Raider Voodoo Priest and kept his right hand off to the side. He kept looking into her eyes while she stared at his hand, and he cupped his hand slightly, curling the fingers very slowly, the woman still staring at his hand, mesmerized, and the woman stopped shaking entirely as she stared at his hand, calm now.

He dropped his right hand to his side, resting his hand on his sidearm, and she stood there in the doorway, unmoving, looking in his eyes now. The house was silent behind her. He told her softly to get back inside and she shuffled backwards, and he closed the steel door and latched it.

Thomas looked up and down the alley.

"We can get him on, right here," he said to me, and he talked into his I-Com, telling Morrone to move up into the alley.

Thoman hefted his light machine gun, the insurgent unmoving at his feet, and shouted to Tex, "On the trucks, Tex, we're rollin'," and Tex hustled toward us, M-4 held from the hip, eyes hard as he rushed up the alley, Thoman checking his six.

Houchek drove up and we threw the insurgent on the back of the truck and swooped west down the alley, gun trucks meeting us on the wide avenue. We rolled hard across town for the Strike Brigade Holding Area, where all insurgents were detained and interrogated.

The skies were blue now and swept with puffs of white cumulus clouds. The insurgent was huddled over near Hero of the Kurds, DJ Rush steady on the Ma Deuce, Zen Master saying to the insurgent,

"You're a real tough guy now, aren't you, you sorryassed motherfucker. You're going down you sonofabitch, you're going down. How does it feel motherfucker, how does it feel?"

The insurgent whimpered and I gave a thumbs-up to Lotto. He nodded and I looked over at Smith across from me and he gave me a thumbs-up and said, "We got this bastard. Let's get his partner in crime. Let's get the bastards!"

"Hell yes!" I shouted and checked our six, and Morrone was right behind us, his sunglasses on, rockin' hard, some twenty meters behind us. I waved to him and he waved back, smiling.

There was a hood over the insurgent, a dark-green sandbag Tex had cut open with his fighting knife. Tex kept one hand on the insurgent as we rode east across the dark blue-green beautiful waters of the Tigris River in the late morning, herds of water buffalo swimming toward a wide sandbank south of us.

We were rocking across the Tigris River on Freedom Bridge, formerly named Saddam Bridge, and one the Kurds had crossed with 10th Group Special Forces commandos as they'd liberated Mosul in early April. Houchek, wicked at the wheel and grooving hard, asked Zen Master, "How's it look back there, Sergeant Lotto?" and Zen Master saying, "We're good, don't wreck us Houchek. I haven't eaten yet."

I could see 3rd-502nd compound north of us, directly north where tall pines and cedar trees and wide-branched cypress trees shaded the eastern banks of the Tigris, saw grass high along the shoreline. Water buffalo grazed across the river in thick green grass, on the western banks, in front of Strike Brigade's headquarters compound. There were nineteen water buffalo, their horns wide to the sky, moving slowly south along the verdant green riverbanks of the Tigris under the bright autumn sun.

Houchek grinned and said, "Mr. Tucker, Sergeant Lotto actually talked today, mark this day in your calendar. The Zen Master has spoken! Hail, Zen Master! Long live Zen Master!"

DJ Rush shouted from the Ma Deuce, "That's so fuckin' punk!" and Tex laughed, warm breezes rushing up from the south as we reached Arab Mosul, Lotto's team in good spirits.

Lotto grinned as we rolled off the bridge and swung a left at a traffic light, grooving left into a heavily developed neighborhood in Arab

Mosul, everyone scoping rooftops and alley corners and balconies, trash fires smoking from heaps of garbage piled on the sidewalks. Iraqi Arab men huddled near a mosque, kaffiyehs around their necks, glaring at us as we rolled on, gray smoke thick on the sidewalks.

Hero of the Kurds talked in Arabic to the insurgent and the insurgent was silent, and I said "Mala Mustafa Barzani, peshmerga, peshmerga." The insurgent bent his head and Hero of the Kurds smiled broadly and slapped me on my shoulders and said, "Oh Mala Mustafa Barzani, peshmerga, Massud Barzani, peshmerga! We must find Saddam and kill him!"

I leaned toward Hero of the Kurds and told him that Strike Brigade commander Colonel Joe Anderson from New York City had told the *New York Times* that he didn't want Saddam captured, he wanted Saddam killed. Hero of the Kurds exclaimed, his eyes aflame, clasping his hands, "Oh, Colonel Anderson, he is the Ancient Warrior! The Ancient Warrior knows—to capture Saddam is a gift to the insurgents. The feydayeen, Saddam, Al Quaeda, Al Ansar Islam, all insurgents opposed to freedom in Iraq, they are all the same—they want a dictatorship to return here. Ancient Warrior speaks truth as the eagle flies in the mountains near Halapja!"

The insurgent hunched down further, shaking slightly as Hero of the Kurds spoke, and Zen Master kept him bent over in the truck, a hand on his back. Bradley armored fighting vehicles rolled by us, bristling with machine guns, and a sand-colored M1A1 Abrams main battle tank followed in the wake of the Bradleys, rumbling by like a great steel lion on the streets of Mosul.

Two Bradleys checked its six, the coaxial machine guns on the Bradleys moving slowly, counter-clockwise, and then back again, clockwise, as the armored column proceeded north away from the Mosul airfield. DJ Rush held the triggers of the Ma Deuce like he was holding onto life itself. He nodded to the last Bradley commander and the commander waved to him, giving him a thumbs-up under blue skies in Mosul, gulls gliding over the Bradleys and the Abrams west of the Tigris.

There were seagulls flying southwest of us now over the rooftops of Mosul and we rolled very fast, Houchek rocking us forward down a two-lane stretch of straight wide asphalt west of the airfield and braking smoothly, hanging a hard right onto Strike Brigade's rear supply base and main Brigade compound, a huge support facility on the southwest reaches of Mosul.

Bombed-out buildings everywhere, rubble and brick and mortar blasted to ruins and ashes over rolling hills, trees blasted into shriveled hulks, branches blackened and bomb craters dotted the gray hills west of the airfield. A few dogs roamed north in the rubble and children played among the few trees that still had leaves, small acacia trees the likes of which I'd seen thousands of in the mountains of Oman, where rugged acacia trees stand green in the cool mountain air in Omani highlands on the Arabian peninsula.

Iraqi Arabs were living in the shells of some of the bombed-out one-floor bungalows, plastic sheets and tin and wooden pallet boards jury-rigged for roofs, rocks piled up near their shacks, walls going up for new rooms.

Now the poorest of the poor were taking over the land, building houses on one of Saddam's former compounds, where the U.S. Air Force had blasted pillboxes and ammunition supply points of the Iraqi Army near the former Ba'athist airfield of Mosul.

And Hero of the Kurds leaned forward, the lines on his forehead deep like trenches, and shouted as we jolted over twisting bumpy gravel trails through Strike Brigade's supply base. "But we must kill Saddam and all Ba'athists who support the feydayeen! Hang them at Halapja!" Riding now in Mosul in the warm early autumn sun past ruins of Ba'athist ammunition supply huts and compounds, Hero of the Kurds told his story.

"Saddam was going to kill my wife if I did not return from Vienna. And he threatened to kill my children. There was only one choice. The Mukhabarat would've killed my wife and children, for sure, had I stayed in Vienna. I was jailed at Abu Graeb when I returned, of course. In prison I prayed we would be free from Saddam. That someday we would be free from his terror. Now the dream is real! Now we are living the dream! Oh these are glorious days, glorious days! America delivered us from our damnation!"

We rode on west past the bombed-out ruins and swung south on dusty gravel and dirt roads, huge convoys of U.S. Army tractor trailers headed for gates a mile west of us, gun trucks well armed with .50 calibers and MK 19s on point and trail for the convoys, dust boiling up under the huge black tires of the tractor trailers. DJ Rush wrapped an olive-green bandana about his face, dust all around us now, hills golden with wheat high for the harvest rolling far in the distance west of us, beyond the barbed wire.

Hero of the Kurds nodded, hand on his chin, narrowing his eyes. "That is why we must win! Our children must never know the horror my generation suffered. We must prevail!" I shook his hand and he smiled, nodding slightly, wind in our faces, wheat fields now golden in the sun and rolling west toward Syria.

We were near the Brigade holding center now, a small one-story concrete building, khaki-and-sand paint thick on its plastered outer walls. A beefy U.S. Army sergeant with no identifying badges waved us in, Thomas leaping off the truck as we halted.

I got out of the way and Lotto grabbed the insurgent and the men cleared the truck. The insurgent shuffled forward, out of sorts, and Lotto slipped his M-4 over his shoulders and grabbed the insurgent and lifted him up and handed him down to Thomas and Smith, raiders scrambling off the other trucks, dust coating our trousers and flak jackets and helmets, men wiping the dust out of their eyes.

McNair, Lotto, Hero of the Kurds, and Thomas walked the insurgent inside, the sergeant with them, leading them into the interrogation center for detainees at Strike Brigade. There were a few pines and oaks shading the interrogation center. The insurgent stumbled as they got him near a heavy wooden door, and Super Scout gripped his shoulder and held him up and they all entered, the door slamming shut behind them.

The raiders cooled out as we waited for the intelligence. Dalip and Nguyen, from Jeremiah Johnson's team, wiped down their M-4s, dusting them off with horsehair shaving brushes, and cleaned and oiled their bolts. Dalip, who loved hanging out in New York City and whom I called, "Downtown." He was ace with the light machine gun and M-4.

Downtown lit up a smoke and handed the pack to Nguyen and Nguyen nodded, fishing a smoke out from the pack and lighting it with a brass Zippo lighter, nodding his thanks as he handed the pack back to Downtown. Hootch was on the back of the truck, catchin' Zs, resting easy, his light machine gun mounted on the all-purpose steel machine gun mount that could fit a light machine gun, heavy machine gun, or Ma Deuce.

Dalip carried a light machine gun and had gone street to street at Karbala, house to house, like his buddy Nguyen from southern California, from April 5 to 8, 2003. They were both with Bravo Company, 3rd-502nd, at that time. I called Nguyen, "Cali."

Cali was a quiet young man from Orange County. His family had emigrated from Vietnam as refugees, in the wake of the Vietnam War. He was agile on raids and patrols, quick to learn, and he listened well to Chapman and Turcotte.

Chapman spoke of Utah as his team cooled out, Turcotte kicking back on the passenger's side, in the TC seat, smoking a Cuban and sipping water from a one-quart olive-green canteen.

You could see the pines in the snow and the hawks over the Tetons when Jeremiah Johnson talked of Utah. And the high ranges and the deep blue skies. You knew he'd walked those ridgelines deep in Utah and seen suns rise and moons fall with his wife and kids.

Chapman had listened to the wind in the pines and the roar of the mountain lions in the highlands and peaks of Utah all his life. He'd hunted many ridgelines in the Tetons in his youth, and he had the true hunter's respect for nature and wildlife that only comes with many hours of stalking and patiently tracking and taking down big game. There was a longing in his eyes when he spoke of his loved ones in Utah.

There, under the sun, waiting for the intelligence to come from the interrogation, believing we'd make another raid in Mosul that early autumn day, Chapman slipped off his Kevlar helmet and tugged their pictures, wrapped in waterproofed plastic, out of his helmet. He kept the pictures taped down inside the bottom of his helmet with olive-green duct tape, the go-everywhere, do-everything duct tape that the men called "one-hundred-mile-an-hour tape."

And Jeremiah Johnson smiled, holding out color photos of his loved ones. His kids were ruddy and blonde, like him and his wife, and they were smiling together with him in the photos. "I really miss my wife and kids, brother," he said softly, and he gazed out west at the fields of wheat on the hills rolling west toward Syria under high blue skies, a few clouds drifting east.

Chapman asked me of my journeys in Northern Thailand and Burma and the hill tribes I'd lived among, the Karen and Black Lahu and Hmong. There were clouds like white buffalo in the skies above Mosul, and I asked Jeremiah Johnson if he'd ever heard of the Legend of the White Buffalo, a Karen hill-tribe legend from northern Thailand.

He called Turcotte over. I sipped my brandy and the Pathfinder offered me a Cuban and I lit it, and Jeremiah Johnson fixed up a cold coffee for me.

The sun was hot on us now and our flak jackets were dry and the raiders eased back. Havana Tiger and Big Hungry shared crackers from an MRE and laid back on the trucks, eyes half-shut, kicking back.

Chapman nodded to me and I set the cigar in a rusted steel tin. The instant coffee was mixed with MRE creamer and sugar—delicious in the noon sun in Mosul.

I thanked them for the coffee and told them the Karen hill-tribe Legend of the White Buffalo, which I'd heard on the Thai-Burmese border in October 1992.

"There was a young Karen hunter, in a village deep in Karen highlands—what is today northern Thailand and Burma. He was an orphan. The older hunters had gone two weeks without bringing home game. Kids were sad-eyed—rice only goes so far. The village headman called the young hunter over. The kid had never hunted alone. The headman told him to go out, solo, and don't come back empty handed. The kid gathered his spears and knives, his hunting gear, and his bow and many arrows. As he was leaving the village, a young and fine nubile maiden cast her eyes on him. She asked the village headman how long the young hunter would be gone. The headman told her, he'll be back with wild game or he won't be back at all. The beautiful maiden thanked the headman and lit candles for the young hunter and prayed for him."

Turcotte nodded. "Victory or death."

Chapman looked at him and nodded. The Pathfinder folded his arms, grinning wickedly now.

"Bring back the wild game or don't come back. Save the village, damned right. Go on, Hawk," Jeremiah Johnson said.

"All right then. Six days the kid tracked. Nothing. No track, no scent. On the morning of the seventh day, he prayed to the gods of the forest, to the spirits of his ancestors, and to the spirits of the earth, rivers, mountains, and sky. This was the ancient way of the Karen.

"As he finished his prayers and got up off the jungle ground, he looked up through a break in the triple-canopy jungle and saw clouds shaped like white buffalo running across the blue sky. Now, the Karen believe that a white buffalo has sacred powers. If a white buffalo is born, it is well kept, protected, and given extra-special attention.

"He saw the clouds like white buffalo and he prayed a prayer of gratitude to the sky god, for making the clouds like white buffalo on that day. He stepped forward and started to cross a stream, toward a glade just above the opposite shore. A white buffalo, its eyes shining golden in the morning light, leaped out of the jungle on the far side of the glade and stared straight at him. The kid froze and then moved slowly forward, crossing the stream and keeping his eyes on the white buffalo. As he stepped on the western shore, the white buffalo bolted back into the jungle.

"The kid carried on up the short steep hill to the glade. As he reached the glade, three wild boars rushed out. He drew his spears and killed two. The boars were mature, very healthy.

"Two mature wild boars meant three days of fresh game for his people. He wrapped the meat in banana leaves and palm leaves and tied it tight with slivers of bamboo. He knew he could make it back to the village by the next dawn, running straight across ridgelines, as the crow flies, if he ran all night. He took off, the meat secured in his leather shoulder bags.

"Dawn came and he saw smoke rising from the morning fires of his village. Crossing a trail, a huge buck came from out of nowhere. The kid speared the buck in the side and it slowed; he drew three arrows and shot it dead. The kid was weary but ecstatic now. He had game for a week, easy, for the village, just with the deer meat.

"He wrapped the venison as he'd wrapped the wild boar meat, filled his last shoulder bags, and hustled back to the village through bamboo stands and wild groves of banana trees. As he entered the village, children came dancing and singing, saying, 'The young hunter is brave, the young hunter is brave! Alone, he entered the mountains! He brings meat for the hungry children! He is Karen and he is brave! Long live the young hunter!'

"Exhausted, the kid handed the wild game to the village headman. He told the village headman he was going back to his hut to sleep and not to disturb him for two days.

"The village headman told him not to sleep just yet. The kid asked why, and the village headman told him to get clean and there would be coffee for him soon. And he told him to build a small fire in his hut, in the way of the Karen.

"The kid loved the village headman like a father, and he nodded his head and walked away to his hut. He bathed with cold mountain water, climbed the ladder to his hut, and changed into clean clothes. As he was building a small fire, he could hear a woman's voice below him, softly singing. He walked out and looked down from his deck and there was the young and fine nubile maiden. She was dressed all in white, in the way of Karen virgins, and she was singing, 'Oh mighty hunter, may I enjoy your company? You are a handsome brave man. Let me enjoy your company, mighty hunter.'

"Now, the kid knew he could only talk to a Karen maiden if she had her parents' approval to talk to him. If the woman had her parents' approval, she'd be carrying flowers from her mother's garden and her father's hunting knife.

"He asked her if her parents knew that she was here. She swore that both her father and mother knew, and they had given her their blessing. She held up flowers in one hand and her father's hunting knife in the other. He folded his arms, smiling, and asked her if she longed for him in her heart, also, in the way the falcons long for blue skies. She smiled and told him that she had cast her eyes upon him many times and prayed for him when he was away, on his solo hunt deep into the mountains. And he smiled broadly down at her and welcomed her up.

"She climbed the ladder and entered his hut and made coffee for him, and together they sat by the fire. She told him she'd lit many candles for him and prayed for his return. He thanked her and held her hands in his, and she asked him of his journey.

"He told her of the long hunt and no track or scent and how he'd prayed on the seventh day, and the clouds like white buffalo in the sky, and she listened to him like she was listening to the wind on a river. He told her of the white buffalo appearing mysteriously from the jungle and the hunt and crossing the mountains home, running through the night, and she held him close and they made love by the fire.

"You are not so tired, she told him as he held her close in the late morning in northern Thai highlands, and he laughed. She told him she loved the story and that the Karen would tell it forever, and that forever, wherever the clouds run like white buffaloes in the sky, the Karen will know good luck is with them, that the blessings of the gods of the sky and rivers and mountains and jungle are with them, night and day."

The Pathfinder and Jeremiah Johnson grinned, nodding. "Much obliged," Chapman said, and Turcotte slapped me on my back. Then the insurgent came out into the bright early autumn sun, stumbling slightly, his head still hooded, McNair leading him toward us. Thomas motioned to Chapman and he walked over, meeting the lieutenant as he came up with McNair and Lotto, the insurgent dragging his sandals across the gravel. Morales hustled up to them, helmet in one hand, M-4 in the other. The intelligence sergeant stood in the shadows cast by some pines on the interrogation room and gave me a thumbs-up.

I waved to him and I heard Thomas say to his team leaders, "Hasty raid, we know where the second one is. The guy talked, he gave up everything, let's roll." The trucks roared alive and the raiders leaped up on the back of the trucks, tossing on their helmets and snapping the chinstraps tight, their faces hard.

It was close to one o'clock and we swung out of the interrogation center, acacia trees swaying in a light breeze, jamming across the dirt roads of Strike Brigade's supply base, spitting dust as we rolled outside the wire, clips jacked in, riding hard and fast through Arab Mosul, wired tight.

I was in the lead truck with Zen Master's team, DJ Rush on the .50 caliber and Tex across from me, the insurgent to my left, his head down, Hero of the Kurds to my right. Zen Master and the Guerrilla Fighter checked our six, each with one leg over the gate, troopstrap firmly secured, dust boiling up behind us, sidewalks empty in the heat.

Big Hungry drove Charlie Team, coming right behind us, Havana Tiger next to him in the front of the truck. I pumped a fist to Sergeant Morales as we rode east across the Tigris under the blinding sun and he waved back to me, barrel of his M-4 over the doorway, pointing south. The great herd of water buffalo was now on the wide sandbank south of Freedom Bridge, milling about, ambling along under blue skies. The massive male buffaloes guiding the herd were moving out to its flanks, striding proudly into thick high wild grass, wide horns glistening in the sun and their heavy bulking black torsos coated with brown mud. Gold crescents and stars, symbols of Islam, glittered far in the distance from minarets and mosques.

All along the shores of the Tigris, saw grass rose wild yellow-green and golden south of Freedom Bridge, and fallow fields greened the eastern banks in Kurdish Mosul. There were no huts or farmers' shacks within eight hundred meters of the sandbanks on either shore, only roaming water buffalo and flocks of seagulls gliding over the Tigris south along the river as we rode to raid, just past one now. We raced north down the streets of Mosul.

Traffic was thick both ways on the wide boulevard north, and Houchek slammed his horn and broke hard and roared away, Iraqi Arabs trying to bum-rush our convoy at times, cutting in front of Houchek without warning, trying to weave between our trucks. And Houchek kept slamming on the horn and speeding up, rocking hard to raid. I called Houchek, "Rock-Steady," he was hell behind a wheel.

Iraqi police at intersections halted traffic and waved us through as two Kiowas swooped over us, heading east, perhaps two hundred meters off the deck, Nabi Younis mosque shining yellow-white in the sun northeast of us. Hundreds of pigeons gathered in the sun on the wide sidewalks below Nabi Younis, and white-bearded men with canes walked along slowly, dropping bread crumbs, pigeons tagging along on their heels.

There were great stands of fresh fruit and vegetables stacked in wooden crates near the Nabi Younis intersection where Blackhawk Mama had swooped down like a *deus ex machina* and rescued Hurt on that rough dark night, the market stand commanding a corner just ahead now. We rocked hard into the corner, Zen Master pointing north to Guerrilla Fighter and saying something quick and low to him, and Guerrilla Fighter nodding and giving Zen Master a thumbs-up. Rock-Steady made the curve smooth and righteous, rolling north off the turn, Iraqi Arab children waving to us, kids beaming in front of heaps of oranges and apples and green beans, and Rock-Steady pouring it on now, pedal to the metal, jamming.

I looked back and Big Hungry was right with us, Havana Tiger waving to us, and we sped down a two-lane road toward two old crumbling brick gates. Rock-Steady hung a hard left through the gates and halted, Zen Master leaping out and Guerrilla Fighter right with him, sun in their faces, Tex bounding off the truck, the insurgent bent over and flex-cuffed still, motionless on the back of the truck, DJ Rush on the Ma Deuce.

I jumped off and ran for a sidewalk perhaps fifty meters in front of us, Morales coming up on my left and saying, "Be careful, *hombre, tranquilo*," and running past me. On a sidewalk directly to our twelve o'clock, nearing the open doorway of an auto shop, Lotto stepped swiftly around stacks of tires and heaps of engine parts on grease-blackened pavement, his weapon shouldered. Iraqis were running away, arms akimbo, as the raiders closed on the shop: Chapman sprinting up with Bravo Team, Turcotte facing east and pointing to Dalip, Stocker and Nguyen setting up a hasty crescent-shaped perimeter eastward, traffic halting all around us, Thomas grabbing Hero of the Kurds and telling him to get down behind a stack of tires.

A big, heavy man in a khaki short-sleeved shirt and black trousers stepped out of the auto repair shop and Zen Master leveled his rifle on him. The man shot his hands up and spoke quickly, his eyes big as saucers. Guerrilla Fighter stepped up and talked with the man, the man keeping his hands above his head, shadows edging out from the stacks of tires on the grease-blackened pavement.

Tex came up and checked Zen Master's six as Zen Master looked over the man's ID, the guitarlike strumming of an oud sounding from a radio down the alley.

Thomas called for Hero of the Kurds and he hustled over and began translating. I heard Lotto say, "It's him, we got him," and Lotto turned back toward Morales and pointed back to the trucks, Iraqis running west down the oil-blackened street. Morales pumped a fist in the air to his team and we ran back to the trucks, raiders moving swiftly now, covering each other, bounding back over the potholed asphalt in bright hot October sun in Mosul, Rush hard on the Ma Deuce, the man flex-cuffed and looking down, thick rolls of flesh bouncing off his belly as Thomas and Lotto hurried him along.

It took four raiders to lift him up and into Lotto's truck. Smith said, "Damn, you are one fat bastard, you sonofabitch!" Houchek laughed and said, "He's headed for the Guantanamo slim-diet plan, oh yes!" Hero of the Kurds laughed, his coal-black eyes shining.

Up on the truck, I asked Tex about the man, and he said, "He told us he threw the grenades. He threw the IED that nearly killed Hurt and wounded Gordy and Chapman. We got the motherfucker. Fuckin'-a punk rock for fuckin' ever."

On point, leading us out of the raid, Rock-Steady drove like A. J. Foyt in his prime. The raiders kept their weapons at the ready and both insurgents sat bent-over under the Mosul sun, sandbag hoods over their heads. The grenade thrower shook, moaning something in Arabic, trembling.

Sergeant York stared at them and I said, "We got the rat bastards, buddy," and he nodded, smiling as we rolled west over the Tigris, water buffalo swimming in one great black herd north along the river, their horns swaying above the dark blue-green currents as they fought their way through the water, headed for the thick green fields in front of Strike Brigade's compound on the western banks of the river, blue-and-green tiles shining now on minarets near Strike Brigade's headquarters where Ancient Warrior lived. The skies were deep blue and cloudless now all over Mosul, and there were seagulls south of us, gliding on the wind on the Tigris as we crossed Freedom Bridge.

"Baghdad?" Morales asked, gripping his M-4 by its black plastic barrel guards as both insurgents came out of Strike Brigade interrogation. Thomas nodded to him. We jumped on the trucks, three thirty now in the afternoon, the men wrapping bandanas around their faces and strapping tight their flak jackets in the midday heat, acacia branches drooping down in the still, dry heat. West, beyond the wire, I could see donkeys ambling up a hill, up a trail alongside a wide field of wheat, and a boy walking slowly behind them carrying a stick.

Charlie Team on point, we drove on through the bombed-out ruins of pillboxes and long, low concrete ammunition warehouses to the Mosul airfield, the insurgents with Zen Master's team on the second truck. We dropped the two insurgents off inside three outer rolls of concertina wire surrounding a makeshift prison, the division holding center for insurgents. A gray U.S. Air Force C-130 landed as we cleared weapons; a guard asked for an ID and I showed him my passport, and the Guerrilla Fighter spoke with him briefly.

The guard, a 101st sergeant carrying an M.203, his flak jacket heavy with 40mm grenades, handed me back my passport and nodded, a convoy of U.S. Army "six-bys" and trucks rolling up behind us, dust coating his sun-reddened face a faint brown.

"Fly the friendly skies with the Screaming Eagles. Oh yes, they'll be in Baghdad before the sun goes down. They had breakfast in Mosul and they'll have dinner in jail in Baghdad, helluva' travel itinerary, don't you know!" Kentucky Rifle exclaimed, his eyes bright in the sun as he set his flak jacket and war gear beside his light machine gun.

His desert camouflage fatigues were plastered to him, wet with sweat. He ripped the cap off a liter of water, guzzled half of it, and handed it to Eureka Kid. Bradley armored fighting vehicles rumbled slowly past us, and the Guerrilla Fighter and Super Scout stepped through the outer strands of razor-sharp, silver barbed wire.

McNair frowned and said, "No rest for the weary, no chow, we've got another mission," deadpan, and Morales laughed, shaking his hand, saying, "Bullfuckingshit, Sergeant First Class, I don't think so. Charlie Team is fuckin' hungry, *hombre!*"

Super Scout grinned and stepped up on the back of the last truck, Watkins reaching out a hand and helping him up. I heard Thomas say to Chapman, "We'll eat at BSA," meaning we'd roll back near the Brigade holding area to Brown and Root's huge reinforced tent, the Strike Brigade rear-area chow hall.

The raiders slipped on their flak jackets and checked the action on their weapons, riding the bolts back and forth, and jacked in clips and laid long links of live rounds in the feed trays of their machine guns. A breeze came up cool from the east. Cedar trees on a hill west of the Mosul airfield bent back like bamboo in a Burmese jungle when wind rushes off a river in Karen highlands.

We made the chow hall in ten minutes or so, dusted off, and the raiders cleared their weapons and checked for any rounds in the chambers. The Scouts were meticulous when it came to accidental discharges and thoroughly checked each weapon every time they came back in the wire—anywhere.

We were sweat-soaked and tired and hungry and the chow was excellent. Steaming mashed potatoes with thick brown gravy, corn on the cob, and steak the Scouts called shoe leather, but soaked in soy sauce it tasted fine to me. There were cold sodas and sweet lemon iced tea, urns of piping hot strong black coffee, and apple pies, blueberry cobblers, and sheet cake topped with thick chocolate icing.

Smith told me I'd be better off in desert camouflage than my civilian clothes: "It's easy for a sniper, or any insurgent, to pick you out. They'll try to kill you first, the way you're dressed. Might think you're

Special Ops. You definitely look like Special Forces, with that vest. You're in combat with us, you need to look like us. We've been talking about it. We think you'll be safer in a uniform."

I'd finished eating and was drinking coffee. I looked down the table. Big Hungry was on his second plate. Morales and Morrone nodded at me, backing up Smith. I told the sergeant I'd wear a uniform.

"Good. Staff Sergeant Smith was on my sniper team. He's stateside now. He left a set of fatigues back at the hootch. He was about an extra-large, I think."

We shook hands and I thanked him. It was damn kind of Sergeant York and the Scouts to look out for me. I drank down my coffee and McNair glanced over at us, from where he was sitting with Hero of the Kurds and Thomas, and nodded toward the door.

With Watkins and the mortarmen and all three teams of Scouts, we walked out to the trucks, Tex and DJ Rush laughing in the bright early autumn sun, tractor trailers and huge six-wheeled open-bed trucks kicking up dust and gravel on a wide dirt road running north to south across the Strike Brigade supply base.

We boarded our trucks and headed for the river, eyes on, clips jacked in, scoping alleys and balconies and rooftops. Mad traffic, thick in the late afternoon, sun a distant western fire on shores Xenophon patrolled north along the Tigris in that long ago. No trash fires now, and the scent of raw sewage was faint on the breeze off the Tigris River.

Gulls glided over the Tigris and the water was wide and dark blue and glimmered in the early autumn sun. I rode with Charlie Team, Kentucky Rifle up on his mounted light machine gun, Big Hungry at the wheel as the Guerrilla Fighter checked our six.

The raiders rode back bolts and cleared weapons and rolled through the rusted light-blue steel gates of 3rd Batalion-502nd compound in Kurdish Mosul, two Kiowa Warrior gunships hovering down on a landing zone as we came through the wire. Dust and fine debris kicked up by the descending Kiowas swirled around us, and the raiders shielded their faces, turning away from the LZ. Morrone slowed our truck near the pines that shaded the saw-grass-thick riverbanks of the Tigris.

Fulks was running in his flak jacket, sweat pouring off him, and he gave us a thumbs-up and shouted "Hua!" as we jumped off the trucks. I could see water buffalo grazing on the opposite shore, dried mud caked brown on their hides as they dipped their horns and dug into the high wild grass on the western banks of the Tigris. Scattered gunfire echoed from the clusters of stone and concrete houses across the river in Arab Mosul, minarets on the western horizon like masts at sea.

Morgan leaned forward in his high-ceilinged quarters on the second floor of the HHC company building, a portrait of his wife on the wall behind him. It was nine in the evening on October 9, 2003; I'd been on patrols with Scouts and Mortars since the raids of October 3. He scratched at his light-brown crew-cut hair, eyes narrowing, reflecting on a question about Al Quaeda in Mosul.

The Commando was solid like a light heavyweight, and he trained in the mornings, slamming hooks and jabs and short, sharp uppercuts into a heavy bag hanging from a chain thrown over a steel beam in back of his quarters.

The three-story building had a flat roof floored with stone and was walled with brick and sand-colored stone. You could see for miles, up on the roof. The Scouts kept four olive-green nylon cots there; it was a good place to rack out. You could see the swift dark currents of the Tigris at night and the stars over the far mountains of Iraqi Kurdistan. East, some six hundred meters, there was an ancient stone mosque, its minarets tiled green and blue, stone an amber color at dusk in Mosul.

Morgan folded his arms, losing his grin, and sat back on his couch.

"Mosques are the conduit for Al Quaeda in Mosul. Mosques are the conduit for Al Quaeda in all of Iraq, no question. They are also the contact point for the Iraqi insurgency. Some mosques definitely have weapons. Feydayeen use mosques as safe havens. It's where initial contact is for feydayeen. The mosques are where everything is happening for feydayeen in Iraq and is still happening. I infiltrated mosques here with my intelligence network."

"You got people inside the mosques, relaying back information on the insurgency and Al Quaeda?"

"Absolutely. I used informants for infiltrating mosques. They'd stay for days, soaking up intel. *The Arab Mind*, by Rafael Patai, had a huge impact on me at Georgetown. My experience on the ground here really echoes his thoughts. You demand, and don't make open-ended promises—veiled threats are common in Arab culture. Stand and deliver and you'll be respected. But you demand respect, more than earn it. That's Arab culture, for real, what you see on the ground over here. I can only analyze off-ground intelligence, human intel. And I have to stress, I've been damned fortunate to gain outstanding human intelligence. Specifically, my guys were looking for anyone with anti-American, anti-Coalition sentiments who were planning attacks. Once I'd get the intel, I could work it. That information was vital to raiding markets, homes, and mosques. You know, if a mosque is being used to plan insurgent attacks, store weapons and munitions, and otherwise support the Iraqi insurgency or Al Quaeda or any anti-Coaltion forces in Iraq, we have every right under Coalition rules of engagement to enter it, search it, and clear it of any weapons or munitions."

He sipped from a mug of fresh-brewed Columbian coffee and set it down. He leaned forward, hands clasped.

"It was very tough, of course, to lose Specialist Derick Hurt to the IED attack. You know we're all pulling hard for Hurt. He's a great soldier, consummate professional, and very well-respected. I've lost two Iraqis, killed in action. The Iraqis I lost were collecting intel. Some do low-level source collection, some are strictly for overt patrolling, in uniform. The patrolling establishes legitimacy, gets people seeing Iraqis are taking over security. It's a solid human intelligence network, which has been crucial in the war. The war, in a way, just started. We're still at war here—it's all operational. This is our generation's war, and it'll be a long, drawn-out war. We must win in Iraq and we must win in Afghanistan. There is no alternative to victory. Here in Mosul, it really and truly became a street fight. Every day is a street fight when you never know what's coming around the corner and you have to hold the corner and move on, keep hammering, never drop your guard, stay in the fight. Recon, patrol, and raid. Raid. I cannot overemphasize the importance of reconnaissance. Reconnaissance is everything in this war. If your reconnaissance is solid, your intel is real good human intel, and you keep improvising, keep innovating, you'll seize the initiative and hold the initiative and you will prevail. I never step back when I box and I never retreat in combat. I believe you must attack and engage and overcome. You must never retreat in war. And you've gotta' out-think the enemy, out-savvy the enemy, be both more patient and more swift to strike— easy to be hard, hard to be smart. You know, one of the Iraqis I lost,

Waleed Ahmed, had been fighting against Saddam for over ten years. He told me, after an attack on us on June 12, 'they attacked you so they attacked my family.' He was fully committed. He was killed in action, trying to get intel on the attack, fighting the fight."

"Where was the attack on June 12?"

"On the police station," he said, gesturing north, upriver.

I nodded, remembering the police station we'd passed many times on patrol, roughly three kilometers north of the Widowmakers compound, a wide, solid concrete building painted white with blue trim, near the Emerald Bank. A huge open-air market was some fifty meters east, and a gas station. North, some fifty-odd meters from the police station, was one of the busiest intersections in Mosul, a T-intersection with concrete medians spreading from it east and west. West of the Emerald Bank, roughly 150 meters, stood the eastern approaches of an old, green, steel bridge spanning the Tigris River. "There was a demonstration on June 12," he said, going on. "In that time, we were incredibly busy. Raiding twice a day, easy. Putting down riots. All the Scouts and Mortars were raiding, raiding, raiding. And patrolling, patrolling all hours, handing out propane, trying to halt the black-market propane and gas. Gas lines were incredible. There was an ambush on a convoy as the demonstration was going down on June 12. The feydayeen had placed insurgents in a mob, near the police station. Feydayeen tossed Molotov cocktails at our convoy. I immediately developed sources and sent NISF [now the ICDC, Iraqi Civil Defense Corps]. I wasn't pulling any punches. I was trying to balance development projects with combat operations against feydayeen.

"Waleed Ahmed was meeting sources when he was killed. It really shook up the platoon. Shook us all up. War is cruel and just hits you in the gut, and you have to carry on. You know, you've gotta' stay in the fight. We buried Waleed Ahmed with full military honors. After three days of mourning, the platoon came back together. Our network got very big. We raided a mosque. I had evidence of people meeting to plan attacks and propaganda printed at the mosque. We raided the mosque and got weapons and ammunition."

He drank from his coffee again and set the mug down.

"Did you build your intelligence network right away, as soon as you'd moved up from Baghdad, on the air assault?" I asked.

He nodded. "Top priority, once we got here. That was the longest air assault in history, from Baghdad to Mosul. Well, for the first sixty days here, late April to late June, no one would talk to anyone else, only to me. Informants weren't giving anything up to anyone but me, not in this sector. I'd get a call and have to race back here, from wherever I was, for a back brief to corroborate the intel. Then, I'd have maybe two to three hours to corroborate before we could make the raid. You develop instincts, a sixth sense, on hasty raids. Sometimes I ran operations so sensitive that I didn't tell anyone. Not a soul, just sketched it out and grabbed Scouts and Mortars and said, 'Gents, we're raiding.' Surprise is everything on a raid, surprise and swift violent action."

"How much of the intel, from right off the street, is bogus?"

He grinned. A prayer call screeched out from what had been dubbed the Mosque of Many Screeching Prayer Calls. We waited for a few minutes, the Arabic wailing out from the mosque. Finally, perhaps on command from the Almighty Himself, the screaming stopped. Morgan cupped one hand under his chin, squinting.

"The culture here makes it interesting. You might think that the Arabs are at ease with you, but they may just be blowing smoke. So much is a face game. Are they telling you something just because it will save them face? They'll tell you things that don't always pan out. For every twenty things, you may get two. It's worth it. Those two things will help you win the war."

He nodded quickly, gulping down the last of his coffee.

"You get some evil perpetrators off the street," he said, going on. "We've nailed key Ba'athists, former generals. There are three kinds of insurgents we've nailed here: former Ba'athist Party regime loyalists who want the status quo back. They want a Ba'athist dictatorship back in place. Saddam gave them whatever they wanted. Women, cars, houses, you name it. Then you've got feydayeen Saddam. These are former Iraqi Army, and also simply Iraqis whose allegiance is still to Saddam. The second group has rudimentary military skills. The first group often hires the second group. They also hire foreign fighters—Syrian mercenaries, for example. And your third group—Al Quaeda and Al Ansar Islam terrorists. Al Quaeda and Al Ansar Islam are building up cell networks through the feydayeen." I paused, getting it down, and Morgan sipped from his coffee. I'd heard reports up north of Al Quaeda's connections to Al

Ansar Islam and the feydayeen from Kurdish military intelligence, but no American in-country had ever stated as such to me.

"Al Quaeda and Al Ansar Islam are coordinating with feydayeen Saddam?"

"Yes," the captain said, shrugging his shoulders, speaking in a calm, matter-of-fact tone. "Which is where the mosques come into play. It's very much a reconnaissance and intelligence war, and Special Operations will have an increasingly large role to play. I bet I can count on one hand the generals from WWII, Korea, and Vietnam who can tell me how to fight this war. By no means in any previous war was an infantry company commander, like myself, fighting like a CIA case officer. Moreover, we've done over two-dozen raids that were strictly joint Special Operations raids with CAG. We've done the planning—they've given me the ability to say no. "The future is down that road—merging line units with Special Operations on a broader scale. All 18th Airborne Corps-82nd Airborne, Screaming Eagles, and 10th Mountain will strike and kill our enemies in Iraq and Afghanistan with greater effectiveness if we integrate our Special Operations elements with our line units. And a vital part of all this, of course, is building strong, solid, human intelligence networks. Habitual relationships between Special Ops, line units, and human intelligence networks must be formed. Working with the Special Operations community, for instance, we use UAVs for aerial recon, real-time recon. As advanced as our technological recon assets are, like UAVs, however, the human intelligence cannot be replaced. There is simply no substitute for eyes-on reconnaissance. Which is why, in this war, your scouts and snipers are invaluable. Many times I've gotten intel with a picture and a ten-digit grid location, exact target location, and been told not to recon—that the human, eyes-on recon, was unnecessary. I disobeyed those specific orders not to obtain eyes-on reconnaissance and I got the eyes-on recon. I confirmed, via eyes-on recon, that the reports were wrong, denied the intelligence, got human intel on the perpetrators, and still carried out the operations. And nailed the perpetrators. I always tell the young lieutenants, and the men, of course, do not avoid reconnaissance. Reconnaissance is absolutely crucial to victory."

"Roger that. Was it difficult to cross-train the mortarmen for Special Ops missions?"

He leaned back, spreading his arms over the couch, and smiled.

"Not really. No, it wasn't hard to cross-train mortarmen for that—they're already bred for those missions, basically, by the army. I told the guys in Mortars that they'd be operating independent of their squads, and as sections, independent of each other. I told them they'd be carrying out what we generally look at as Special Operations missions, sure. I told them this back at Fort Campbell, long before we deployed—'Don't ever think for a fuckin' moment that you're not going to be doing it on your own.' We trained hard at Pat Cassidy Urban Warfare Training Center at Fort Campbell, and thank God we had Sergeant First Class Clark with us. And, of course, First Sergeant Fulks. Both veterans of the Battle of Mogadishu. Both these warriors have more combat wisdom in their little pinky fingers than the Atlantic's got salt, let me tell you.

"When First Lieutenant Joe Thomas became Scout Platoon leader, after we got up to Mosul, that gave us three veterans of Mogadishu in one company. Which merged into one Special Ops platoon, essentially, Scouts and Mortars together. Incredibly good fortune. When we got up to Mosul and got into the street fight, all that training back at Campbell came into focus. I got six more trucks once we were in Mosul, and extra machine guns. The trucks and heavy guns have been vital to our success. Now, with Scouts and Mortars combined as a raiding and reconnaissance element, I've got a thirty-man infantry platoon with .50 calibers, M240B machine guns, SAWs, MK 19s, M.203s, M-4s, and, of course, the 81mm mortars if we need to use them. If you properly train any infantryman for raids and reconnaissance, he can carry out the mission. I've seen it happen, I know it can be done. We did it. It's a testament to the resiliency and ingenuity and steadfastness of our fighting men, at the end of the day. They adapted. They improvised. They overcame. I am very, very proud of these men. It's an honor to command them and to lead them in combat."

"Einstein of Special Ops thinks SOCOM can operate here as long as they're needed—likely, roughly five more years. Do you agree with him?" The Commando nodded, cupping his chin with one hand.

"First Sergeant Fulks is a canny operator, always thinking ahead. He is a huge, huge asset to us. All of us, we deeply respect him. He is coming up on eighteen years on active duty and ten of it has been deployed. Well, with respect to what he said, SOCOM can handle whatever they're tasked with over here, sure. They are definitely going after Saddam, night and day. They nailed Uday and Qusay here, of course. Scouts came on and supported that mission."

"Do you remember the call you got, for that mission?"

His eyebrows shot up and he nodded.

"Day like that you'll never forget. I pulled together the Scouts and they supported the raid. More than that, I really can't get into. What I can tell you is that the men, all our men on that raid—Coalition Special Ops, 101st, everyone—really impressed the hell out of me. Now, we're going very hard after Saddam."

"On Saddam," I said, "Einstein of Special Ops told me he thinks we'll nail Saddam, as he put it, 'Before Christmas, in or around Tikrit, joint Special Ops mission/4th ID.' Do you agree with him?"

He leaned back, squinting, and folded his arms, nodding slowly.

"Saddam's Al Tikriti tribe. Well, that's the heart of his power base—Tikrit. Old dogs, new tricks. And dictators are all the same, really, their pride is their Achilles' heel. First Sergeant Fulks may be right—that's typical of the First Sergeant, to think that through in that way. It's a tough fight in Tikrit. My hat's off to 4th ID [Infantry Division, commanded in Iraq by Major General Ray Odierno]. One of our men, Private First Class Jesse McClure, has a brother in the fight there."

I nodded to him and sipped from my coffee. I kept my leather satchel, camera gear, and war gear in McClure's hootch and was fortunate to call him a friend of mine. I'd nicknamed him "John Grady Cole," after the hero of Cormac McCarthy's classic novel, *All the Pretty Horses*. Like the young, ardent-hearted cowboy in that magnificent novel, Jesse McClure was from deep in West Texas, from the town of Bronte, in the heart of cattle country, roughly twenty miles north of San Angelo. He'd often speak of his brother and their days under the sun on the far ranges—"I reckon I've saddled a horse or two, in my time, yessir. That's a mighty fine book," he'd told me when I'd met him in late September, pointing to my weathered paperback copy of *All the Pretty Horses*. "Doggone shame that young cowboy had to lose the beautiful Mexican girl, but that's love and war, I reckon."

On that evening of October 9, John Grady Cole was up on the roof listening to George Strait sing over Mosul from his small portable stereo and talking with Big Hungry and Havana Tiger.

"That's right. God bless the McClure brothers. Captain Morgan, can you tell me about the Whorehouse Raid?"

He busted up laughing.

"How'd you know about that?" he said, shaking his head, grinning.

"Havana Tiger and Einstein of Special Ops filled me in over the last few days. On patrols and back here, cooling out."

"My wife will kill me! Sergeant Morales and First Sergeant Fulks are not blowing smoke. Yes, Virginia, there was a whorehouse raid in Mosul." He sipped from his coffee, grinning wildly now.

"Einstein of Special Ops told me you'd suspected that Ba'athist loyalists were meeting there. Havana Tiger said the men doubted that it was actually a whorehouse. Scouts and Mortars thought the intelligence was bogus. But the men were quite enthusiastic, nonetheless."

His eyes brightened. He shrugged his shoulders, grinning.

"Right on all counts. The men were enthusiastic when the word came down in the mid-afternoon. This is so many raids ago. I think it was July. It was my personal goal to raid a whorehouse because whorehouses were used as meeting places for Ba'athists during Saddam's dictatorship. Also, Ba'athist-connected whorehouses were known storage areas for weapons and drugs. I was also targeting drugs on this raid. This particular whorehouse was frequented by many Iraqi and Turkish truck drivers. I worked the human intel and wrote up the op order. Nobody actually believed that I'd order the raid. You could hear the men talking, as we got on the trucks to raid. Everyone was upbeat and I stressed to the men that they had to stay focused and treat it like any other raid— anything can go down. We rolled out and got there in the early darkness. Big Carter from Mortars, he stormed in with the battering ram. Scouts cleared the whorehouse, checking all the rooms. It was wild. Johns were trying to get out the back, grabbing at their shirts. Arab women were walking around buck-naked. "When I got word from the Scouts that the whorehouse was cleared, I entered and checked things out. There was a balcony on the second floor and I remembered the doubts of the men. I stood on the balcony and shouted, 'Men, this really is a whorehouse!' The men cheered. I draped one of the bras off the balcony. It was all over the radio. I'll never forget my transmission to Brigade: 'Roger. I have in my custody eight Iraqi males, four young children, seven whores, and two AK-47s, over.' Leaving the joint, the madam was trying to talk to me and her tongue kept darting out. I was trying to explain to her that we were only going to question her daughters, and then, likely, release them back. Her sons, by the way, recruited clients to have sex with their sisters. Well, the madam started pointing at her tongue. First Sergeant Fulks laughed when she was doing this. Hell, we all laughed. She kept pointing to her tongue. We turned to leave and she told the translator that she was a diabetic. She asked in Arabic, 'Can you put some sugar on my tongue?' First Sergeant Fulks had a bag of M&Ms in his pocket and he handed it to her and she thanked us. No doubt made some truck drivers unhappy, for a few hours. The men talked about it for days, of course."

Early autumn rushed by in a haze of sunlight and dust and screeching loud prayer calls from mosques. The fields opposite the main gate began to brown in the autumn that came fast to Mosul, leaves scattered brown and gold on the streets and along the banks of the Tigris. We rolled on long night patrols down sewage-fouled narrow streets, stench abominable from the streams of raw sewage and refuse. Dawn counter-IED patrols and night "presence patrols," which the Zen Master called "contact patrols": "Division calls them presence patrols, but that's bullshit. They're contact patrols; we're inviting contact, rather than initiating action."

3rd-502nd raided a huge open-air market with Alpha Company, Bravo Company, and Scouts and Mortars on October 13, 2003, a raid for two thousand AK-47s that netted one AK-47 and one Iraqi insurgent. The intel had come in the day before that roughly two thousand AK-47s were in crates, brand-new, still packed in grease, at a huge market some one thousand meters east of the police station, very close to the Nabi Younis mosque.

There were Kurdish children swarming over Kentucky Rifle as he held down a corner, at raid's end. I talked to them in Kurdish and praised Mala Mustafa Barzani, and they erupted with cheers, shouting "Amerikee, Amerikee," leaning down out of windows and grinning madly at us, jubilant and all smiles.

I kept in touch with Kurdish military intelligence and General Zebari throughout my journeys among American warriors. As October went on, the Kurds strongly advised me to get to Fallujah: "American commandos there are striking at the Ba'athists, at all insurgents. Keep strong, brother, and be safe. May the spirit of Mala Mustafa Barzani and all peshmerga be with you. Raid with the Americans in Fallujah!"

Gray clouds began drifting daily over Mosul. The nights grew colder, and there was no word from the 101st on the war crimes reports I'd filed on September 27, the Gizi and Soriya war crimes massacres. I inquired at battalion and division level and received no reply; what particularly troubled me about the Soriya massacre was that the perpetrator, First Lieutenant Abdul Kharim Jahayshee, was widely reported by Kurdish military intelligence to be walking free in Mosul under protection of his fellow Ba'athists. The Kurds, most unfortunately, had no jurisdiction in Mosul; all they could do was hand over intelligence reports to the 101st and pray. And Abdul Kharim Jahayshee, who'd led the slaughter of Kurdish Chaldeans and Kurdish Muslims at Soriya on August 16, 1969, a village ninety minutes drive north of Mosul—and who was a confidante of the captured Saddam loyalist, Tarhar Yaseen Ramazhan (number eight on the list of Coalition's "most-wanted" in the "deck of cards" list of fifty-five)—still walked scot-free in Mosul. This caused me to reflect on just how intense and committed Petraeus was to capturing or killing prominent Ba'athists in northern Iraq.

As Ramazhan was in Coalition custody, I could not fathom why he was not being interrogated about Jahayshee. If the Kurds were right— and it was Kurdish peshmerga who'd captured Ramazhan in Mosul on August 20 and handed him over to the 101st in the first place—Jahayshee likely was leading insurgent cells in Mosul. All the more reason to raid and arrest him. The survivors of the Soriya massacre were still alive, and, as I write, remain alive in Dahuk and Kurdish villages north of Dahuk. I reckoned, as October drifted toward November, that prosecuting Ba'athist war criminals doesn't fall under a financial formula for winning a counter-insurgent war. But justice is better ammunition than money in war.

On October 21, the Scouts told me that enemy activity in 3rd-502nd sector had dropped off dramatically since I'd attached to them. The battalion commander, Lieutenant Colonel Alfonso Ahuja, joked with me about it, telling me, "Whatever mojo you've got, don't mess with it, the feydayeen disappeared after you came."

The lieutenant colonel was a tall man, hawk-eyed and easygoing, and he wore his M-9, 9mm sidearm on his right hip. He'd taught at West

Point in 2001 and 2002; in early 2003, he'd deployed with the Screaming Eagles and crossed the berm from Kuwait early in the war.

Near dusk on October 21, I was lifting weights with McClure and Fulks came toward us, his eyes hard in the early dusk.

We hailed Fulks and he told us, "3rd Platoon Bravo is raiding seven klicks north of Nimrud tomorrow. Air assault. Expecting heavy contact. Intel says there are three thousand mortar rounds—at least—in a cache. Two insurgent targets—one insurgent cell leader, one assistant. Feydayeen have been telling imams [Muslim clerics] at mosques in and around that village, 'We have many weapons and we are ready to spread them around.' Small village on the Tigris. There's a seat for you on one of their choppers, I reckon," he said, looking at me.

I asked Fulks who I needed to talk to and he told me to see Ahuja. McClure wished me luck and I shook his hand and thanked him, and thanked Fulks for looking out for me.

The colonel was in his office, a white-tiled, high-ceilinged room with the windows covered in layers of clear plastic and secured with one-hundred-mile-an-hour tape. He was talking with Boykins.

The colonel advised me to make sure that both plates were in my flak jacket before we headed out in the morning. I thanked him and cleaned my camera, checked film, and secured the plates in my flak jacket. There was some coffee, thanks to DJ Rush, who was standing radio-watch that dusk. I poured a cup of strong black coffee, grabbed my steel canteen, and listened to Norah Jones singing beautifully up on the roof from McClure's stereo. She was playing piano and singing ballads that had all the feeling of dusk in the desert in Arizona, when the reds and golds of twilight meet the first stars flickering softly in the blue of the evening.

Charlie Team came up on the roof and Havana Tiger told me that Bravo 3rd Platoon was solid in the street fight in Karbala that past April, and they were good men to be with, steady under fire. Eureka Kid nodded quickly, listening to Havana Tiger, and added, "Bravo Company is hard core, Mr. Tucker. You're with tough dudes, those guys. The professionals. Damn straight."

The Deerhunter, Staff Sergeant Charlie Everhart, had the Robert Fagles translation of Homer's *The Illiad* in his hand, and he joined us on the roof as Kentucky Rifle told us that 3rd Platoon Bravo had a new platoon leader, Second Lieutenant Bromberger, and that he was well regarded by the men. The Deerhunter nodded.

"Third Platoon's all right," Everhart said, his team nodding, some with their hands on their hips and others with their arms folded, looking at him as he spoke. "That new lieutenant is sharp. Just keep your powder dry and your head low. And don't get in front of them. Stay up with them, hell, stay up near point the way you like to, but don't get in front of them. I'd be carrying at least double combat load, myself, on this air assault."

I thanked the Deerhunter and he told us he was heading back downstairs, reading Homer in the evening as was his habit in Mosul. Morrone asked me about Burma, and I told him the magnificent Karen guerrilla fighters were true warriors—they'd saved my life on that long-range reconnaissance patrol deep in Karen highlands, behind Burmese Army lines.

Morrone nodded, and a thoughtful, musing look came over him and he said, "But you sure as hell don't miss the chow. Monkey meat is a taste you didn't get around to acquiring, by God!" We all laughed, up on the roof, Thoman passing smokes around.

McClure let Norah Jones play on, and he exclaimed, eyes big as saucers, "Hellfire, she sure can sing!" We lit up smokes and the men talked of their women and their dreams and journeys they'd made and raids in Mosul, of marrying their sweethearts and college on the G.I. Bill.

McClure asked me about Spain, and I told him of the Casa del Campo in Madrid in the spring, when sheep flood the golden green meadows and shepherds hail you as you run by their flocks, tipping their weathered hats and bowing slightly in passing and calling you *campeon*. And how the winter in Madrid is precious, flamenco bars and jazz bars open late in the night, winter skies clear and cold at midnight, mountain sun brilliant in January dawns. And the beaches of the Costa Brava north of Barcelona under the deep blue summer Mediterranean sky, boulders and sand and sea.

McClure smiled and told us he'd journey to Spain one fine day as the first stars brightened over the Tigris River and Orion glimmered in the eastern skies over the far ranges of Iraqi Kurdistan. There was no wind and the night was quiet, streetlights from Freedom Bridge casting yellow and white poles of light on the Tigris.

◉ ◉ ◉

The Tigris glistened wide and blue and rolled in sweeping serpentine curves south under high sandstone cliffs and through pure desert and endless fields, date palm groves dotting the desert in green clusters. Specialist Boggs shouted above the roar of the Blackhawk's blades at one thousand feet, "I'm carrying three times my combat load, Mr. Tucker! We all are!" Around him, his comrades nodded, pointing to their flak jackets and loam-and-green camouflaged assault rucks. We were maybe five minutes in from the LZ and three Blackhawks strong.

We veered west over rolling harvested fields and hardscrabble scrub desert, donkeys meandering about below us, and swept over mud-hut villages linked by goat and sheep trails.

Kiowa Warrior gunships flanked us, and they darted east as we shot down to the river, waves blurring and a fine mist sweeping off the waves as we swooped into the LZ, a long berm east of us. There was a field beyond the berm and a village on a cliff above the field, mud huts and concrete houses looming some one thousand meters east of the LZ on the eastern banks of the Tigris.

Boggs nodded to his comrades, lines in his forehead deepening, and they nodded back at him. I unlocked the five-latch safety harness and slipped it off my shoulders.

The Blackhawk landed smoothly and we all hustled off; I jumped onto hard-packed dirt, whirling dust and bits of harvested wheat coating us all in a fine powder, and Boggs came up around me and nodded, running, hunched over as the blades whirled above us. There were cliffs rising about a thousand meters east of us, beyond a wide flat wheat field, and I could see a mosque on the cliffs through my binoculars.

Boggs led us into a field. He was carrying an M.203 and we ran, setting in a hasty perimeter near a berm, his fire team taking cover behind the berm and bushes and taking a knee, scoping the fields and the village beyond. The choppers lifted and swooped west, blades beating a heavy thumping whirling sound like ceiling fans in a long narrow hallway on a hot summer day.

Bromberger, a keen-eyed man and about six foot two, had told me before we boarded the Blackhawks in Mosul that the Wahabi Muslim imams in the village had been calling for the deaths of Americans and Kurds. He called Sergeant First Class Stone, his platoon sergeant, over. I hustled over to them. I heard him say to SFC Stone, "satellite fucked

it up, we're at the wrong LZ, southern approaches aren't on the map."
Ahuja was taking cover behind a berm south of us and I waved to him
and he pumped a fist. He was with Bravo's company commander and
their first sergeant. Due east at our twelve o'clock, a Kiowa hovered on
the northern approaches to the village, a crowd gathering some three
hundred meters south of the Kiowa. Perhaps thirty people, and I could
see men in dishtashas through my binoculars, arms folded, scowling.

Stone, a burly, tall man carrying an M-4 assault rifle and an assault
ruck sagging with live rounds, gazed east at a line of scrub brush and
acacia trees perhaps one hundred meters east of the berm. Between the
acacia and the village, only one three-foot-high dried mud berm stood—
nothing but open harvested field to the cliff.

North, fallow fields with high wild grass and bushes ran some one
thousand meters. Boggs had set a light machine gun behind a rock on a
dirt mound, covering us to the north, the gunner prone in the dirt, eyes
on the high grass and bushes. A whitish-gray donkey wandered a hundred meters north of us through the bushes, a bell around its neck clanging in the mid-morning heat.

South, a dirt trail cut through the last berm and ran southeast and
snaked up the cliff to the village. There was a cypress tree south of us, soli-
tary near a junction of jeep trails. Flocks of sheep grazed perhaps four hundred meters due south of the cypress tree, two small boys in jeans and
loose baggy jerseys, heads wrapped in kaffiyehs, walking behind the flock,
a sheep dog big as a wolf tramping along beside the two young shepherds.

I could see Specialist Kemp with a mine detector strapped on his
back and a light machine gun scoping the junction, assault ruck over his
shoulders, covering down on the southern approaches. The Tigris
wound wide and beautiful and swift perhaps eighty meters west of us.
Kemp and his comrades all carried shovels, their weapons, and ammo;
their flak jacket collars were dark with sweat.

"Sir, the cache may be south of us," Stone said to the lieutenant. The
lieutenant nodded quickly, stuffing his satellite imagery map in his pocket.

"Map is no fuckin' good to us, now. All right. Let's set in on those
trees, recon for the cache."

Stone grinned.

"Roger that, sir."

The lieutenant rose and spoke quickly into his I-Com, then pulled his radioman over and talked into the handset as Stone gestured to his squad leaders. We rushed east for the tree line, setting in ten meters apart, Boggs getting his raiders in good fighting positions, setting up hasty fields of fire, the men scanning over their barrels into wide fields of plowed brown dirt and the crowd motionless in the village. Both Kiowas were swooping in swift S patterns over the village, water buffaloes rolling in the mud on the banks of the Tigris.

A gun truck from 3rd Battalion-502nd Delta Company rolled up in support. Dust thick on its olive-green fiberglass hood, it came down a jeep trail south of us and peeled off, heading west, and set in, a gunner on a Ma Deuce swinging the barrel around and covering our southern flank. I asked the lieutenant about the gun truck and he told me we had four in support, and that the other three, on the eastern edges of the city, were set in a loose crescent. Two were MK 19 gun trucks and two were armed with .50 calibers, he told me, motioning to his radioman and wiping sweat off his brow.

Boggs waved me over and I ran to his fire team, the men steady behind their guns, sun a furnace in the cloudless skies.

We were seven klicks north of Nimrud, on shores Xenophon and his light infantrymen had patrolled on their journey back to Greece, and Boggs gave me a thumbs-up as I took a knee behind the berm. The donkey moseyed along west toward the river, bells ringing and clanging. I could see a herd of water buffalo across the river and a farmer walking with them, a Kurdish turban wrapped around his head. I waved to him and he smiled and waved back.

"We're setting in here. All day, holding the berm. Over there," Boggs said, pointing toward the cypress tree, "is where the cache likely is."

The lieutenant was walking toward the cypress tree, radioman off to his left. The lieutenant had a M-9, 9mm sidearm in a black nylon holster strapped around his right thigh, and he walked fast, striding out, eating up ground. His radioman jogged beside him, hand mike at his ear as they moved toward the trail junction.

Kemp and his comrades had their mine detectors out, headphones on, sweeping the ground, inching forward, Kemp five meters ahead of his comrades, his brothers making a loose V behind him. There were three mine detectors. The infantrymen, who were not trained sappers but who were doing a damned fine job as sappers on a combat mission, would sweep the ground, halt, and move on. I told Boggs I was headed over to the minesweepers, and Boggs nodded as he kept eyes on the village, Kiowas swooping low over it. There were farmers threshing wheat to our south on the edge of a field, and the strong, refreshing scent of wheat and dust drifted on the breeze across the fields now.

A machine gunner grinned and said, "Call us Boggsy's Raiders, Mr. Tucker," and Boggs and his comrades laughed, steady behind their guns, sweat beading on their necks and foreheads.

Boggs shook my hand and wished me luck, and I wished the same to him and his comrades. I stayed low along the berm and hustled up to the minesweepers and heard Kemp say, "Sir, I've got something."

Kemp stood motionless.

Bromberger said, "Don't move, Kemp, easy now," and he stepped carefully over to Kemp as all three minesweepers held in place, Bromberger glancing anxiously at Kemp.

"Listen, sir," Kemp said, and he handed his headphones to his platoon leader. The lieutenant nodded his thanks and listened and he grinned. "Well-done," he said to Kemp, slapping him on the back, and gave him a thumbs-up. The lieutenant marked the spot with a white stake and gestured to the men to move forward slowly, and they came forward, inching through the deep, thick dirt, dust drifting up on them as they swept the ground. I took a knee and scoped the crowd. Three men were sprinting east, away from the crowd. They were young and bearded and the last man kept glancing back at us as he dashed away, east into the heart of the cliff-top village. The crowd clustered near the mosque now.

"Sir. Strong signals. Deep and strong, very clear," said one of Kemp's comrades in a low, calm voice. The donkey ambled along near the river west of us, bell ringing out. The water buffalo were in the river now, mucking about in the muddy waters and rolling around on the western shoreline of the Tigris. The lieutenant marked the position with another white stake and Kemp said, "Again, sir, over here," and the lieutenant moved up ten feet and marked Kemp's finding.

"Get the shovels out," the lieutenant said as he stepped toward the berm, scanning the fields and the village beyond, the company commander nodding.

Kemp and his comrades unstrapped the mine detectors and started digging, the soft loose dirt piling up quickly, the men digging furiously as their mates provided security. Stone talked with Bromberger and looked toward the southern reaches of the village.

"I know I'm going to hell, but I'm not in a hurry to get there today." It was Kemp, and he was some six feet deep now, his shovel in one hand, sweat pouring down his beet-red face. The tip of his shovel was wedged in hard between two mortar rounds. He looked up at us, hands at his sides, sweat pouring down his face, eyes intense. "Sir," he said, glancing at the lieutenant.

Bromberger kneeled down on the edge of the hole, keeping his eyes on Kemp.

"Go easy, Kemp. Lift that shovel out slow. Real slow."

Kemp lifted the shovel out like he was pulling up a weighted fishing line from deep blue sea and he breathed out, all of us shaking our heads, damn relieved there in the autumn sun in Iraq. He laid the shovel down in the dirt and leaned back on the edge of the hole.

"Well, sir, it ain't Vegas but it's definitely a jackpot," he said, a wild smile on his face, and his comrades grinned. Kemp leaned over and pulled out a white plastic case of 82mm mortar rounds. There were six mortar rounds in the case. I could see white plastic jagging out below where he'd pulled out the mortar rounds, more white cases piled deep in the ground, mortars jutting out, like looking at the jaws of a shark.

"Goddamn!" the lieutenant exclaimed and we all busted up. The water buffalo were cooling out in the mud and the donkey was standing still, flicking its tongue out at flies, and flapping its tail. I waved to the Kurdish farmer as he sat in the shade of three date palms across the Tigris, and he waved back to me and raised a hand high to the sky, as in salute. He was leaning back in the shade, smoking, his Kurdish turban lying to one side.

I sipped some water from an olive-green plastic canteen and congratulated the men, and Bromberger said, "I think we've got a helluva' lot of digging, no question."

And they damned sure dug, the men soaked with sweat as the morning went on, digging in shifts, the pit widening and deepening and mortar rounds in white plastic cases, both 60mm mortars and 82mm mortars, stacked about thirty meters north of the pit. There was no breeze, and long, wide green palms hung down from high brown pillars of date palms along the river in the windless dry Iraqi heat by the Tigris, men sipping their water and being damn careful not to waste it. By day's end, Boggsy's Raiders dug out some twenty-four hundred 60mm mortar rounds and six hundred 82mm mortar rounds from the pit.

We'd gotten a tip from the Kurds that the mortar cache was in this field, and I remember thinking that everything I'd seen of import, every capture of an Al Quaeda terrorist or Ba'athist loyalist, every raid that had taken down major targets in northern Iraq had come from the Kurds.

The August 21 capture of an Al Quaeda terrorist in Dahuk—the terrorist Abdul Kharim of the Al Quaeda Hamburg cell, who'd infiltrated northern Iraq through Syria—was possible because of a Kurdish barber, Kurdish police, and Kurdish military intelligence. The August 20 raid on Tarhar Yaseen Ramazhan in Mosul—a raid that likely contributed to the eventual capture of Saddam—occurred because Kurdish peshmerga nailed him. They got their own intel, worked the intel, and made the raid at a moment's notice. The Tarhar Yaseen Ramazhan raid by Kurdish peshmerga on August 20, 2003, in Mosul is a classic example of how to maximize ground intelligence in war and how to execute a hasty raid.

And the Kurds did it completely on their own—no satellites, no radio or telephone intercepts, no UAVs or super-sophisticated spy gadgetry, just good old-fashioned hard-core warrior reconnaissance, patrolling, and raiding.

As well, the successful capture of the two Iraqi insurgents on October 3, on the Payback Raid, came because of Kurdish sources.

Now we were uncovering a huge Iraqi insurgent mortar cache, and again, it was thanks to the Kurds. Each one of those mortars, placed in an IED, could kill at least one Coalition soldier or civilian working for Coalition Provisional Authority (CPA), or anyone else aiding us in our cause.

By day's end, we'd raided the village and captured one Iraqi insurgent. Boggsy's Raiders were brilliant, uncovering RPGs, mortar sights, cleaning rods for mortar tubes, magazine pouches, yellow detonation cord, an Iraqi Army field telephone, bandoleers full of 7.62-caliber bullets, bandoleers packed with magazines already filled (thirty rounds to a magazine, ready to be handed off and fired), a machine gun bipod, maps, and brand-new wooden stocks for AK-47s in freshly painted green wooden crates marked GHQ JORDAN.

There was a pipeline to the insurgents in this village in the heart of Ninevah province, governed by the prominent Ba'athist and former general under Saddam Hussein, Ghanim Sultan Abdullah Al Basso. Petraeus had appointed Ghanim Al Basso as Governor of Ninevah and Mayor of Mosul in May 2003 over the vehement objections of General Babakher Zebari, now a senior advisor to the Iraqi Defense Ministry.

Zebari, and many other Kurdish leaders, had vigorously protested the governor's appointment, telling Petraeus in May 2003 that the Iraqi insurgency would take close note of the appointment and increase attacks throughout all Iraq.

Later, on April 13, 2004, in Dahuk, Zebari told me that Ghanim Al Basso was forced to resign in late March 2004. U.S. Army Special Forces discovered that Ghanim Al Basso had been aiding Iraqi insurgents.

Gabe (a pseudonym), a U.S. Army Special Forces reservist who'd seen action in northern Iraq since late March 2003, and 10th Group Special Forces in northern Iraq reported to Coalition forces in northern Iraq that Ghanim Al Basso's brother, a key Iraqi insurgent leader, was funding and distributing weapons, munitions, and ammunition from Syria and Jordan to insurgents throughout northern Iraq.

Ghanim Al Basso had been giving information on Coalition forces to his brother and aiding anti-Coalition forces in every way possible since Petraeus appointed him as Governor of Ninevah and Mayor of Mosul. This was according to 10th Group Special Forces warrior Jake (a pseudonym), who had fought in Iraq from March to April 2003 and January to May 2004. Zebari, KDP commanding general for northern Iraqi Kurdistan, and Faisal Rostinki Dosky, director of KDP military intelligence, had previously informed me in late February 2004 that their grave reservations about Ghanim Al Basso's appointment by Major General Petraeus had been all too justified.

The American counter-insurgency specialist, 10th Group Special Forces warrior Jake, stated, moreover, that both General Zebari and Faisal Rostinki Dosky's assertions about Ghanim Al Basso's aid and support to the Iraqi insurgency since his appointment by Major General Petreaus were "accurate and complete; we took down Ghanim Al Basso and he was not shy about telling us he'd been aiding the insurgency all along. He was handing his brother everything he could and banking him with what he could. Ghanim Al Basso directed Coalition funds to the insurgents. That's fact. He was proud of it. Smiled when he told us. Our only regret is Ghanim Al Basso got off so lightly; if it was up to me, both he and his brother would be dancing with the seventy virgins in the Great Hereafter. General Zebari and Faisal Rostinki Dosky told it straight and true, Hawk. Accurate and complete. Ghanim Al Basso was dirty from jump street. And the Kurds understood that. No one knows northern Iraq like the Kurds, believe it. Kurdish intelligence holds top hand in this neck of the woods. Not listening to the Kurds here is like ignoring a hunting guide when you're stalking a bighorn ram in Colorado. Unwise. Especially when you weren't raised on this turf, in these highlands. Chrissakes, the Kurds have survived here for six thousand years. But Petraeus never really listened to the Kurds, and after a while, they realized that further conversations were pointless."

Both Ghanim Al Basso and his brother were Ba'athists under Saddam's dictatorship, like Abdul Kharim Jahayshee and Tarhar Yaseen Ramazhan.

Kurdish friends and comrades of mine complained bitterly about the appointment in the summer of 2003, noting that Ghanim Al Basso's strong Ba'athist ties were well-known to all Iraqis.

As the deeply respected Iraqi Kurdish artist, Seerwan Shakkur of Dahuk, told me on July 28, 2003, "Ghanim Al Basso was one of Saddam's generals. How can the Americans trust Saddam's generals? Why do you think Uday and Qusay thought they'd be safe in Mosul? They knew General Petraeus had decided that Mosul and all Ninevah should be governed by a Ba'athist, a general under Saddam.

"Saddam feydayeen and all Iraqi insurgents are overjoyed now, I have no doubt. The Ba'athist stronghold of northern Iraq now has a prominent Ba'athist in power. I thought America came here to destroy Saddam's dictatorship, not reinforce it. Petraeus made an incredibly stupid decision. It saddens me tremendously because we will pay for it; all Iraqis will pay for it in blood—the insurgency will grow now, mark my words. Why did Petraeus do this? Why? He understands nothing about Iraqi culture and history and politics and he spits on the graves of all Kurdish peshmerga who fought to free this land from Ba'athism."

Boggsy's Raiders flew back on Blackhawks. I rolled back to Mosul in a gun truck, with Delta Company gun trucks on point and trail. We were sweat-soaked and feeling good, and Iraqi Arab children shouted to us, "Amerikee, Amerikee," as we passed their mud huts and cinder-block shacks by the sides of jeep trails, rolling east for the main road north to Mosul.

All I knew on that bright, hot afternoon in a field by the Tigris was that without the Kurds, three thousand Iraqi insurgent mortar rounds never would've been discovered. We had no other human intelligence on the feydayeen cells in that village, none whatsoever. Each one of those mortar rounds, placed in IEDs, would've killed or wounded at least one of our comrades in Iraq, and thanks to the Kurds there are three thousand crosses that will never be planted in American and Coalition cemeteries.

As we came back through the wire, Ahuja told me that the Screaming Eagles would soon be on "redeployment operations," preparing to return to Fort Campbell, Kentucky. Days to come, I decided that it was high time to get to Fallujah. Boykins told me to contact Major Shervington at 2nd Brigade Headquarters, across the Tigris River from 3rd-502nd compound, for the Blackhawk south.

It was a strange, bad time in Mosul in the last week of October 2003. There were five days of mad gunfire across the river, like clockwork, morning attacks on Strike Brigade compound, from October 24 to 29. Americans would rush out, jacking in clips and carrying sniper rifles and light machine guns and M.203s, trying to get line of sight on the insurgents across the Tigris River, gun smoke drifting over the Strike Brigade headquarters compound like a thin gray mist.

The attacks varied in length and intensity. But we were not sending out raiders—moreover, reports came in of mortars being launched from the sandbanks south of Freedom Bridge, where I'd seen water buffalo grazing many times. I checked if counter-mortar patrols would be sent out and riverine patrols, to hunt down and kill the insurgents who were using the sandbank to fire mortars at Coalition forces in Mosul. But no counter-mortar patrols went out, no sniper and scout teams went out, no attempts to strike and kill the enemy before he could attack us were made.

And in the early dusk on October 29, 2003, after I'd secured approval for eight weeks with Task Force 1Panther in Fallujah from Major Watson, Task Force 1Panther XO, John Grady Cole talked about his own frustrations in the street fight in northern Iraq.

We were listening to George Strait sing from McClure's small portable stereo up on the roof in Mosul, gulls flocking over the Tigris and scattered single-shot AK fire echoing from north of us on the western banks, from 1st Battalion-502nd sector in Arab Mosul.

"Sounds like celebratory fire, bud," McClure said, frowning, lifting his binoculars and scoping the minarets and rooftops across the Tigris, remarking on the Iraqi habit—common throughout the Middle East—of firing off live rounds from pistols or rifles in celebration of feasts or weddings.

Live rounds abide by the law of gravity and can easily kill or wound people. But in the name of respecting Iraqi culture, celebratory gunfire is allowed by Coalition forces; made no sense to me, on the ground where AK-47s kill infantrymen and other Coalition forces. Made no sense to McClure either, and he was also no fan of the Coalition Provisional Authority ruling that all Iraqis are allowed one AK-47 per household.

"First, you're telling the Iraqis, in the middle of a war, 'Go ahead, keep your AK-47,' which is an assault rifle, a weapon of war. 'And get all the ammo you want, and by the way, shoot them off whenever you damn well please.'"

John Grady Cole knew rifles and he knew war and he spoke with a combat veteran's quiet confidence. He had teamed with Specialist Hurt in the actions north; Hurt was the sniper and McClure was his spotter. A spotter must be an excellent sniper, and, actually, the spotter will often be the more experienced and more accurate marksman of the two.

McClure, gesturing with his hands and leaning forward, George Strait singing from the stereo as minarets dimmed on the Mosul skyline in the gathering darkness, mist rising off the Tigris in the night, further explained how Iraqi insurgents use Coalition rules of engagement to lure in Coalition forces in the guerrilla war in Iraq: "Second, it's an easy way to suck us into an ambush. The genius who thought up this rule in Baghdad, like the genius who thought up the 'Sure, keep your AK-47' law, has never been in combat—I guarantee it. Nobody who's seen action would've even thought of, much less insisted on, either of these asinine laws. Look, the insurgents can fire off a barrage of celebratory gunfire and get our attention, fire off another barrage and suck us into the area, then hit us with RPGs and IEDs. See, they *know* we have to check out gunfire. But they also know, of course, that we can't fire unless we're directly fired on. The insurgents understand the rules of engagement we're under and use them against us. But they can fire any damn time they please. We're stacking the deck against our own men with the rules of engagement we have in Iraq. And I'm with Commander Marcinko, hell yes! You listen to the man who has seen action; that's the man who knows war! That's the man who can tell you how to *write* rules of engagement, because he's *lived* rules of engagement—in combat! Hell yes, the SEALS are wise! How can you write it if you haven't lived it? I reckon Commander Marcinko is right, bud: 'Rules of engagement are there because of lawyers, they aren't there because of war. War says kill the bad guys.' And we're for damned sure at war! Hurt nearly died because of major combat. That was a coordinated near-ambush by well-armed, experienced feydayeen. AK-47s, machine guns, and IEDs. They had the kill zone marked. Former Iraqi Army, likely. Our scouts are only alive by the grace of God, let me tell you."

He sipped from a can of Coca-Cola and set it down.

"Saddle and ride for Fallujah. All right then. Brother you keep your powder dry and your head down. You take damn good care out there. I reckon I'll be seeing you in West Texas, pardner."

We shook hands and McClure went down to his hootch. Morales came up on the roof later and handed me a Kukri fighting knife, the long heavy curved blade carried into battle for centuries by Ghurka light infantry of the British Army, warriors of Nepal. It had a wooden handle and it was original, of Nepal, and perfectly balanced. Morales lit up a Cuban cigar and handed me the Kukri.

"Carry it in Fallujah. *Vaya con Dios, companero,*" he said.

FALLUJAH

"We're at war here. It's all about winning the war. We have to make victory top priority, nothing else. And the true heroes are the eight men I've been privileged to lead at war here. The eight men in my squad. Combat sappers. For them to carry out the missions I've seen them execute, without hesitation, without any illusions that they'll be recognized for their service, is extraordinary."

Staff Sergeant Jeremy Anderson ("Street Fighter")
Combat Sapper, 82nd Airborne
Fallujah, western Iraq, February 4, 2004

● ● ●

I FLEW TO BAGHDAD IN A BLACKHAWK FROM MOSUL on November 9, 2003, thanks to Major Shervington, Brigade Air Officer for Colonel Joe Anderson's 2nd Brigade of the 101st. Just after dawn we ran for the chopper in Mosul, a hard driving rain soaking me and a captain, and lifted off from a landing zone near the eastern banks of the Tigris River. We swooped through thick gray skies and followed the Tigris south to Baghdad, the heavens clearing over central Iraq as the machine gunners held steady on their guns. Our choppers had been hit hard throughout late October and early November, and it was difficult to get air transport south from Mosul. The tragic downing of a U.S. Army CH-46, shot down by Iraqi insurgents near Fallujah on November 2, 2003, was the worst, with seventeen Americans killed.

I landed at Coalition Provisional Authority headquarters at noon on November 9, tried for three days to link up with the 82nd Airborne, and on November 13 met Lieutenant Colonel Brian Drinkwine in Fallujah, whom I nicknamed "Spartan Six," and his intrepid paratroopers of Task Force 1Panther (1st Battalion-505th Parachute Infantry Regiment), 82nd Airborne Division, at Forward Operating Base, Volturno. The colonel carried a 9mm sidearm in a tan leather shoulder rig with four clips. The 1st-505th had named their base after a classic action in Italy in WWII at the Volturno River.

In early October 1943, the 1st-505th had fought hard against Nazi German units at the Volturno River in Italy and had driven them back, seizing and holding key terrain. Their battalion symbol is a black panther. In the dust and sand outside his concrete hut on Volturno, I reminded Spartan Six of what the Black Lahu hill tribe from northern Thailand say: "If you would be a great hunter, watch the panther and learn." A stocky, amiable man, the colonel grinned and said, "Good to have you on board, we are a battalion of great hunters and I'm damned proud of my men."

It was good to be in Fallujah. I was certain that Kurdish military intelligence was right, just from the attitude and bearing of Drinkwine's men I ran into on that thirteenth day of November. These were hatchet-faced men with hard eyes who carried sidearms snug on the front of their flaks in quick-draw rigs and cut-down light machine guns strapped over their shoulders, same as the light machine gun Thoman had carried in Mosul. Special Forces were among them, lean, their eyes on fire like Thomas on missions in Mosul. They had Heckler Koch MP-5 submachine guns jury-rigged with mountaineer's D-clips and parachute cord to their flaks, magazine pouches full with clips as they perused maps and satellite photos under camouflage netting near the battalion operations center. Their boots were thick with dust and they wore khaki-and-green-checked kaffiyehs wrapped around their necks. I kept my mouth shut and grabbed a coffee, as is my rule whenever around Special Forces. But I was happy. I wanted to be with Americans who were striking hard at the people who'd killed my friends, Kurds, and who'd supported Saddam's brutal campaigns against the Kurds. From all I saw that first day on Volturno, I was sure we were targeting, tracking, and taking down Ba'athist generals, Iraqi insurgent cell leaders, and insurgent financeers, among them former Ba'athists who'd been key to Saddam's campaign against the Kurds.

Fallujah has never been a place of tranquility, though its clusters of date palms on both shores of the wide brown currents of the Euphrates and its fields of wheat are enchanting to the eye and truly beautiful, especially in dawn and dusk light by the river. Through the centuries, it has thrived as a haven for pirates of the desert, a crossroads for smuggled goods, and a refuge to pimps, horse thieves, bootleggers, and other criminals throughout the Near East. The Ba'athist Party—which, as Morgan noted in Mosul, controlled prostitution in Iraq—made a mint on Jordanian, Syrian, Iranian, Turkish, and Saudi truck drivers at brothels in Fallujah.

Too, it was near Fallujah that Xenophon and his Greek mercenaries, in the pay of Cyrus, Prince of Persia, made their stand on the eastern banks of the Euphrates, escaped annihilation at the hands of Artaxerxes, King of Persia, and began their epic March of the Ten Thousand through the heart of Iraq. Xenophon fought near Fallujah in September 401 B.C., seventy years before Alexander the Great led Greek chariots through Mesopotamia and into Central Asia.

In more recent times, Fallujah has been the base for smugglers who trade in illicit goods of all size, kind, and make, from Syria and Jordan to Iran on the west-to-east route, and from Saudi Arabia to Turkey on the north-to-south route. Stolen European cars, for instance, hustled from Turkey to Saudi Arabia and Iran (and from Saudi Arabia to other nations of the Arabian Peninsula, such as the United Arab Emirates, Oman, and Yemen) get handed off in Fallujah. There is a joke in Al Ain, United Arab Emirates, among Bangladeshi and Indian immigrant auto repair technicians: the Mercedes you're working on got pregnant in Fallujah and gave birth to a customs official's new house at the Saudi border. Fallujah sits dead-smack center on main highways running through the heart of western Iraq, which eventually reach all countries that border on Iraq. It is a major river-crossing and ancient crossroads. It is, in military parlance, strategic terrain, key terrain: terrain that if lost, will aid an enemy enormously.

Fallujah is where the deals go down in western Iraq. It's where the sheikhs and imams take their cut from international smugglers and issue their threats, promises, and praise. To imagine the kind of power the sheikhs and imams of Fallujah wield, in all of western Iraq, consider the Cosa Nostra in the metropolitan New York area of the United States prior to World War II, when the Cosa Nostra controlled the waterfront, prostitution, numbers, rackets, and pretty much anything they had an eye for. Then, multiply that power by a factor of ten, exponentially. That is the kind of power the sheikhs and imams in Fallujah possess: deep, wide, and deadly. Which, on reflection, may account for the visceral hatred that Fallujah sheikhs and imams have had for the Coalition's presence in Iraq and for their deep support of the Iraqi insurgency and Al Quaeda in Iraq.

To the sheikhs and imams of Fallujah, the Coalition is more threat than opportunity. Dictatorship favored the sheikhs and imams and ensured their prosperity. A democratic Iraq, where their power and influence is diminished considerably—and where rule of law, eventually, would decrease their illicit holdings—is no doubt viewed by the Fallujah sheikhs and imams as a grave threat.

Saddam Hussein ruled Fallujah by killing sheikhs who did not give him enough of the cut and by heavily rewarding sheikhs who joined the Ba'athist Party and did his bidding. The sheikhs who survive in Fallujah today are those who gave Saddam what he wanted and were themselves either prominent Ba'athists or strongly supported Ba'athism—on the sly. It has been said of Iraqi Arabs that the only politics they know are politics of violence, fear, and brute intimidation. That is unfortunate but in Fallujah, I saw little to persuade me that it is untrue.

The most powerful and influential sheikh in Fallujah and western Iraq, Sheikh Gazi Al Bowisa, of the Al Bowisa tribe, is a prominent former Ba'athist and long-time confidante of Saddam. Sheikh Gazi's business empire stretches from the Mediterranean to the Persian Gulf. One U.S. military intelligence specialist, Sergeant Ruben Quinones of the 82nd Airborne and Fort Lauderdale, Florida, would later tell me the following about Sheikh Gazi, on February 4, 2004: "Sheikh Gazi financially supports 85 percent of anti-Coalition forces in Fallujah and western Iraq. Absolutely. He is dirty and he was deeply connected to Saddam. His loyalties have not changed, not in the least, despite Saddam's capture."

Quinones built his own intelligence network in Fallujah. He was on the street every day and at all hours. He and his U.S. Army military intelligence team were on countless raids and patrols. I called him "Serpico."

Like that brilliant and brave New York City detective, Quinones is a warrior for the truth. He was the only Coalition Forces soldier, enlisted or officer, who was willing to go on the record—name, rank, and unit—about
Sheikh Gazi Al Bowisa's deep support of anti-Coalition forces and Al
Quaeda in Fallujah and western Iraq. One Coalition officer had this to say
about Sheikh Gazi Al Bowisa, on November 24, 2003: "It was my rec-
ommendation to kill Sheikh Gazi. We had enough on him to warrant not
just a raid to capture him, but to strike at him with deadly force. I called
for an air strike at a known location, and we had real-time intel. We had
eyes-on, he was there. Higher authorities canceled the mission, and the authorities were not military. When I asked who specifically canceled the mission, I was told not to inquire, or it would be my career.

"I would bet you the Brooklyn Bridge and all the East River beneath
it that Sheikh Gazi Al Bowisa was a prime CIA source during Saddam's
reign: he traveled throughout the Middle East and Europe, he is a
Ba'athist, he was tight with Saddam, and after Saddam, Uday, and
Qusay, he was the richest man in Iraq. Meaning, he's now the wealthiest
man in Iraq, no question. He has extensive ties to Syrian Ba'athists, and
Syria is a well-known sanctuary for feydayeen and Al Quaeda. I have no
doubt, now, that he remains well connected to the CIA. Otherwise, we
would've carried out the air strike. And you're right about Sergeant
Quinones: he has the only human intel network in Fallujah that doesn't
run off paid sources—he has solid ground intelligence, phenomenal
ground intel, in my book."

Serpico and his men and women knew Fallujah like fall knows harvest, and they never paid informants. Unlike the CIA in Iraq, Quinones
refused to buy intelligence: he got it the old school way in Asia—he
earned it.

As Quinones would later explain on February 4, 2004, in Fallujah,
"If you go spreading money around, especially in Asian cultures, people
believe they can tell you anything that will save face for them, first and
foremost, and in some way please you. Remember, the most important
thing in Asia is saving face. We are in southwest Asia. Will paid information be the intelligence you need to kill the enemy? No, it will be the information that does two things: saves face for the informant, and keeps
the informant paid. And at that point, the informant doesn't care about

you saving face. Because you already *lost* face, hugely—you already showed you have a lame, *money is all important* attitude toward understanding the culture. What's the worst thing in Asia? Losing face. Now you can see why the CIA, with its *money buys everything* operating schematic, is so disrespected and also, simply incompetent, when it comes to working the intelligence. It's easier to hand over money and sit in an air-conditioned office than it is to infiltrate a terrorist cell. It's also the worst way to gather human intelligence—to think you can buy intelligence. Especially in Asia. And once you lay those dollar bills in a source's hands, then *he's* played *you*: he's suckered you into keeping him on your payroll, and he knows that you don't know, or care about, the culture or the street.

"Know this: The CIA, with all its money and technology, did not provide the primary intelligence that nailed Khamis Sirhan and Abu Shihab [two key insurgent leaders captured in mid-January 2004 in western Iraq]. We did that, with solid human intel from sources in my network. How did we nail Uday and Qusay, Saddam, and practically every major raid in this country, successful raids, main target killed or captured? With solid human intel and tips off the street from Iraqi Arabs and Kurds, not paid informants. Same—same right here on the street in Fallujah. We're in a war here. All the intel I get, I get because my network knows one thing: I am here to kill or capture anyone who is funding, supporting, leading, or fighting with Iraqi insurgents, Ba'athist loyalists, Al Quaeda, Al Ansar Islam, or any other anti-Coalition forces. The worst is Sheikh Gazi, by far. He buys the majority of the RPGs and IEDs, pays people to make the attacks, and pays people to build insurgent cells. He is evil and he is slick. He was in bed with Saddam for years. Make no mistake, he is very clever."

Sheikh Gazi Al Bowisa's power in Fallujah is further instructive of Ba'athist power in Iraq.

Sheikh Gazi Al Bowisa's ties to the Ba'athist Party reflect how Saddam used Ba'athism, a pan-Arab nationalist political theory formed by three Syrian intellectuals (Michel Aflaq, Zaki al-Arsuzi, and Salah al-Din al-Bitar) in the early twentieth century, to his own ends. Ironically, the word *ba'ath* in Arabic means rebirth, yet little was born from Ba'athism in Iraq but terror.

Sheikh Gazi Al Bowisa, like many prominent Ba'athists, supported Saddam's dictatorship out of both greed and fear: Greed for the treasure

Saddam promised to prominent Iraqi businessmen, sheikhs, and imams if they became party members. Fear born of Iraqi Ba'athists' well-earned reputation for violent reprisal, fear of losing money, fear of a knock on the door in the middle of the night from the Mukhabarat. If one wanted to attain positions of status and privilege in the dictatorship, Ba'athist Party membership was mandatory during Saddam's reign. Saddam's brand of Ba'athism relied heavily on three- to seven-member cells, which held enormous power at a neighborhood and village level. However, individual cells rarely knew one another, which made Saddam's power, flowing from the top down, even more cunning; outside of Kurdistan, *anyone* could be a Ba'athist informant or spy. Even in Kurdistan, where resistance to Saddam's reign was the strongest, longest, most organized and most active, there were turncoat Kurds who were Ba'athists and made out very well from their connections to Saddam, though they are not enjoying life too terribly much since April 2003.

Further consolidating his power by placing Al Tikriti tribal members in many key positions throughout his dictatorship, Saddam wove an intricate web of Ba'athist power that had all the trappings of Arab nationalism, including an intense and virulent hatred of Israel. Al Tikriti tribe was Saddam's tribe, of course, from his hometown of Tikrit (where he was eventually captured on December 13, 2003, by U.S. Special Operations commandos and elements of Major General Ray Odierno's 4th Infantry Division, as predicted by Fulks).

Saddam struck at Israel first, with Scud missiles, after invading and occupying Kuwait in August 1990. The Palestinian Liberation Organization, which at the time was led by Yasser Arafat, backed Saddam's invasion of Kuwait to the hilt. This was despite Arafat's large debt to ruling sheikhs of Kuwait, whose signatures on contracts with Arafat in the early 1960s guaranteed huge income for Arafat, which he immediately used as the foundation money for Fatah, the military arm of the PLO. But Arafat knew in the fall of 1990 that Saddam was an ally against Israel, and that's all Arafat really needed to know. The Israelis had no doubts about Saddam's designs on Israel and had, nearly a decade earlier, launched a daring air strike against Saddam's nuclear facilities in 1981.

I am writing in late November 2004, over a year since I was fortunate to join raids and patrols in Fallujah with Lieutenant Colonel Drinkwine and his paratroopers and the light infantrymen of 10th

Mountain Division, supported by M1A1 Abrams tanks and Bradley fighting vehicles of the Big Red One (First Infantry Division, U.S. Army). First Marine Division, which relieved the 82nd in western Iraq on March 27, 2004, has been heavily engaged in Fallujah. Following the murders of four Blackwater Security personnel—who were not mercenaries, as some ill-informed media reported, but retired U.S. career military guarding a food-service convoy, one of whom was a retired Navy SEAL—in Fallujah on March 31, the Marines took heavy fire on patrols and firefights escalated to a siege.

Two American corpses, blackened and charred by fire, were hung from green-painted steel girders on the eastern side of one of the main bridges in Fallujah on March 31. The April fighting was fierce and some six hundred insurgents were killed, with many Fallujah residents fleeing the city.

It is still unclear why or who pulled the Marines out of Fallujah in mid-April 2004, when heavy fighting had gone down and two-thirds of Fallujah had been cleared by First Marines. But the city was lost to the rebels until early November 2004, when First Marines, aided by elements of the U.S. Army 1st Cavalry Division, Big Red One, U.S. Army Special Forces, U.S. Navy Seabees, The Black Watch Regiment of the British Army, Iraqi Army 36th Commando Battalion, and Iraqi SWAT teams, assaulted and cleared Fallujah. At last count, Coalition and Iraqi forces killed at least twelve hundred Iraqi insurgents and foreign insurgents, and intermittent skirmishes continue as I write from my home in a fishing village on the west coast of Malaysia in autumn 2004. In the November fighting for Fallujah, I was reminded of advice from a paratrooper sniper, Staff Sergeant David McGillivary, on December 13, 2003, deep in the western Iraqi desert some three hours southwest of Fallujah.

McGillivary is from Newberg, Oregon, built like a strong safety, and like many of his brothers in Fallujah and Mosul, a veteran of both Afghanistan and Iraq. Twenty-seven years old in the fall of 2003, Ranger/Airborne qualified, he led a Scout/Sniper team in Fallujah. I called him "Boss Sniper." He was very keen on desert reconnaissance. He carried the Barrett .50-caliber assault rifle and a 9mm sidearm, and he was an expert on all sniper systems.

"You needed a brigade, at least, just for Fallujah," McGillivary said, drinking coffee under high blue cloudless desert sky in western Iraq.

"And the rules of engagement: war. Now, you'd need a division. To clear, hold, and secure Fallujah, now, you really should use a division. Tanks at every major intersection and snipers in hides. Bradleys in support. Air support. Choppers. Special Forces. I wouldn't do it with less than a division now, honestly. We lost a tremendous opportunity to secure Fallujah in April 2003—even in May. The door was wide open," he said, shaking his head slowly. "And we gave it away, which is unforgivable in war. You can't hand your enemy a spear and pretend he's not going to use it. It's not a battalion-sized mission, either, but that's how the Coalition is fighting it. Examine western Iraq and a question develops very quickly: Why didn't we clear, hold, and secure key terrain in western Iraq when we had the opportunity, in April and May 2003? We had momentum. We had the guns. We had the warriors. And we had them on the ropes."

Sipping coffee and reading the haiku of Basho, a legendary Japanese poet, I felt a tap on my shoulder. It was Major Bottiliegere, whose deep-set eyes were red-rimmed and whose voice was hard and low. He reached out a hand and nodded toward the massive silver urn of coffee.

"Damn glad to meet you. Come on in, let's talk about the hit. Grab a refill if you'd like, plenty of coffee night and day brother," he said, and I followed him to the ops center. We entered a small room lit with long fluorescent tubes, the walls covered with satellite photos.

A map of Fallujah and surrounding environs covered one wall, the black-and-white map dotted with small, plastic red flags. I asked him what the red flags were for and he told me, "Each one means the raid went down solid, main target captured or killed." Eighty percent of the raids in Fallujah, as it turned out, were solid: main target captured or killed either by U.S. Army paratroopers, Special Forces, Coalition Special Operations commandos, or 10th Mountain light infantrymen. Big Red One was often with us, thank God.

The major grabbed a thin black pointer, long as a riding crop, and jabbed at a spot in the southwestern sector of the city, a cluster of indistinct gray buildings on the wall-sized photo of Fallujah.

"We make the hit on November 18 on Chemical Evil Fat Mama—Kurdia Turki Ali Halif, a Ba'athist. She was Chemical Ali's secretary. You're tight with the Kurds, I heard. Buddy, you came to the right place.

She's building feydayeen cells here. We'll hit her and her cell hard. Vegas—that's Captain Caliguire, Alpha Company commander—Vegas is dealin' jokers wild! Vegas is gonna' make the hit. Combat ops are top priority here." He folded his arms, squinting as I nodded to him. He wiped at dark reddish-brown circles under his eyes, two captains stepping aside as the Major—whom I nicknamed "Count Bottiliegere," for his Count Dracula-like sleep-deprivation ways—gestured toward a wide whiteboard hammered into the rear stone wall. "Kurdia Turki Ali Halif" was written in large blue letters on the whiteboard. I knew her name well, and also that of her boss—Chemical Ali.

It was Chemical Ali (General Ali Hassan al-Majid) who'd been hand-picked by Saddam Hussein to use weapons of mass destruction against the Kurds and Shi'ites. He was very close to Saddam. General Ali was in the Revolutionary Command Council; Commander, Ba'athist Party region, northern Iraq; Ba'athist inner circle; presidential advisor; and head of the Central Workers Bureau. He'd been in Coalition custody since August 21, 2003, nailed on a raid by Coalition Special Operations. Kurdia Turki Ali Halif was his secretary, had access to all his documents, and was despised by the Kurds for her deep Ba'athist connections and unashamed belief that the chemical weapons dropped by Iraqi jets on the Kurdish town of Halapja on March 18, 1988, and fired from Iraqi Army mortars on countless Kurdish villages—villages I'd walked through in the summer and early autumn of 2003 and met Kurdish survivors of Ba'athist-planned massacres—were entirely justified. From that moment forward, the missions I joined in Fallujah became very personal.

Bottiliegere pointed to a list of the missions for Task Force 1 Panther in Fallujah and western Iraq, tapping at the whiteboard: "Now, get your gear squared away, take it easy today. Recon going out tomorrow night and you'll be on it. Recon for Chemical Evil Fat Mama Ba'athist. Gotta' make the hit! Utilize our night fighting assets. Mr. Tucker, I want you at every targeting meeting and every operations order, unless you're on a mission," he said, setting his hands on his hips.

I went on outside. The Special Forces commandos had swooped. I stowed my gear and read Xenophon outside the ops center. The coffee was strong enough to fuel a fighter jet, and I met Command Sergeant Major Bryant Lambert, Sergeant Major Curtis Regan, and Major Timothy Watson.

Lambert was the battalion sergeant major; he shared a hootch with Drinkwine. Regan was the battalion operations sergeant major and shared a hootch with the Count and Watson, who was the battalion executive officer. Lambert, a giant of a man, was one of the last Grenada veterans still on active duty; he'd carried an M-60 machine gun and jumped into combat at Grenada in October 1983 with the 82nd Airborne. He had a wife and daughter in Fayetteville, North Carolina, and had served damned near everywhere in his long career. He'd earned his bachelor's degree on active duty. He had a dominating presence. I called him the "Judge." The Judge carried an M-9, 9mm Beretta sidearm in a shoulder holster, that day; on patrols and raids, he also carried an M-4.

He shook my hand and told me that he had to head over to Forward Operating Base St. Mere, the 3rd Brigade headquarters base, for a meeting with 3rd Brigade Command Sergeant Major Burgos. Paratrooper and light infantry called FOB St. Mere, "MEC," and like one-hundred-mile-an-hour tape for olive green duct tape, it was one of those U.S. Army slang words that defied questioning. Specialist Van Dyke, a hard-eyed paratrooper with Popeye forearms, walked up to the Judge and talked briefly with him. Van Dyke was Ranger/Airborne qualified, an Afghan veteran, and the Judge's driver in Fallujah. Van Dyke carried an M-4.

"Good to have you here, Mr. Tucker. We're riding to MEC; make yourself at home," Lambert said and rolled on with Van Dyke. Regan, carrying a 9mm on a black leather shoulder holster and six clips, poured himself a cup and talked about John Steinbeck under the heavy gray green-and-sand-colored camouflage netting. He very much enjoyed John Steinbeck's work, especially *East of Eden*. He also handed me histories on the 82nd Airborne and 1st-505th PIR, damned thoughtful of him, and asked me loads of questions about the action up north. I called him, "Mark Twain." Regan had the devilish wit you find in Twain's work, and like Twain, he was from the heartland of America. He was a native of Oklahoma.

"Are you sure you came to the right place?" he said, grinning like a madcap as I got up to go jogging. I told him it was good to be with American raiders in Fallujah and he nodded and said, "Keep your powder dry and your head down. If you drink the last cup of coffee, make the next pot, or you'll be on the next chopper up north, by God. Good to see you."

● ● ●

Late in the afternoon, I was fortunate to meet three U.S. Army soldiers who'd been in Fallujah since the first week of June 2003. Of all Americans in-country, these men had seen the most action in Fallujah.

They were U.S. Army reservists from Ohio who'd been in-theater since March 2003; they remained in Fallujah until March 2004, conducting psychological operations and aiding U.S. Army military intelligence in Fallujah and western Iraq. I called them "the Desperados": Staff Sergeant Grey Wettstein, a chain-smoking, affable gentleman with a wife stateside and more than sixteen years in the army; Sergeant Eric Viburs, the "Gladiator," a cheerful Midwesterner with real insight into Fallujah, like his fellow Desperados; and the young warrior, Sergeant Nicholas Browning, who'd been called to war from college.

The Desperados were on the prowl at all hours, meeting Iraqi Arabs in set appointments and on the street, roaming Fallujah night and day.

From their beloved city on Lake Erie, Cleveland, they journeyed to Kuwait on March 7, 2003, and were ordered to cross the berm on April 17 at two thirty in the morning. After chow on November 13, 2003, we sat around a dust-covered wooden table at dusk in the sand near their small concrete hut, and I listened to the Desperados talk of Fallujah's early chaos. "We moved here from Kuwait with five trucks and met up with a larger element in Al Nasiriyah, at Tallil Air Base. Iraqis were looting everything they could around Al Nasiriyah—fencing, guardrails, everything. I saw incredible poverty. I saw women in the desert scraping salt off the ground. Burned-out Iraqi Army tanks and blown-up, eviscerated armored troop carriers," Sergeant Viburs said.

Browning lifted a hand, raising his eyebrows. Viburs nodded to him and Wettstein lit up another smoke, breathing out slowly. "Every piece of equipment in the wrecks was looted," Browning said. "Yet there were no villages nearby, not even goatherds' tent caravans, *nothing* for miles around." Browning shrugged, laying one palm out. You could read in his eyes that he still saw that poverty. Would see it forever. Wettstein glanced at him quickly. "Roger *that*," Wettstein said, Viburs nodding slowly. Browning leaned back as his staff sergeant spoke.

"Everything was sketchy, it seemed, at that time," Wettstein said, going on. "The original plan of the war was that 3rd ID [3rd Infantry

Division] was to push up from Kuwait and cordon off Baghdad. 1st Cav [1st Cavalry Division] was supposed to actually take Baghdad. Now, it was supposed to take 3rd ID ninety days just to move on Baghdad. 3rd ID wasn't supposed to be on Baghdad's perimeter until June 20. June 20 was D-Day, as planned, for 1st Cav to swoop up and begin taking down Saddam in Baghdad. 1st Cav was supposed to move up on the ninetieth day; they would've been held, fresh and strong, strictly for that mission, until June 20." He rubbed out his smoke and lit another.

"Yet Baghdad fell after a twenty-one-day campaign," Viburs added, Browning and Wettstein nodding quickly, Wettstein squinting hard. "And 1st Cav, as a division, never moved. It's funny in a way now: our orders still read, "Attached to 1st Cavalry Division." We, us three Ohio wildcats, were supposed to roll up to Mosul and Kirkuk and serve with 18th MP Brigade. Never happened. We hung out in Baghdad, waiting."

Wettstein folded his arms. Browning nodded to him and Viburs sipped from his coffee. "April 28 was Saddam's birthday," Wettstein said, gulls high over acacia trees west of us, headed for the Euphrates. "The 82nd Airborne was in Fallujah that day. They were the first Coalition forces actually in Fallujah. It was godawful hot at that time. And it got hotter."

Browning's eyes skated toward him and Wettstein nodded to him, Viburs resting easy now, a black crow rushing up over a small concrete shed perhaps twenty meters behind us.

"Our paratroopers were shot at during a demonstration by Iraqis in Fallujah," Browning said, hands on his knees, leaning forward. "Some civilians were killed. The 82nd paratroopers were part of Task Force Gauntlet, which held Fallujah down for two weeks, then left."

Viburs, his face hard, set his coffee down.

"Uprisings went on," Viburs said, Browning nodding to him. "At this time, late April and going into May, we lived in Baghdad right across from the Hands of Saddam. Unbeknownst to us, 3rd ID was planning to move to Kuwait."

Wettstein put away his smokes and folded his arms, glancing around at all of us.

"A key thing to understand about Fallujah is the depth of affection for Saddam, and for Ba'athism," he said, Viburs and Browning nodding very slowly and looking at him. "Most of the people in Fallujah worked in some way for Saddam's regime. They cheered Halapja in this town, and they still would. The fascist brainwashing was on a Hitler-like scale. That's a huge part of the fight here, really, in the entire country—outside of Kurdistan.

"Well, when we toppled Saddam's Ba'athist regime, we eliminated the cash cow. We took down the dictator. Not everyone is happy when you take down the dictator; the people who were fed by the dictator, who took the money and bowed to the dictatorship and turned a blind eye to Saddam's terror, those people are right here in Fallujah. They want the Ba'athists back. They want their cut. It was easy money and they didn't care where it came from. Of course, if we'd rolled hard into Fallujah great guns and laid down the law, right away, I am convinced things would be very different right now. I honestly believe that we would not be here; it would've been resolved. And it would've had a great impact on the Ba'athist strongholds. That would've sent the right message to all Iraq: We are striking at the Ba'athist strongholds."

Browning nodded quickly, grinning slightly, and said, "The Thunder Run."

Viburs gave him a thumbs-up and Wettstein nodded once.

"That's right," Viburs said, sipping his coffee, "3rd ID had it all planned out. Massive operation. This would've gone down in May 2003. They called it Operation Thunder Run."

"Operation Thunder Run," Wettstein repeated, speaking each word slowly, carefully. He lit up a smoke, poker-faced.

"Third ID," he said, going on. "The Big Throwdown. Take Fallujah. Seize all bridges, crossroads, and junctions. Shut it down. Declare martial law. We will not take any more of your Ba'athist feydayeen shit. If 3rd ID had struck with the sledgehammer on Thunder Run, we wouldn't be here right now. And it was during that time frame, May into June, when Fallujah was wide-open for weapons caches, foreign fighters, Al Quaeda cells. Anti-Coalition forces organized, planned, stored weapons, munitions, and ammunition, and made all their connections to the imams and sheikhs in May and June 2003.

"Now, complicating all this, of course, is that every swinging dick in 3rd ID had been told in Kuwait, 'Your ticket home is through Baghdad.' So when 3rd ID got their orders to roll to Fallujah, the news didn't exactly boost morale in the ranks. The guys in 3rd ID were spent, bat-tle-weary. Exhausted. Third ID had seen action night and day. They'd put a lot of live rounds downrange. Look how they hammered down, fought 'round the clock, and drove on Baghdad. Incredible. Third ID went balls to the wall. And you try and take a unit who just laid waste to whole Iraqi Army units, and turn them into a peacekeeping unit? Bam! No, it doesn't work that well. Third ID was handed a damn difficult mis-sion here in Fallujah, after they'd helped secure Baghdad with the Marines. Fallujah is a key Ba'athist stronghold, and unlike Mosul, for in-stance, there is no ethnic group in Fallujah that strongly welcomes the Coalition as liberators, such as the Kurds. Well, the road home for 3rd ID didn't lead through Baghdad, it led to Fallujah. Putting myself in the boots of those guys, my comrades in the army, who had to deal with that—I can understand their frustration and their anger. And the wives and girlfriends, stateside; their men's lives and their family's concerns were directly affected by all this. You need clarity from leadership. We need leadership that speaks clearly and backs up what they say, at all lev-els. I've seen the strength of straight talk in the combat I've seen in my life. I've seen the wisdom of leadership that provides clarity."

His comrades sat bolt upright with his last words and Viburs ex-claimed in a hard, strong tone, "Roger that." Browning nodded to both of them and Viburs nodded to Wettstein and spoke up.

"Well, there was a FRAGO cut [fragmentary order] that released us from 18th Brigade and attached us to 3rd ID. We were sent to 2nd Brigade Combat Team, 3rd ID," Viburs said.

"Our first patrol in Fallujah was on June 8, 2003," Wettstein added, fishing out a smoke. He lit up and continued, grinning a bemused grin now. It was a grin I'd seen before, in Spain and Burma, the slight grin of a man who has seen action and survived and is grateful, and somewhat amused even, to still be around.

"We were with mortarmen from 1st Battalion-64th Regiment, an armor battalion. We got a call that there was looting. Mad dash, we rolled out the wire, headed for Route 10." He glanced at Viburs.

"Most affirm," Viburs said, wincing. "Iraqis were looting the former Ministry of Agriculture. All kinds of farm equipment there: tractors, ro-totillers, shovels, all kinds of tools. There were hundreds of people and no less than fifty big, open-bed trucks. Looters were on forklifts, putting pipes on trucks, stealing everything under the sun."

"We had three Bradleys, four M-113s, and two gun trucks. We rolled up and the looters scattered like flies," Wettstein added, lighting up another smoke.

"I leveled my weapon at a guy on a tractor," Viburs said in a flat and low tone, calm, folding his arms. "He jumped off the tractor and it kept rolling and slammed into a wall. He ran away."

"We detained about twenty people," Wettstein said, breathing out a long stream of smoke, his eyes merry. "We flex-cuffed them. And we found Iraqi guards on the site. They had AK-47s and plenty of live rounds. They were all in one corner of a small building, hunkered down, hands over their faces. You know any weapon is useless without courage. The looters didn't scatter entirely. A crowd of looters gathered outside the gates to the warehouse, knowing our rules of engagement prohibited us from detaining them."

Viburs raised a hand to him, palm open, and Wettstein nodded. Browning was sitting back now, one leg crossed over the other, a hand cupped under his chin, reflective.

"Now, we'd been there eight hours, easy," Viburs said. "Damn hot. And the mortarmen had pulled solid duty, done quite well. The mortarmen had secured the looting site, captured looters, and prevented the crowd from returning to loot the remaining tractors, tools, and equipment. Then their battalion and brigade command ordered, 'Release the detainees.'"

Wettstein sat up, shaking his head. Eyes fierce—you could feel his anger. It was palpable, even months after the incident.

"We were shocked," Wettstein said, still shaking his head. He breathed out hard, leaned back, and lit up another smoke, snapping his Zippo lighter shut very hard, the steel on steel click cracking loud.

"The mortarmen were really pissed off. Here they'd put it on the line to nail these guys, rolled up hard and quick, carried out their combat orders, and then had it all thrown away by their very own commanders. The lieutenants and senior enlisted men on the looting site realized, after this day, 'We might as well let the Iraqis in Fallujah loot, because our battalion commander won't let us arrest them.'"

I raised a hand and he nodded to me.

"Didn't that send the worst message possible to Iraqis in Fallujah and all Ba'athist strongholds?" I asked him, and he nodded quickly, eyes wide now.

"No question," he replied, and his comrades looked right at him.

"Sent an awful, awful message to Fallujah," he said, going on. Viburs and Browning leaned forward, eyes on their staff sergeant.

"And yes, to all Ba'athist strongholds," Wettstein said. "What it said to the law-abiding Iraqis in Fallujah, those who were hoping for real change in Iraq, was the Coalition doesn't care; it doesn't matter if you want to live by the rule of law, because the looters rule Fallujah. As time progressed, basic criminal activities increased considerably. Like stolen cars and stolen gas. For a long time, they'd sell it right out of the ten-thousand-gallon tanker trucks—Ministry of Transportation tanker trucks. And 3rd ID did not arrest them. The message in Fallujah that Iraqis received was, 'American soldiers roll over. You can do what you want and the Americans will do nothing.'

"I got my ass reamed by a captain and a lieutenant on a psy ops patrol. My guy on a heavy machine gun spotted an Iraqi on the street with an AK. Violation of Coalition law. I had a Scout squad supporting me. I went after the Iraqi with the AK. Later I was told that I'd led the Scouts, and my own team, into a dangerous situation. After the captain and lieutenant finished chewing my ass, I told them that I know it's a dangerous situation, we're at war, and we're making it more dangerous by pretending it's not a war. Their philosophy was that if it doesn't happen directly in front of me, right in front of my patrol, it doesn't concern me.

"Right before 3rd ID left Fallujah, the first IED went off in Fallujah on July 18, 2003. Third ID's response was to cordon off the area, on the western side of the old bridge. [Author's note: The old green steel bridge in Fallujah, near the riverside market, is where four Americans—Blackwater security personnel guarding food convoys under contract to Sheikh Gazi Al Bowisa in Fallujah—were butchered; two of their charred corpses were hanged from steel bridge beams on March 31, 2004.] The IED went off right across the bridge, on the western side. Third ID sent a tank platoon and Bradleys. It was a two-day operation. We were with them. Ten RPGs were fired at us, at one point. There was no response from the tanks or Bradleys. After the eleventh RPG, one tank fired back at the insurgents. Brigade, essentially, did nothing to engage the enemy. The Fallujah insurgency knew, from that day forward, 'if we set off IEDs and fire RPGs at the Americans, the Americans will drive away. They will not attack and destroy us.' If you're an Iraqi on the fence in Fallujah and you see that, are you going to have confidence in the Coalition? I think not.

"At that point, the anti-Coalition forces in Fallujah—foreign fighters, Saddam feydayeen, Al Quaeda, and your basic straight-up gangsters; criminals in that wave of 250,000 prisoners released by Saddam—knew that Fallujah could be an operations center and staging area for anti-Coalition forces, based on 3rd ID's weak response. And, therefore, the insurgents in Fallujah have been able to influence the population here in ways we cannot, because the Iraqis here remember the inept response of Coalition forces in Fallujah from April to late August 2003. In contrast, examine how the 82nd has handled the situation. When attacked, the paratroopers secure the area and call in a larger force to search and destroy. The paratroopers do not retreat. They do not back down. The 82nd doesn't negotiate with the insurgents, and that's wise. You need to keep raiding, keep hammering at them, and show them that we are here to kill anti-Coalition forces. Either they can join us in a new day for Fallujah and all Iraq, or they can make damned sure their wills are in order."

Viburs reached out a fist and Wettstein tapped it, Browning nodding to both of them.

"There was a pipe factory in Fallujah," Viburs said as Wettstein sipped coffee. "Manufactured the huge water pipes, and so on. When we first got to Fallujah on June 8, 2003, looters were on it like white on rice. And every time you went by the pipe factory, people were looting it. Even taking aluminum sheathing off the walls. Within three weeks' time, complete concrete buildings in the factory compound were gone. Only the foot-high remains of cut I-beams were left; the factory became a wasteland."

I raised a hand and he paused and I asked him, "You mean they even cut all the I-beams, tore apart the whole girders of the building? Beaucoup welding torches, gas—that's considerable money, taking down girders. Who could pay for that?"

"Sheikhs would be the only people in Fallujah with the finances to back that," Viburs replied. "Right, day in, day out—that is some expense." Browning sat straight up now and glanced quickly at his comrades. Viburs nodded to him.

"They saw no one would stop them," Browning said in a matter-of-fact tone. "They knew they could get away with it. And they got away with it." He folded his arms and leaned back.

"Looting and banditry have historically been ways of life in Fallujah," he said, going on. "This whole area, all Fallujah and western Iraq, has been a smuggler's paradise for centuries, a sanctuary for bandits running anything and everything from Syria to Iran, from Turkey to Saudi Arabia. It's where all the bandits meet and make their deals and hand out the cut to sheikhs and mukhtars. [Author's note: *Mukhtars* are neighborhood leaders who have great influence in Iraqi society; mukhtars are nominally under the control of a mayor, but in reality, they operate independently from any governing authority.] So the basic attitude of Iraqis in Fallujah, the ruling conviction, has always been, 'Where's my cut?'

"Like Staff Sergeant Wettstein said, the whole idea of doing the right thing has never applied here. The culture in Fallujah has always encouraged corruption—sanctified corruption. The imams have done nothing, historically, to change that. The Iraqis call Fallujah the city of mosques, but the imams in the mosques have done nothing to end the corruption. Imams have incredible power in Muslim societies. Nothing prepares you for a place like Fallujah. You can't get the faintest grasp of it until you're deep in it, on the ground, around the clock; until you walk the streets and listen to the imams preach their hate. Can you imagine churches blaring monster loudspeakers five times a day in Chicago or Minneapolis, 'You must go kill the police, they are the evil keepers of the law, they are the Devil!' But that's Fallujah, that's what we're up against. The imams in Fallujah are stridently anti-Western, which only exacerbates the difficulties involved in standing up a government here. The imams, too, want the dictatorship back; they prefer having the Ba'athists back in power. Until the imams either clean up their act or get cleaned up, nothing will change here."

"And the sheikhs? They must know what deals are going down and where the feydayeen stacks arms and munitions. Sheikhs have serious power in Arab Bedouin culture, no?" I asked.

"No doubt," Wettstein shot back quickly, nodding. "Sheikh Gazi has the most power of all the sheikhs. We're trying to get him on our side. The 82nd has done a damn fine job of raiding professionally, swiftly, and precisely—very high success rate here on raids, about 80 percent. They've rocked hard! Real aggressiveness. They've sent out the message to all Iraqis in Fallujah: 'If I risk my life to tell the 82nd key intelligence on anti-Coalition forces in Fallujah, the 82nd will come through, the paratroopers will nail the bad guys and get them off the street.' That's a tribute to Sergeant Quinones, also, of course. He knows Fallujah rock-solid and has been on the street; hellacious patrolling, great human intelligence network. I must say, there is a great difference now with the 82nd in town. The paratroopers make it happen; if you commit crimes against us or against Iraqis, we will hunt you down, we will capture you or kill you."

Browning nodded and slammed a fist against his knee. "The raids by the paratroopers get it done! They are exact. The paratroopers and 10th Mountain are tenacious. They are shrewd. And the people in Fallujah see that we are keeping our word, they see that we mean business." Viburs gave him a thumbs-up and Wettstein smiled, eyes merry again.

"The biggest thing, as my comrades have been saying, was that in the past, the insurgents in Fallujah knew they could fire on us and get away with it," Viburs said. "But since the 82nd came, the paratroopers ended that. And 10th Mountain—hell yes. Excellent battle coordination and execution, with Attack Company light fighters and the paratroopers. I continue to be incredibly impressed with their aggressiveness, their professionalism, and their calmness under fire. We really had to fight with 3rd ID, trying to get them to listen to us. That has not been a problem with Task Force 1Panther, with anyone from the 82nd or 10th Mountain.

"You know, I don't really care if people like my opinion. I'm here to win a war. We haven't won it yet, and we must win. But as long as you consider what I have to say, in a targeting meeting or operations-order meeting, in any meeting aimed at winning this war—beautiful, I know that my input is useful to the planning process. And Lieutenant Colonel Drinkwine has treated us all with great respect, very much so in this regard: He has carefully listened to our advice and our analyses. We're very much a part of the operational planning here now, and it makes our duty considerably easier, considerably more worthwhile. You really feel like you're making a contribution, when Lieutenant Colonel Drinkwine listens to you and takes your counsel into consideration. The key word here is respect. And it's good to have a commander who understands that, especially in Arab Bedouin culture in Iraq. Lieutenant Colonel

Drinkwine has a pretty solid grasp on the culture here, and it's helped him in dealing with the sheikhs.

"Of course, Legendary Medic is phenomenal; the colonel gives credit where credit is due, and he credits Legendary Medic's insight as crucial to the street fight in Fallujah, city of mosques and many sand fleas. And a few sheikhs. Well, the sheikhs are on notice: if we have hard evidence they are supporting anti-Coalition forces in any way, we're coming after them."

"Kurdish military intelligence told me Sheikh Gazi Al Bowisa was tight with Saddam. And that all his tribe is Ba'athist," I said.

"Right. Sheikh Gazi was a confidante of Saddam. And the Al Bowisa tribe is Ba'athist. As I'm sure you're aware, the Ba'athist Party was officially outlawed by Ambassador Bremer. A solid move by Bremer, one I personally would like to shake his hand for and thank him, but one that the Ba'athists have made an end run around, with their Return Party. Ba'athists are now well ensconced in the Return Party. They want a return to Ba'athist dictatorship, of course. Sheikh Gazi is like the John Gotti of Fallujah, he is the big Mafia don of western Iraq. Sheikh Gazi is the power in Fallujah. I see it like this: it's like John Gotti in New York City—unless you could prove it, you can't just go and get him. Without the hard proof, we can't just go and detain him. But we suspect he is behind anti-Coalition forces in Fallujah. It's no longer a secret, that's for sure. You know, the FBI and everyone else investigating Gotti made sure they had a very solid case before they finally nailed him. That's how I see Sheikh Gazi: We have to build a very solid case of hard evidence before we can detain him."

Viburs folded his arms. "*If* we can swing him around to our side, that would be fantastic. Will that happen? That's up to Sheikh Gazi. We must be very firm with people like Sheikh Gazi. They wield a helluva' lot of influence in Iraqi society. And he is the richest man in Iraq. Sheikh Gazi is the wealthiest man in the country. He has 80 percent of the contracts on American bases in western Iraq also, including the base we're on right here at FOB Volturno. Sheikh Gazi has the contracts on the food-service convoys, for instance, that supply our bases. Those food-service convoys are guarded by Blackwater security personnel. Nearly all the contracts on our bases in western Iraq are controlled by Sheikh Gazi. And Sheikh Gazi has his hands in nearly every business in western Iraq—vast power in this immediate area of operations. His business empire stretches from Syria to Saudi Arabia, throughout all the Middle East—from the Mediterranean to the Persian Gulf. So he deals with the Syrian government on a fairly regular basis; I'm sure he has deep ties to the Ba'athists in Syria. There are strong indications he is financially supporting the anti-Coalition forces in Fallujah and western Iraq. He's like a Mafia don, like my comrade said. If we take him down, we must be certain we have the goods, hard goods, on him," he concluded, leaning back now.

"Is there any one operation that really stands out, for the Desperados? One mission you'll never forget?" I asked.

Viburs grinned as Wettstein laughed and Browning chuckled softly. "The Abbas brothers," Viburs said.

"Absolutely! The raid on the Abbas brothers," Wettstein said.

Browning sat up, not smiling now. "It was the one good thing 3rd ID did here," he said. "They really ran the raid well, they carried out that mission tremendously well. Left the youngest Abbas brother without a smile, however."

"He was deflowering his virgin bride," Viburs said. "He turned his head and saw us, rifles pointed at him, and our translator told him, 'Get dressed, you're going to jail.' He kept humping away. Meanwhile, his wife saw us, of course, and she started screaming and kept humping. The translator told us, 'She is telling him, as long as you make love to me, the Americans cannot pull you out of me. Stay inside me, you must stay inside me!' Finally, one of the 3rd ID soldiers put his rifle on the guy's back and that convinced him he had to end the big fun. His wife screamed at us and our translator told us, 'She says she did not climax, you must give her another chance, you must let her climax!' Definitely not in the field manual."

"The Abbas family had stolen flatbed trucks full of looted bags of concrete mix on that compound," Wettstein added, lighting up a smoke. "We came for the brothers, however. The concrete was gravy. The Abbas brothers had been using video equipment to tape staged harassment of Iraqis in Fallujah. The Abbas brothers were dressing up in American uniforms and hassling Iraqis. Then they'd turn over the tapes to Al Jazeera. Al Jazeera aired those tapes for real, broadcasting them worldwide, with their correspondents proclaiming that all this was evidence of anti-Arab, anti-Iraqi American brutality in Fallujah."

"The Abbas brothers are career criminals," Browning interjected, Wettstein nodding to him. "Three brothers, all told. The oldest brother was the worst felon of them all. Saddam released him, like so many criminals released in the last throes of the Ba'athist dictatorship here, to wreak havoc and chaos."

"We found out that the youngest Abbas brother was getting married," Viburs said, Browning grinning slightly. "We worked our sources and determined that there was indeed going to be a wedding. Their neighbors confirmed the wedding, and also confirmed that the Abbas brothers were involved in terrorist activities in Fallujah. We showed up at sunrise, morning after the shindig. Third ID led the raid, Bradleys in support, heavy metal. Came in hard and fast. Surprised the hell out of the wedding party, no doubt.

"It must have been a helluva' wedding reception. There were stomped-down beer cans and empty bottles of Jim Beam and Wild Turkey and champagne bottles tossed all over a great big lawn. There were men and women coupled in the grass, clothes in heaps. You could smell the liquor in the air, the place reeked of booze. Eerie, really, to be raiding the drunken ruins of a wedding party at dawn in Fallujah. We were walking over drunken Iraqis as we made the raid.

"Inside the house, after we'd arrested all the Abbas brothers, we found two RPK machine guns, four AK-47s, one hundred thousand dinars [about $10,000 U.S.], linked ammo, and tin-can Molotov cocktails, all rigged, ready to be lit and thrown. When we asked the youngest Abbas brother if he thought he was going to throw the Molotov cocktails at us from inside a jail cell, he said, 'Oh no, those aren't bombs, they're candles. We use these tin cans full of gasoline and metal shavings for candles, all the time. We love the tin-can candles.' He was a real class act."

Rockets slammed into our compound around nine that evening, the whoosh and roar and thud of the 122mm rockets causing Captain Zawachewsky and Captain Huston to rush up to the roof, where you could see into the desert beyond the walls of FOB Volturno. A counter-battery fire mission went out, 105mm artillery rounds called down by Staff Sergeant Steinmeyer, an artilleryman and bear of a man from Michigan, to kill the insurgents who'd fired on us. Steinmeyer used radar and the Count was by his side in the ops center, calling down the counter-fire. Later, Steinmeyer told me the insurgents had likely fired from the bed of a truck and hightailed it.

November 14 was quiet; a meeting at the mayor's compound was moved to the November 15, and I readied my gear for the night recon.

"Desert Yetis fear no terrorist and crush Al Quaeda! Desert Yetis recon! Chemical Evil Fat Mama is going down! Call me Radio Free Yeti. I'm Specialist Richard Dean. My Ranger Warrior Platoon leader is up front. He's a father of two and my wife's pregnant, it's our first—hooeeee it's fuckin' cold tonight! Heading out the wire! Gonna' take a little trip into Fallujah, yessir! Fat Mama Chemical Ali's secretary, oh yes, she's evil! Ain't no doubt about it that's one fat evil mamasan! Whooeeee, going out the wire and it's past midnight! Recon, recon, Rangers lead the way. Go 82nd! Oh where are you tonight, oh where are you tonight, you can run but you can't hide! Fat Mama Chemical Evil! Whaddya say, El-tee?"

Thus I met the Desert Yetis, 1st Platoon Alpha Company, the pride and joy of Second Lieutenant Matthew Leclair, a mustang officer and former U.S. Army Ranger sergeant. We were on a mounted reconnaissance patrol in the wee dark hours of November 15, 2003, in Fallujah.

Four trucks strong, we rolled out the wire, men pounding gloved hands in the cold and dark. Specialist Cane from Detroit was on a mounted heavy machine gun on our lead gun truck, on point, brass 7.62-caliber metal-jacketed live rounds hanging down from his heavy machine gun barely visible in the darkness ahead. I called Specialist Cane, "Detroit City."

Radio Free Yeti had introduced himself as we rolled out the south gate, heavily armed paratroopers with shotguns and sidearms waving us on. We had a Ma Deuce on trail, .50-caliber gunner wearing an olive-green balaclava over his face and black leather gloves on his hands in the cold autumn night, gripping the triggers.

Leclair glanced back as Radio Free Yeti ended his breezy welcome and said, "Dean, we're eyes on now, out the wire. And don't call me Ranger Warrior Platoon Leader again! Just 'cause I had five years in the Rangers doesn't mean you have to advertise it to everybody. Radio Free Yeti, when God made you, he broke the mold! Mr. Tucker, I heard you were Marine infantry."

I told him that he heard correctly and our driver, the "Fallujah Wheelman," Private First Class Kevin Bozzelli from New Jersey, grinned.

"Mr. Tucker, we won't hold that against you."

All of us laughed now, heading into the darkness, stars ablaze in the far night skies, distant lights of Fallujah few and glowing a faint yellow white in the zero dark cold. A shooting star flamed through Orion's belt in the eastern skies over Baghdad. There was a gunner above us, in the open turret of the hardtopped truck, desert winds blasting cold in the deep night. He was "Patton," Staff Sergeant Christopher Smith, with an M.203. You could feel winter coming on in Fallujah. The moon was waning and high to the east, and it was zero dark thirty—one thirty in the morning.

South of us, as we rode a long two-lane asphalt road west toward Fallujah, the desert was a dark wide sea, scattered palms and groves of cedar trees amber in the darkness. The north-south highway, Route 10, was dead empty in the desert cold. Stars flooded the sky. The men were wide awake, scanning the night, eyes on, solid on the recon. I sipped coffee and adjusted my Kukri on my flak jacket as we crossed an overpass, city now starkly visible, a blue-tiled minaret lit up in the night. The men had their night vision goggles on, looking like they were going to hunt Godzilla of Fallujah.

Considering how Kurdia Turki Ali Halif had helped Chemical Ali murder the Kurds, I remember thinking that we well and truly were hunting Godzilla Woman.

There was a curfew on and it was being honored; the streets were desolate, occasional trash fires smoking on empty concrete sidewalks as we rolled through slowly, the scent of raw sewage strong on the wind now and wild dogs scattering as we approached. Strangely, the dogs didn't always bark; some of them would just freeze and then dash away, running off into alleys between half-finished cinder-block walls and mud huts and cinder-block houses roofed with tin and wood.

Rolling on empty streets in the city of mosques, we swung off to the west and crossed an empty field, garbage heaped along the sides of stone and concrete huts and houses, slowing down now. Our breath misted in the cold, the Fallujah Wheelman banging on the heater to no avail, Dean laughing as he gazed out at the night through the high-tech, green-lensed nightscope on his M-4. I said to Leclair, "If you guys are the Desert Yetis, does that make you the Jedi Knight, lieutenant?" [Author's note: The Desert Yetis got their nickname from the Yetis in the *Star Wars* films, produced and directed by George Lucas.]

The lieutenant grinned and said, "Before you say anything Dean, know this: *only* Mr. Tucker can call me the Jedi Knight. *You* still have to call me Lieutenant."

"What, can't we call you, 'The Jedi Knight,' sir?" said Bozzelli as Leclair scanned a row of houses west of us, on the edge of the field. A taxi came up out of the east, one light on, and heading toward us. It was some two hundred meters away, rolling slowly, dust trailing behind it like foam on the wake of a skiff at sea. It must have been blaring Arabic music because even two hundred meters away, you could hear the tabla drums beating and a woman's voice drifting over the field.

"No can do, Bozzelli. Only Lieutenant. Listen to Bozzelli, Dean, he'll set you straight. None of that Ranger Warrior Platoon Leader crap from him, Dean! Bozzelli, there's hope for you yet. I have faith in you. Friggin' New Jersey wild man. Truly you are the Fallujah Wheelman. Out of earshot, call me anything you damned well please. I'm sure you do. Mr. Tucker, check this out, Dean, hand him your NODs," said the Jedi Knight, and Radio Free Yeti took his radio handset off first, then slipped his night vision goggles off, and I scoped the field and the row of houses in the darkness.

The night became lime-green and alive through the lenses. By the third house down in the row, I could see a kid coming out of an open gate. I could see a cat prancing along a brick wall, the cat eyeing us as we eyed it, and the kid stepped back inside the gate and left it open. Inside there was a Mercedes; it looked new, the finish gleamed in the daylight-bright glow of the night vision goggles. The night vision goggles were lighter, tougher, and worlds' improved since my time in the Marines in the late 1980s, when our night vision goggles were damned heavy and awkward. Our nightscopes also, back then, were not much improved since the Vietnam War. It was good to see that some real investment had been made since then to get decent reconnaissance gear to our troops.

We headed southeast down wide potholed streets and dirt roads, through the maze of Fallujah's mud huts and cinder-block walled compounds, toward desert jeep trails, our reconnaissance complete on Chemical Ali's secretary. Four trucks rocking hard now, the Fallujah Wheelman in a good mood, saying, "O Jersey Girls are the finest, Lord, Lord, but my platoon leader married a Southerner, yes indeed! Lieutenant, it's not fair, I should be able to call you 'The Jedi Knight, sir,' sir!"

"Bozzelli, if life was fair, you and I would be on a beach with our women and not kickin' up dust in a city full of terrorists, deep in the heart of Ba'athist Merry-Go-Round. You've been around Dean too much. He's taught you those Radio Free Yeti ways. Mr. Tucker, I love my wife and our two sons. My wife's in Savannah, Georgia. I call her every chance I get. Drives her crazy. Patton, I'm coming up. Bring down the .203. You must be freezing up there, Patton."

"Roger that sir," said Smith as we entered desert, Bozzelli braking gently as we rode over a hump of dirt, Cane on point just ahead of us, up on his heavy machine gun, riding into the moon deep in the night. Patton, a big cat at six foot four, massive like Zen Master, came down out of the turret and handed the .203 to the lieutenant.

Leclair covered down for us, scoping the night with his NODs, Dean checking something on his radio pack and saying, "Patton, I reckon I'll call the Grizzly now. Call us in?"

"Hell yes, Dean, we're headed back. That's our first sergeant, Mr. Tucker. First Sergeant Dunn—the Grizzly. We used to call him the Rattler, because he'd sneak up on you like a rattlesnake—you could never see him coming. But he didn't like that one, so we call him the Grizzly, 'cause his voice sounds like a grizzly bear roaring. Vegas didn't cotton to us calling our first sergeant the Rattler, either. So it's a good thing we've got Radio Free Yeti. He thought Grizzly fit. Damn it's cold. What do you think, Mr. Tucker? Godzilla Woman in Fallujah? That kid at the gate never turned his head. We got lucky, right there. Mercedes wasn't there a few nights ago. We've got the raid locked on, brother. I think she's here."

"Kill or capture Godzilla Woman, hell yes. The Count planned it, Vegas fine-tuned it, righteous. Long live the Desert Yetis."

We were deep in rolling hardpacked sand now, huts of goatherders and shepherds looming out in the night. Seeing those huts in the desert was like being on the Chao Phraya river in Thailand, up-country where the river is wide and empty deep in the night, and seeing bamboo rafts floating all by their lonesome in moonlight. A dog howled and we rolled on, Radio Free Yeti calling in our position to the Grizzly. Dunn affirmed our reconnaissance, his voice like a bear roaring on the field radio.

The Fallujah Wheelman guided us over highway guardrails that had been crushed by tanks to allow easy access to the desert. That way, American raiders and other Coalition forces could enter and leave Fallujah without using overpasses and the cloverleaf. Our warriors in Fallujah called the main east-west junction, where Route 10 meets Highway 1, the Cloverleaf of Death. Patton's comrade, Staff Sergeant Paul J. Johnson of Alpha Company, had been killed with a command-detonated IED near that cloverleaf on October 13, 2003. It was also where many IEDs had killed our warriors on convoys, which rolled through it on their way to either the Syrian border or Baghdad.

Near the south gate, heading back through the wire in the zero dark desert cold, a paratrooper raised his shotgun and waved us in. A second paratrooper with a light machine gun raised a hand as Detroit City cleared his heavy machine gun ahead of us and the Jedi Knight cleared his .203. Leclair's men fished out their smokes and lit up, grinning now, scent of burning tobacco strong in the chill Iraqi desert air.

We halted in a gravel-filled depression and the men got out and everyone did a weapons check, flashing handheld mini-Mag flashlights and high-illumination flashlights attached to their M-4s and .203s on each other's chambers, making sure. A 100 percent cleared weapon check ended the reconnaissance patrol.

The Fallujah Wheelman dropped me off back at the battalion ops center and the men cheered and hollered, "Desert Yetis rock!" and I yelled back at them, "Fuckin'-a!" and the Jedi Knight gave me a thumbs-up and shouted "Hua, Airborne!" as they rolled away.

In the morning I rode for the mayor's compound, escorted by First Lieutenant Walton and his gang of supply honchos, the Supply and Transportation unit within Headquarters Company. It was ten in the morning on November 15, a beautiful sun-shot day, high cumulus clouds like puffs of cotton blossoming over the minarets of Fallujah.

Captain Huston, massive like a defensive end and a kind man whose wife was expecting that November in Alabama, and Captain Zawachewsky, a fellow Afghan vet who'd led deep reconnaissance patrols on the Afghan-Pakistani border due east of Khandahar, had a meeting at the mayor's compound, the former Ba'athist Party headquarters building in the heart of the city. I called Captain Huston the "Voyager," for he'd seen many lands and seas in his youth and in his career in the army. Due to his remarkable actions on long-range reconnaissance in Afghanistan, I called Captain Zawachewsky, "Scout of the Far Afghan Hills."

Walton occasionally liked to drive lead truck on his convoys, as I came to find out, "because it takes the load off my guys. They drive everywhere, they're always on point when it comes to IEDs. My guys have to roll from the airport to Ramadi hell for leather. IEDs are always on their minds. If I'm behind the wheel, it takes some of the heat off them." I called Walton, "Steve McQueen." Steve McQueen was about six foot one and outgoing, with a great sense of humor inside the wire and a hard-core, "get it right the first time" demeanor outside the wire.

Caliguire's Commandos, Alpha Company paratroopers commanded by Vegas, Captain Terrence Caliguire, rode with us, the paratroopers up on their guns, vigilant, scanning the desert in all directions. Shepherds and goatherders waved to us as we rode past a huge junkyard full of rusted, decrepit cars and trucks and motorcycles and military vehicles, paratroopers steady on their heavy guns, flak jackets loaded with grenades and clips and fighting knives and mini-Mags. The shells of cars and trucks and blasted remains of open-bed trucks and tanks seemed to stretch south for miles. Date palms rose from mounds in the center of the fields, irrigation canals leading like spokes in a wheel from the date palm groves out into the harvested wheat fields, wheat stubble jutting out from the dark brown earth on the eastern outskirts of Fallujah.

There were thick metal sheets welded into the sides of the trucks. Like nearly every truck that paratroopers and light infantrymen rode on during combat patrols in Fallujah, it was "up-armored"—doors made of thick steel that had been jury-rigged to fit a Humvee and armor welded into the open rear bed and under both front seats.

"Caught a lot of IEDs here, near the overpass, Mr. Tucker," the .50-caliber gunner shouted into the wind as we swung up the on-ramp, speeding up, heads tucked down, men holding their rifles and machine guns between their legs.

Our .50-caliber gunner stood tall like DJ Rush on the Ma Deuce as we crossed Route 10 and swung off the hardball (asphalt road) onto a rugged, bumpy jeep trail. Uptrail, I could see a blockhouse standing about one hundred meters northwest of a gas station; the blockhouse looked like many I'd seen up north, destroyed by U.S. Army 10th Group Special Forces and Kurdish peshmerga.

I could see two holes cut out through the thick blockhouse walls, each hole roughly twenty feet off the desert floor—ideal for snipers. As we rode uptrail toward Highway 1, the main drag in Fallujah that runs east from the Euphrates straight out to the Cloverleaf of Death, I realized that a sniper in the blockhouse would have line of sight on anything going north or south on the jeep trail; looking east, a sniper would have line of sight on anything moving on the highway and also in the fields that stretched to FOB Volturno.

I asked our .50-caliber gunner if they'd ever taken sniper fire from it and he told me, "Negative. But it'd be a smart place for a sniper to hole up in, those walls look four feet thick, at least. Probably need a tank round to take 'em out. Whaddya' think we should do?"

"Set charges on it and blow it in place. Deny the enemy the cover and concealment. How often do you ride on this jeep trail?" I shouted to him, above the wind, Steve McQueen rolling hard now as we neared Highway 1, auto repair shops crowded with Iraqi Arabs busy on that mid-November morning. I waved to the Iraqis and shouted "*Asalaam Ah Laekkum*" and a few waved back and replied, "*Wa Laekkum Asalaam.*"

"We ride it a lot. It keeps us off the Cloverleaf of Death. Just set charges and blow the shit out of it, sir?" our .50-caliber gunner said as Walton sped up quickly, jamming like Rock Steady Houchek, grooving west onto the main drag. A mosque bigger than any I'd seen in Oman or the United Arab Emirates came up on our right some three hundred meters away. Iraqi Arabs tried to bum-rush our convoy as we rolled hard for the mayor's compound, trying to cut in behind us in BMWs and taxis. Garbage was scattered in heaps all along the road and the stench was as foul as any in Mosul.

"What, is there a sign on your compound that says, 'Break glass in event of war?' Deny them potential sniper positions, hell yes, if it's not a public building," I said. "That's an Iraqi Army blockhouse, built by Saddam. Saddam's on the run, his Ba'athist dictatorship no longer exists, set charges and blow it to kingdom come. Send the feydayeen in Fallujah a message: We're not waiting to be attacked."

"Hua! Fuckin'-a, sir, you're speaking our language, fuckin'-a right! Airborne! 82nd! All the way!" he shouted as we slowed, passing the mosque, a four-way intersection just ahead. There was an Iraqi policeman in the middle of the intersection, even though a stoplight was working; some drivers were ignoring both him and the stoplight and whipping past, racing though the intersection.

Walton hit his horn and shouted to the cop, everyone steady on their rifles and .203s and machine guns. I scoped the mosque and saw a man in a minaret and he ducked.

"There's a guy in a minaret, the mosque behind us."

"Keep eyes on. Can you see a weapon?" asked Walton.

"No. Negative on weapon," I said and the man popped back up.

"Keep eyes on," he said as the cop finally opened a way for us, just wide enough for our trucks to get clear now. Walton put pedal to the metal and we shot forward, convoy right with us, and he shouted back, "All trucks up?"

"We're good, sir," a .203 gunner shouted to him and Walton replied, "Roger that! We have passed through the Stoplight from Hell and we are nearing the Land of the Bizarre, also known as the mayor's compound. Mr. Tucker, be advised, the police here are fuckin' crooks, buddy. I am not bullshitting you. Do not trust the fuckin' police in Fallujah. Not for a fuckin' cup of coffee, even."

"Roger that, Steve McQueen!" I hollered and the men laughed, steady on their weapons, good on all their fields of fire, weapons shouldered and everyone up on their gun. Tabla drums and piano and oud rocked from taxis moving west downtown and we rolled in the gate. Iraqi police in black leather jackets, unsmiling, waved us past concrete barriers and Hazelit earthen barriers that were piled all around the outer walls of the former Ba'athist Party headquarters in Fallujah. I greeted the police at the gate in Arabic and they did not reply—a bad sign. If an Arab does not respond to *Asalamm Ah Laekkum*, it's a classic Arab insult and shows deep disrespect. Hazelit barriers are about six feet high and constructed of thick gray plastic and filled with earth and stone. You'd see them throughout Iraq, at all Coalition forces buildings and all interim Iraqi government buildings, such as the mayor's compound in Fallujah. Concertina wire would be placed atop the Hazelit barriers and rolled atop the outer walls of the compound. A burned-out, two-story sand-colored building commanded a view of rooftops in all directions. Sand-bagged fighting positions lined the rooftop, green sandbags bursting at the seams.

Just east of the burned-out edifice stood an L-shaped, white concrete two-story building, not quite as tall, with parking in the mud behind it. Iraqi Arabs, in dishtashas and kaffiyehs, meandered around a door. Fallu-jah police carried paratrooper-stock AK-47s—the folding metal stock ver-sion of that 7.62-caliber assault rifle—from the pistol grips.

Walton slowed and stopped near a western wall up on a rise; his .50-caliber gunner had outstanding overwatch for us—eight hundred meters west, down Fallujah's main drag. Smoke drifted gray toward us from heaps of burning trash on nearby streets and alleys, and our .50-caliber gunner lit up a smoke, eyes on his fields of fire. I told Walton that I was headed for the roof of the burned-out building and he said, "Solid, just make sure you're on my truck, heading back. Get with Staff Sergeant Corcione, 1st Squad leader, 3rd Platoon, Alpha Company. He's got the roof," and I hustled through the mud to a smoke-blackened doorway, sandbags piled up waist-high on the outside of the door.

"Call me Naples, sir, I'm Specialist Napoli. Follow me up on the roof, fuckin'-a 82nd all the way!" I heard from behind me.

There was a light machine gunner, NAPOLI on his flak jacket, about five foot ten and stocky, coming toward me. Paratroopers were coming up fast behind him, bent forward slightly, assault rucks on their backs, weapons shouldered at quick-action, clips jacked in their rifles.

Naples had a small loam-and-green ammo bag, like Kentucky Rifle up north, feeding live rounds from up under the machine gun and an assault ruck on his back, like his comrades. He carried a massive blade on the right front side of his flak jacket, a black-nylon sheathed fighting knife jammed blade-down on his flak, knife handle strapped down. He was sweating and moving fast in the heat in Fallujah, sunlight streaming cathedral-like through grenade-shattered windows in the smoke-blackened rooms.

Napoli rushed forward, past piles of blackened, burnt-up documents and bullet-scarred walls all gray and black from smoke. You could tell the building had been torched recently, it had a strong heavy soot smell to it, like blackened charred wood in a sandpit the morning after a bonfire in a desert.

East toward the Stoplight from Hell, an Iraqi man in a dark gray dishtasha with a red-and-white-checked kaffiyeh draped over his head herded sheep along the road, cars careening around him, the sheep oblivious to the traffic congregating at the Stoplight from Hell. A policeman blew his whistle and got no one's attention, cars and trucks making their own way past him, unmindful to both the light and him.

The "Godfather," Staff Sergeant Corcione, came over to Specialist Napoli, Napoli nodding to him as he neared. The Godfather was tall, broad-shouldered, and he was carrying an M.203. Dull brass-jacketed 40mm rounds for his .203 covered an olive-green vest draped over his flak vest; his squad held the rooftop, all Caliguire's Commandos, the paratroopers under command of Vegas. The sun was hot now and there were scattered gunshots northwest of us—Napoli thought they were roughly three hundred meters away.

"You good on rounds, Naples?"

"A thousand 5.56, Staff Sergeant. I'm up."

The Godfather nodded and scanned the roof, checking his men.

"Stay focused, buddy. Holler if you need anything."

Napoli, a fireplug of a warrior who looked like he could walk through a brick wall, nodded to him and kept his eyes on rooftops northwest of us, concrete and stone compounds lining dusty streets behind the mayor's compound. I wished him luck and walked with Corcione as he walked the rooftop, checking the fighting positions and fields of fire of his men and talking to his squad about their fields of fire and their rounds and grenades. There was a fire station some 150 meters due east of the mayor's compound, just north of the Stoplight from Hell, and I could see three men on the rooftop as Corcione talked with a light machine gunner. The men looked at us, turned, and gestured, behind them. I tapped him on a shoulder and he turned his head slightly, and I told him about the men on the rooftop of the fire station. He got down on one knee and motioned for me to get down.

"Morales, rooftop of the fire station. What ya' got?"

"On it, Sergeant. Three guys. Black leather jackets. Looking this way," Specialist Morales, a light machine gunner from Puerto Rico, answered as he aimed at the fire station.

"Keep eyes on and watch for weapons. Mr. Tucker, we took fire from that fire station on the Halloween Siege. So did Bravo Company,"

Corcione said, pointing toward it, his men up on their weapons, in the prone behind sandbags, rifle barrels and machine gun barrels laid over concrete walls on the rooftops in all directions, securing the captains' civil-military affairs meeting with sheikhs, imams, and the mayor of Fallujah. Iraqi police milled about below us, smoking, para-AKs grasped by the pistol grips, barrels pointing straight down to the mud, rifles just barely out of the mud.

I asked Corcione if he knew about the Iraqi police attack on Alpha Company paratroopers on the night of October 13 and he nodded, squinting, keeping his eyes on the firehouse. An acrid chemical scent drifted with the smoke off trash fires, and we wrapped bandanas around our faces until it passed, men steady on their fields of fire, scoping minarets and rooftops and alley corners.

"We had a squad out on the northern edge of Volturno, securing a checkpoint. This was about eight thirty in the evening. Dark. There was a law—there still is a law—about carrying weapons in vehicles. We'd fuckin' made it clear to Iraqi police that they could not fuckin' ride with mounted rifles or machine guns. We'd fuckin' told them that many times. It's a feydayeen tactic, to mount a machine gun on a fuckin' pickup truck. Technicals, like Mogadishu."

He shouldered his weapon and scoped the firehouse and the men bolted and he said, "Rat bastard motherfuckers. Checking us out. Keep eyes on the firehouse, gents."

His men nodded, up on their guns, and Napoli shouted, "Feydayeen motherfuckers don't fuck with Alpha Company!"

The Godfather grinned and gave Napoli a thumbs-up. He scanned the rooftop, nodding to his squad. A black plume of smoke shot up from an alley just north of the firehouse. I scoped the alley corner and an Iraqi Arab woman rushed out, a little girl in ragged light-blue overalls tugging at her long billowing black dress, and together they hustled toward the Stoplight from Hell, the woman glancing back hurriedly and rushing with the child away from the alley. Corcione nodded down and I took a knee as he did the same, cradling his M.203 in his arms, squinting in the bright sun.

"If you ride as feydayeen, you die as feydayeen. The Iraqi police on the night of October 13 fired at us. We engaged. We lit them up. Under Coalition rules of engagement, we had every right to shoot. Mounted machine guns are illegal, and the Iraqi police knew that. But who the hell are the Iraqi police, anyway? Especially in Ba'athist strongholds. This is Fallujah—who's the police here, really? Who are these clowns? Their only loyalty is to their tribe. You'll never clean up this town as long as the sheikhs run Fallujah. They have no history of respecting any rule of law, and the rat bastard motherfuckers sold out to Saddam, hands down. The Kurds had the fuckin' balls to say no to Ba'athism. These rat bastard motherfuckers in Fallujah loved the dictatorship. The only way you can get any kind of fuckin' law enforced here is to break the power of the sheikhs.

"We took fire here right from the fuckin' firehouse on Halloween Siege. Bravo Company took fire from that firehouse, too. Right where we're standing, we held. Dig this: we paid those firemen, we met with them, our commanders dealt with them. Why did the insurgents, some of whom are actually fuckin' Iraqi police and firemen, target this place? Who ran the show on this compound, for Saddam in Fallujah? The sheikhs, who were Ba'athist. This is Ba'athist turf. Who could fuckin' pay the Iraqi police to attack us? The sheikhs could, no question. Are the IPs here the same ones our captains are meeting today, from the same tribes as the sheikhs? Same-same, buddy. And Al Quaeda is in this fucked up town of Fallujah, for fuckin'-a they are here. What happened on September 11 is not going to fuckin' happen again, not if me and my brothers have any fuckin' thing to do about it. And you can fuckin' bank on that, buddy. Fuckin'-a!"

With his last words, Caliguire's Commandos cheered, keeping their eyes on their fields of fire, cirrus clouds striping the high, deep-blue skies north of Fallujah. I thanked the Godfather and told him I'd check out the meeting downstairs, and he reminded me to get on Walton's truck, going back to FOB Volturno. I headed to check out the captains' meeting with the local higher-highers, sheikhs, and imams of Fallujah come to discuss money from Coaltion Provisional Authority (CPA) allotted for Fallujah and other civil-military affairs.

The meeting was a cauldron of unhappy sheikhs, uncaring Fallujah bureaucrats (save for one woman who actually thanked Captain Huston for chairing the meeting) and U.S. Army officers: Captain Ross (who later picked up his Major in January 2004), Zawachewsky, and First Lieutenant Bruznicki, an air defense artillery officer who was a jack-of-all-trades when it came to civil military operations. "Legendary Medic," a master of Bedouin dialects and Arab culture—his real name must be kept confidential—translated, keeping his calm when sheikhs shook their fingers and pouted and glared at the U.S. Army officers.

Near two in the afternoon, the meeting ended. I greeted the Iraqi police as we walked out, saying "*Maass Alaamah,*" the Arabic for "and may God go with you," and they did not respond, again a straight-up insult in Arab Bedouin culture. We rolled back to Volturno, hanging a left at the Stoplight from Hell and riding down a wide dusty trash-ridden avenue. Children cheered us as we swooped toward the train station.

Iraqi men on the sidewalks glared at us and refused to reply to my greetings in Arabic. Walton rocked hard behind the wheel, his .50-caliber gunner solid on the Ma Deuce.

Mosques were blaring anti-Coalition sermons and it was two in the afternoon—very strange. Arab Bedouins in the United Arab Emirates told me that the loudspeakers on mosques are turned on only for prayers and for the Friday sermon. Living in the United Arab Emirates and traveling in Oman, I heard Muslim prayers five times daily and the regular, forty-five minutes to an hour, Friday noon sermons.

But here in Fallujah, it was clear the imams were targeting us—the mosques were being used as communication bases for the feydayeen to announce our location and rally the Iraqis against us. In the middle of the strangely timed sermon, I heard the loud voice proclaim, "Osama Bin Laden, Osama Bin Laden, Al Quaeda! Enshallah, Al Quaeda!" We drove on, smoke drifting over us from trash heaped in alleys, plastic jugs and cartons and cardboard and refuse of all kinds piled up and burning now in the November sun. I could hear, faintly, tabla and drums and Arab voices from the northeast as we neared a T-intersection.

At the T-intersection, train station directly north at our twelve o'clock, we rolled right and east toward a soccer field. The field was some fifty meters off-road, left of us as we rode hard toward an overpass, and I shouted Arabic greetings and the Iraqi greeting, "*Shlaoww Nekk,*" and none of the children and young men on the field replied. The Iraqi Arabs looked at us and stared and said nothing.

It was telling. Up north there was huge respect and affection from the Kurds, and some Iraqi Arabs didn't hesitate to respond with appropriate greetings when I'd meet them on patrols. Even on raids.

Not so in Fallujah on November 15, 2003. Not at all. I remember thinking, there is no love for the Coalition in Fallujah, no indeed.

After getting off the truck back at Battalion Tactical Operations Center (TOC) and thanking Walton and his men, I thought that all the sheikhs and imams in Fallujah want is a return to Ba'athism.

Corcione, Viburs, Wettstein, Browning, Thoman, and Morrone all had been at war in Iraq longer than me, and they had all come to the same opinion on Ba'athism in Iraq: There is no compromise with Ba'athism; you have to slay the dragon of Ba'athism, not throw money at it. Guerrilla war theory teaches that the center of balance is the populace. But the center of balance in Fallujah is radical Islam, coupled with resurgent Ba'athism. The sheikhs fear the imams in Fallujah, and the imams do not fear the Coalition.

The Count chaired the targeting meeting at seven in the evening on November 16, 2003, in Fallujah.

Serpico set his coffee aside and told us Chemical Evil Fat Mama, Kurdia Turki Ali Halif, was in town. His sources in Fallujah had confirmed the Desert Yetis' ground intel gained from the eyes-on mounted recon deep in the night. Serpico also reminded us that Chemical Evil Fat Mama and her Ba'athist feydayeen cell were responsible for the Iraqi insurgent IED attack on two U.S. Army EOD specialists in Fallujah roughly two weeks earlier, on November 2, 2003. The IED had killed both our comrades.

The Desert Yetis recon in the wee dark hours had gone undetected. "She's at that house and we can nail her," Quinones said, his face grim. "Let's take her down and her feydayeen cell. All six Iraqi police in that house are her boys. They're all dirty and we need to take them down," he went on, hands clasped on the wide table in the ops center, dark eyes intense as he spoke, glancing around the room at Scout of the Far Afghan Hills, Captain Love (1st-505th intelligence officer), the Count, Major Cool, Vegas, and the Gladiator, Sergeant Viburs.

Sergeant Olson, a petite and brave woman who coordinated military intelligence with Quinones and whose husband was also at war in Iraq, sat next to Viburs, a determined, focused look on her face. Viburs handed her a document just after Quinones finished discussing the updated intelligence on the raid, and she glanced at the document and nodded to Quinones.

Vegas looked up quickly at a satellite photo on a wall and then to the Count. Vegas sipped from a Coke.

The Count raised his eyebrows as if to say, "Go ahead, Vegas."

Caliguire set down his Coke. He squinted, eyeing the photo, folding his arms. The captain pointed to the black and white satellite photo, indicating where Chemical Evil Fat Mama's house was, and he stood up and drew a circle around the entire block with a black magic marker.

"We are taking down Fat Mama. Vegas owns this block."

The Count grinned.

"Vegas owns this block. Don't play cards with Vegas! He'll take your shirt. Well, she can get reacquainted with Chemical Ali in prison. Let's do it right, gentlemen. Sergeant Quinones, well-done."

The paratroopers nodded to the Count and he got up and we followed him out, Zawachewsky and Caliguire conferring as the targeting meeting closed.

Zero dark cold at one in the morning on November 18 in Fallujah. No moon and pitch black in the desert. Stars blazed like ten thousand fires, and we rode to raid Chemical Evil Fat Mama and her six Iraqi policemen who were actually feydayeen. I was in a truck with the source for the raid, a middle-aged, silver-haired Iraqi Arab man in a gray-wool three-button suit and expensive, polished black loafers. Staff Sergeant Young from Massachusetts, "the Minuteman," checked our nine o'clock, his M.203 shouldered. Riding west for Fallujah in the zero dark cold, he talked about the origins of the Vietnam War. He was convinced it was a terrible mistake to listen to the French in 1945.

"Who the fuck were the French to give us advice in 1945? For Chrissakes, we pulled their chestnuts out of the fire twice in the last century, before 1945 ever said hello. Either we had no one in the field or we ignored whatever ground intelligence we had. Ain't no fuckin' way we could've fucked ourselves like we did in Vietnam unless we burned our own sources, hell fuckin' no."

We were riding hard in the night, Captain Huston with us, and I told the Minuteman of Major Archimedes L. A. Patti and the Deer Team in northern Vietnam from June 1945 to September 1945. The Deer Team had linked up with Ho Chi Minh, General Vo Giap, and the Viet

Minh near the Chinese border and raided Japanese supply lines running from southern China south to all Southeast Asia—denying the Japanese those supply lines made Japanese resupply very difficult. The Deer Team had also carried out joint search-and-rescue operations with the Viet Minh for downed Allied pilots. The Minuteman kept his eyes on his fields of fire and he was quiet for a spell, dust flying all over us, the faint scent of goat and sheep manure drifting on the night winds in the desert.

"Everyone at State and CIA oughta' serve four years, mandatory, combat arms, before they get selected. Enlisted. In the fuckin' ranks. They'd know for a fact not to fuck over the infantry, if they'd fuckin' served on active duty where the knives are honed and the spears are thrown."

The informant kept his head down, trying to shield himself from the thick billowing dust streaming off the sand, and the men tugged at bandanas and balaclavas wrapped about their necks and over their mouths, gun truck jolting hard over the ruts and bumps in the desert near Fallujah deep in the night.

Specialist Hanley was steady behind the wheel, the raiding party a long convoy of gun trucks and raiders and antennas bending back in the wind as we rode to raid. Our truck was tail-end charlie for the convoy, and our .50-caliber gunner had his gun turned around, facing east as we rode west, steady on his gun in the cold night, moon a far crescent glow in the darkness blanketing the desert.

Huston pounded his black leather gloves, breath fogging in the cold, and we swooped off the overpass into the desert, rutted jeep trails jolting us and the men joking and talking about home and women and good times.

Far to the west, lights blurred in the night like the last sparks of a flickering fire over the rolling hardscrabble desert. Orion was glittering high in the eastern skies. Orion always moved east to west over Fallujah after midnight.

In the desert the raiders stayed up on their guns, reflective, quiet. We were eyes on all sectors, and the Voyager held three o'clock, his M-4 outboard, rifle shouldered, taking the jolts and bumps on the ride in stride, his sidearm holstered under his left arm. The Iraqi source winced as Hanley revved up, the convoy speeding up now on the southern reaches of Fallujah, wind blasting us in the late autumn desert darkness.

Hanley stayed within fifty meters of the truck ahead, tactical lights (tac lights) shining a dim red and green on every truck. I could make out the truck ahead by the dust drifting over its rear gate, and its tac lights were like stoplights in the desert. The men could see the night like it was high noon in the desert, eyeing the sands through their powerful nightscopes.

Dust swarmed over the truck ahead of us and it disappeared at times as the jeep trail swerved and dipped over the rolling desert, Hanley hollering, "Fuckin-a, where'd the fuckin' truck go!" and the Minuteman saying, "Hanley, take it easy, just don't drive us into the Euphrates, wise one." The men chuckling as we rode to raid deep in the night, the Iraqi source huddled beside Huston.

Twin spires of mosques lit up the sky northwest of us, perhaps two thousand meters northwest, and the men grew quiet. All of us except the Iraqi wore olive-green gaiters and scarves tied bandito-style over our faces. The horizon lines west of the city, beyond the Euphrates, were a purple-black in the starlight. The red tac lights of our raiding party grooved through the desert like a long line of fire racing west on Xenophon's trail.

Over a great hump in the desert we slammed down, dust clearing in front of us and mud huts and cinder-block houses lining a potholed road just right of us, convoy roaring down the road. Houses loomed west, stark in the starlight, massive in the night like boulders along a mountain trail deep in Karen highlands in Burma, two- and three-story concrete and stone houses like small fortresses within their sand-colored, walled compounds.

Hanley broke hard and we leaped out, the Voyager leading the source west down a narrow, jagged lane, streams of sewage and refuse pooling near an alley corner some thirty meters ahead. The Judge joined us and asked me, "You all right, Mr. Tucker?" and I thanked him and told him I was fine, and he replied, "Solid, keep your head down buddy, stick with me." Huston moved on with the source, heading fast up the alley, the Iraqi keeping his head down, two kaffiyehs draped over his head. I could see Drinkwine, whom I called "Spartan Six," up ahead, his M-4 at the hip, rushing forward up the alley in the darkness.

The Grizzly, about six foot two and built like a middle linebacker, came up behind us as Caliguire's Commandos swept past, staying close to walls on both sides of the alley, hustling up, securing alleys, scoping rooftops, moving fast in the darkness.

The Grizzly said, "Come with me," and we hustled up through mud and dirt and sewage to the southern end of the alley, where it met a field. Right of us, some thirty meters immediately to our north, fire teams gathered along the wall, one team on each side of a wide, heavy, green steel gate, the gate we'd seen open on the Desert Yetis reconnaissance patrol.

A blast boomed in the night north of us, perhaps a mile away. Dunn nodded, a sidearm on his right hip and cradling his M-4.

"Charlie Company, no doubt. Just set off their raid. Going after the bastards that shot down the Chinook. Most affirm." As he spoke, four paratroopers and Scout of the Far Afghan Hills approached us, towing along a middle-aged man in a long white dishtasha.

They halted and the Grizzly talked with Scout of the Far Afghan Hills, their voices low in the darkness, raiders swarming up toward us, both fire teams leaning forward now on the house just north of us. I waited with Staff Sergeant Tormale Grimes, a shrewd and tough raider whom I nicknamed "Shaft," and Detroit City, who had dismounted his heavy machine gun, the M240 Bravo 7.62-caliber machine gun.

Shaft carried an M-4 and he had it shouldered for quick action, flak loaded with thirteen clips, as we held fast by the corner. He took a knee and I did likewise, Detroit City covering the west and south for us, in the prone on his heavy machine gun.

"He knows where she is," said Scout of the Far Afghan Hills, pointing to the man in the white dishtasha.

Shaft scanned the night and rose off one knee and looked toward the house. The Grizzly said, "Stay with Captain Zawachewsky, stay with him," and I nodded to him as we all moved together, Staff Sergeant Jeremy Anderson leading the sappers on the assault, two sappers working on the gate, and Anderson said quickly, "Battering ram, do it Tommy, fuck it up!"

Specialist Thomson rushed hard at the gate, battering ram in his arms, slinging it forward all in one swift hard rush and the gate busted open and Caliguire's Commandos rolled in hard, rifles shouldered, tactical lights on their rifles flashing in the night like fireflies in the Burmese jungle on a night with no moon, second-fire team rushing in, raiders shouting in the courtyard "Move, get the door, do it!"

I fell in with the second-fire team and the captain bolted up, coming from behind me, and pointed to shadows along a wall and said, "Over here, get here now." I got in the shadows and he told me to wait.

Zawachewsky held his rifle down slightly and moved forward with the assault team, shouting back over his shoulder, "Mr. Tucker, move with 2nd team," raising his rifle as he stepped into the house, his voice carrying from within the house, "Go Morales, go go go!"

The second-fire team rushed in and I fell in behind a light machine gunner, raiders scoping the dark halls and rooms with their rifles shouldered, shouts of "Clear, clear," and "There's a kid in here, take it easy, just a kid," coming from within the dark house, lights flickering on in the early morning.

The odor of kerosene was strong in the hallway, paratroopers separating the men from the women and children. Velvet paintings, like those you'd see of Elvis in his Vegas years, hung from concrete walls. Horses in the paintings ran through the desert, nostrils flaring, carrying men with rifles and leather bandoleers strapped across their chests.

Caliguire's Commandos pulled a man from a rear room and came forward with him. The man wore a black leather jacket and on one sleeve was the Iraqi police identification badge. He kept his head down and was silent and they rushed him forward out to the courtyard. I could hear Napoli say, "Fuckin'-a, he had this halfway out from under the bed, fuckin' submachine gun," as I entered the room. Napoli stood by the side of a sagging mattress, a long wooden closet behind him, holding a Sterling wooden-stocked submachine gun in his left hand. Corcione checked it out as his men continued to clear the room, searching through closets and in small bedside tables for pistols, ammunition, rifles, det cord, plastic explosive, mobile phones—any of the common weapons of war that the Iraqi insurgency used to kill and maim and wound our warriors in Fallujah.

"Got AK clips," said Morales in a hurried tone as he grabbed AK-47 magazines from out of a dresser. "Live rounds, 7.62." Morales's wife, who was in Bayamon, Puerto Rico, was pregnant. I called Morales the "King of Puerto Rico." He was a dynamite light machine gunner, and like DJ Rush and Kentucky Rifle, you always felt better when Morales was on a raid with you.

Corcione nodded. "Throw them in here," he said, ripping a pillowcase off a pillow and handing it to the King of Puerto Rico.

Morales, his light machine gun slung over his back, tossed ten AK clips and heaps of loose 7.62 rounds into the pillowcase, the Godfather holding it open for him. Napoli was checking under the mattress again, making sure. The Godfather scanned the room and said quickly, "Clear, are we all clear here?"

The raiders answered as one, shouting, "Clear!"

Corcione nodded and said, "Good, because there's one more room, let's go," and he led us to an adjoining room, the rich scent of fragrant perfume strong as we entered. There were silk dresses smothered in gems hanging in wooden closets, and perfume everywhere. The King shouted, "More ammo, more clips, *hijo de la chingana!*" and the God-father grinned.

"Ain't no doubt, this house is all wrong. Chemical Evil Fat Mama fuckin' well ought to hang. Good job Morales," he said. He opened a closet and there were about twelve more AK clips stacked on shelves.

"Supply safe house for feydayeen, Mr. Tucker," he said as he grabbed the clips and tossed them into the pillowcase. I nodded to him; no doubt, he was right. There was way too much ammunition and war supplies in this house for two or three feydayeen. Corcione leaned over and listened to his I-Com and he raised his eyebrows, grinning slightly.

"Solid. We're coming out," he said into his I-Com. He looked around as the raiders glanced up at him and asked, "Clear, are we clear?"

His raiders shouted, "Clear!" Carrying pillowcases full of AK-47 ammunition and clips, Caliguire's Commandos rushed out of the room, flashing their tac lights in the darkened hallways. The scent of burning kerosene was strong now in the hallways, and the thick smoky scent hung heavy in the night air.

In the courtyard, Zawachewsky was talking with Caliguire. "Right here, we got her," Zawachewsky said, pointing just outside the gate, raiders at all compass points in the courtyard, a low metallic rumble coming from our trucks beyond the courtyard.

Chemical Evil Fat Mama was babbling in Arabic, great jowls flapping on her fat sagging cheeks as two raiders tried to flex-cuff her, two other raiders watching over her, M-4s at the ready. Paratroopers were everywhere, rushing to their trucks, shining neither flashlights nor tac lights, sweat steaming off them in the zero dark cold.

Kurdia Turki Ali Halif was short and obese and the black scarf over her head was shining with rubies. Her black gown was huge on her, like tossing black sheets over a boulder. Her eyes were rheumy and she stank of perfume. There were gold and diamond rings all over her fingers and diamond earrings hanging from her massive earlobes. She looked me in the eyes and shouted, "Saddam, Saddam, Saddam!" I held her gaze and smiled and shouted back at her, "Mala Mustafa Barzani, Mala Mustafa Barzani, peshmerga, Kurdistani, Kurdistani, peshmerga!"

She flinched, and her head shot back. And she froze, her loud babbling Arabic ceasing, a confused look in her eyes. I reckon the last thing she thought an American in Fallujah would say to her were Kurdish praises. The raiders finally flex-cuffed her and all four of them heaved her up in a truck, one raider exclaiming, "The bitch is evil! Watch her, she'll try to bite. She tried to bite me. She'll fight, watch that Chemical Evil bitch!" A raider slipped a green sandbag hood over her and she began babbling again in Arabic, and I remembered the Kurdish women of Gizi, whose village was attacked with chemical bombs and grenades on August 26, 1988, in Kurdistan. I remembered Halima Mohsen, a survivor of the Gizi massacre, telling me on August 3, 2003, in Kurdish highlands deep in northern Iraq, "Why did the world wait so long to defeat Saddam, why?" Held at gunpoint, she'd watched the Mukhabarat and Iraqi Army soldiers beat her husband and son to death with wooden clubs and steel cables at the Dahuk prison in late August 1988.

While Ba'athists like Kurdia Turki Ali Halif applauded the chemical death Saddam Hussein and his Ba'athist dictatorship used to murder Kurds, the women of Gizi watched their village destroyed with chemical weapons and their livestock killed and their men tortured and murdered by Ba'athist secret police.

It was good to know that we'd nailed her and her feydayeen cell. I knew I'd come to the right place. Six dirty Iraqi police would no longer be spies for the Ba'athist insurgency in Fallujah, and Chemical Evil Fat Mama would be joining her old boss in a concrete cell.

Morales slapped me on the back and said, "We're rolling, bro, good job, *que va*, we got the evil devil bitch!" I thanked him and jogged back, passing the Grizzly and the Judge as I made my way to the Minuteman's truck, raw sewage streaming down the alleys—god-awful stench. Raiders held gloved hands over their mouths as they leaped up on their trucks, and the Jedi Knight gave me a thumbs-up as I hustled by, saying, "Don't forget that Geritol tonight, buddy," the Desert Yetis busting up as Bozzelli revved the engine.

We saddled up and moved out down the deserted streets, generators thumping in the night where wild dogs roamed the alleys and streets of Fallujah. Machine gunners scoped alleys and snipers in support looked hard through their high-tech nightscopes at minarets, eyes on for snipers in the zero dark cold.

Entering the desert, as we headed east for Volturno, "Flash, Flash," stormed over the radio, and Hanley from the Granite State of New Hampshire listened closely, the rest of the transmission lost to us in the bed of the truck as the wind roared in the darkness. Dust drifted thick over us from the long line of Alpha Company trucks, Headquarters Company trucks, and commanders' trucks rolling hard through the desert in the darkness.

Hanley shouted, "Charlie Company got the bastards, a crate of AK-47s, beaucoup ammo!" The .50-caliber gunner shouted "Hua!" and the Minuteman said, "Fuckin'-a! Charlie nailed the bastards who shot down the Chinook on November 2. Got feydayeen ammo and AKs, too. Crates. Feydayeen in this town have resupply, all kinds of resupply. Kill the feydayeen! Charlie Company, hell yes!"

Damn happy, we rolled in the wire, on trail for the raiding party, paratroopers at the gate giving us a thumbs-up as we returned, men clearing their weapons and scoping each other's chamber with their tac lights inside the wire, three in the morning in Fallujah.

Back at Battalion TOC, I thanked Spartan Six for the privilege of being on a raid that nailed a key Ba'athist, one who had staunchly supported the deaths of my friends and comrades in Kurdistan.

He nodded gravely, sadness in his eyes. I told him I thought Charlie Company must've carried out their raid with precision and fury to have not only captured the insurgents who'd killed seventeen of our comrades on November 2, but nailed the crate of AKs as well.

The colonel was sweating, even in the cold, and he wiped a green bandana across his forehead, a grin lighting up his face now. "She was one evil Ba'athist, no question. Good that we rolled up her cell. Solid raids tonight by Alpha and Charlie. Alpha's got a counter-IED patrol going out, early on the nineteenth. Are you game?"

I told him I'd be on it. We shook hands and he returned to a commanders' meeting, Private First Class Joshua Gordon and Specialist Cothern, a comrade of Gordon's, listening intently to Steinmeyer in

the Battalion TOC. The commanders stayed up until four in the morning analyzing the raids, going over their after-action reports.

We rolled out the wire on the counter-IED patrol, zero dark thirty in
Fallujah, November 19, 2003. It was four thirty in the morning and the
Desert Yetis led the way. Zero dark thirty is a term we used in Marine infantry to mean any wee dark hour of the morning, anywhere in the
world, between midnight and dawn when it's dark and black and you are
on a mission.

Sappers rolled with us, mine detectors laid outboard in their trucks
like oars in a skiff before it's launched to sea. We had gun trucks on point
and trail—every truck on the patrol save our MK 19s had a machine gun
mounted. The sappers rode with heavy machine guns mounted on their
gun trucks, Private First Class Vincent Carter manning one 7.62 machine for the sappers and Private First Class Brown from Pasco, Washington, manning another, waving to the machine gunner on my truck as
we rolled out the south gate.

The Jedi Knight was in the TC seat, riding like the Guerrilla Fighter
in Mosul on the passenger's side up front. Specialist Cook was driving;
we were trail truck on the patrol and the men were scoping the darkness
with their superb night vision devices. Quiet out the wire as we rolled far
to the west and north down hardpacked dirt jeep trails through fields of
harvested wheat and cotton. Donkeys roamed the fields on the outskirts
of Fallujah in the wee dark hours.

Patton was with us, in the back of the truck, and Doc, the platoon
medic, and Specialist Jake Eller and Specialist Stephen Carmac, paratroopers all. I called Eller, "Jake the Snake," and Carmac, "Longstreet,"
after Confederate General James Longstreet. Jake the Snake and
Longstreet were both from North Carolina, though Longstreet liked to
say of his buddy, "Southerners don't claim Jake the Snake. He's a rare
breed. Definitely not from North Carolina," to which Jake the Snake
would swiftly reply, "Don't listen to him. Longstreet is long on ammunition and short on brain matter. I am a son of the South, and I will
surely profit in time, due to my Southerners' wisdom and natural grace
and charm."

Eller said that once again in Fallujah as the sun rose over fields and
irrigation canals east of us. Patton laughed and said, "Jake the Snake, the

only grace and charm you'll ever find is standing in front of Graceland getting charmed out of your pocket money by some Memphis hustler!"

Carmac busted up laughing, eyes on, steady on his light machine gun. Eller rolled his eyes and said, "That's Patton. Lord. Patton! We got hit on September 13, a date forever engraved in the memory of the Desert Yetis. Firefight lasted an hour and a half. Patton tells us, in the middle of all this, us trying to keep our heads down in the desert and praying we'd survive, 'Men, this is what it's all about! Remember this night. This is it, movement to contact, movement under fire. Kill the enemy!' And he's standing there, AK fire all around us, RPGs flying, and I said to him, 'Staff Sergeant Smith, my God, since when did you become Patton?' And he just looks at me and says, 'Jake, conserve your ammo.' So after that night, we all called him Patton."

Longstreet grinned and nodded to me and I asked him if Jake the Snake was bulljiving me or telling it straight. Carmac's eyes hardened as he scanned the long plowed rows in fields of harvested cotton and he nodded and said, "Truth. Jake the Snake was praying the 23rd Psalm as we rode into that firefight. He was speaking for everyone on that truck. That night, yes indeed, that's when we started calling Staff Sergeant 'Patton.'"

Dawn warmed us and we swung southeast off a jeep trail onto hard-ball, headed toward the Dam Road, a busted-up, potholed road that runs southwest out of Fallujah past mud huts and cinder-block compounds. The road continued alongside a few massive, well-constructed concrete villas before passing through saw grass fields and swamps on the eastern banks of the Euphrates, date palm groves green along its eastern shores.

A car pulled out of a driveway some fifty meters behind us, and as it neared the road, six other cars pulled out with it, all spread out roughly fifty meters apart. I noted this to Patton. He said to the Jedi Knight, "El-Tee, we've got feydayeen. Seven on our six."

"Keep eyes on. Any weapons on the vehicles?" the lieutenant asked.

"I've got it, sir," Eller said, eyeing the seven vehicles trailing us. He scoped the vehicles with his M-4. They were all still about fifty meters apart. We sped up and hung a right near a junction of dirt roads and hardball and our convoy halted, Desert Yetis leaping out, shouldering their rifles and machine guns at quick action.

The seven cars, still equidistant, slowed down as we stopped and Carmac faced west, his light machine gun at the ready. One car slowed some fifty meters west of us. Eller shouldered his M-4 and came up alongside Carmac, and the car sped up, driving on, not following us anymore. I counted the vehicles following it; all six drove on, still equidistant.

Everyone dismounted, paratroopers securing alley corners and scoping rooftops in the warming dawn, gulls swarming over heaps of smoking trash near the junction. The sappers carried mine detectors, sidearms, machine guns, rifles, and assault rucks. They swept the ground for IEDs, paratroopers securing their flanks, mangy dogs barking at us from nearby mud huts.

The sappers cleared the junction of IEDS and hustled back to their trucks, led by Staff Sergeant Jeremy Anderson and Staff Sergeant Snyder, both Afghan veterans. I called Anderson, the "Streetfighter," and Snyder, "New York Warrior." The Streetfighter was fearless on raids and backed his sappers 1,000 percent. He was clever and stoic and his men respected him.

New York Warrior volunteered on September 11, 2001, for rescue crews at the World Trade Center. For three days he pulled rubble and steel and rock out of the ashes with the Lady in the Harbor watching over him. He'd been home on leave that September and he was riding in a car on Long Island when the news broke of the first plane striking the first tower. A year later, with the Streetfighter, he was in Afghanistan, going cave to cave, searching for Al Quaeda weapons caches and Al Quaeda terrorists.

I got back on Leclair's truck and rode with the Desert Yetis on the Dam Road, patrol slowing as two M113s joined us. The M113 is a wide-bodied, armored fighting vehicle that first saw action in the Vietnam War. A machine gunner stood up in the turret. The M113s were from Big Red One, and it was great to see them in the brightening morning. Iraqi insurgents had set off many IEDs in the "Boneyard" section of the Dam Road, where Big Red One rallied to us on that dawn, M113s rumbling slowly. Iraqi children raced out of mud huts and cinder-block houses to wave to us.

We halted in the Boneyard and the sappers rushed forward, on point, sweeping the dirt shoulders of the Dam Road with their mine detectors, Anderson and Snyder in the thick of it.

Grimes and Staff Sergeant Rodrick Hodges secured the sappers' flanks, flicking hand-and-arm signals to their men and to Anderson and Snyder, Hodges leading his squad on the eastern side of the Dam Road.

The sun was high and stellar-bright in hazy blue sky, and I asked Leclair if I could move up with the sappers. He nodded and said, as I hustled up the road, "Remember, our truck number is twenty-seven," pointing to the white-painted numbers on the dark-green side. I jogged up to combat sapper Private First Class Vincent Carter on left flank, some fifty meters east of Big Gus and the Woodsman.

Carter, whom I nicknamed "Ultimate Gunner," carried his light machine gun, wide black nylon strap slung over his back, sweat pouring down his face in the hot desert morning. Ultimate Gunner was the only sapper issued two machine guns, both the SAW 5.56 and the M240B 7.62 caliber. Carter was from Virginia Beach, Virginia, not far from the Cape Henry lighthouse my great grandfather had passed all his life as a boat pilot, guiding clipper ships and freighters up the Chesapeake to Baltimore. When I told him this, in the dust and heat of Fallujah on that morning, Carter grinned and said, "I know that lighthouse. We're both a long way from the Chesapeake, brother. Solid to see it again, for real." The desert sun was burning now in the Boneyard, a great herd of water buffalo moving slowly through marsh and saw grass three klicks south of us, near the Euphrates.

"Keep eyes on for wires and det cord, Mr. Tucker, anything that might be for an IED, trash, plastic bags, anything," and I nodded and scanned the dusty rubble-strewn Boneyard, road curving slightly about one hundred meters ahead of us. Behind us, our counter-IED patrol convoy was inching forward, trucks at a crawl. Leclair talked on his radio to his squad leaders, one hand on his sidearm, Dean right by his side, his M-4 at the ready. Looking east, it was a concrete wasteland, with dilapidated shells of concrete buildings all around us and stumps of rusted I-beams jutting up from bare concrete foundations. Starlings and sparrows flitted about in what shade they could find in the Boneyard, chirping in shadows cast by concrete boulders. A thin haze of smoke drifted from the trash fires over all of us, and the scent was unpleasant, though not nearly as foul as the raw sewage in the streets of Mosul and Fallujah.

"Move, move!" Carter shouted, grabbing my right shoulder and heading east and we ran, hustling some one hundred meters. Carter looked back and then glanced forward and pointed behind two boulders.

We dropped down behind the boulders, trash blowing around us. Directly west, Big Gus and the Woodsman were standing still, mine detectors held over the loose dirt and gravel on the left shoulder of Dam Road. Everyone on the patrol had taken cover—Leclair was behind a truck, listening to his handset, nodding. Dean checked their three o'clock, rifle shouldered. Patton covered their six, M.203 shouldered, on one knee, facing north, his flak jacket stocked full with 40mm grenades.

Samurai, Staff Sergeant Hodges, had his squad well deployed, set in behind boulders and walls, securing the eastern reaches of the Boneyard. Some two hundred meters west of us, Grimes's men were spread in a loose crescent, waving off children as they neared, the children unknowing of the danger, smiling and waving to Shaft and his men as they scanned the wide dusty field that reached to concrete houses and villas beyond.

Anderson and Snyder walked up quickly to Big Gus and the Woodsman and began digging at the dirt with their hands. There was an EOD specialist with them, a big, lean warrior carrying an M-4, flak stocked with scissors and knives and det cord and clips, fatigues dusty and grease-stained.

He leaned down and snatched a wire from the dirt and ran, threading the wire in his left hand and shouting, "Got wire! Come on." He pointed to a paratrooper nearby who was carrying a light machine gun and the machine gunner ran with him, following the wire into the Boneyard. Seeing my camera, the EOD specialist yelled, "No pictures, no pictures," and I held both arms up, keeping my hands away from my camera. He nodded and ran hard through the rubble, wire in his hand.

"IED, Mr. Tucker! We've got one. C'mon Big Gus and Brownie, get outta' there sapper brothers," Carter said quickly. Ten Iraqi children ranging perhaps from four to eleven years old were standing about thirty meters southwest of the IED, gathered in front of a mud hut, holding their hands to their foreheads, shielding the Fallujah sun from their young eyes. Carter explained to me that the battery charge on a camera, set off when the picture is taken, could detonate an IED.

Big Gus and the Woodsman stepped back as Anderson and Snyder disarmed and pulled out two huge artillery shells from the ground, dust swirling up out of the hole, the shells lashed together with baling wire.

They slowly and carefully pulled the wire off, M113s covering them, Leclair talking into his handset as Dean raised his M-4 and scanned houses just west off the Dam Road, Samurai and Shaft talking into their I-Coms, Patton checking Leclair's six and listening to his I-Com. Patton nodded slowly, M.203 at quick action, as he kept eyes on the trucks behind him and the road beyond.

"They're 155s. Daisy-chained. When they're wired together like that, daisy-chained. Feydayeen are evil. They would've killed those kids, too," Carter said, pointing to the children. I thanked him for finding us the good cover and he said, "No problem." Anderson and Snyder carried the 155mm artillery rounds away and set them in the back of one of the sapper's trucks.

The EOD specialist shouted, "Got a hole!" He stood, shaking the wire over a hole dug in behind boulders, roughly 250 meters east from where the feydayeen had buried the IED on the shoulder.

"Command detonated. Whoever set in that IED was going to sit in that hole and kill us himself. Punch the button and the wire would've sent the charge and blown us to hell and back. Woulda' killed those kids, too, Mr. Tucker, or at the very least, scarred them for life. The feydayeen don't have any regard for life. Ba'athist motherfuckers. They won't hesitate to kill Iraqi civilians if it means they can kill or maim us," Carter said as we rose up, patrolling south through the Boneyard, continuing the counter-IED patrol, echoing Thoman in Mosul.

I told him of Kentucky Rifle and his agreement with Ultimate Gunner and he said, "That's right. Kentucky Rifle understands this war. Screaming Eagles. Those cats have a lot of time on the ground here. Crossed the berm and fought north. Screaming Eagles. Kentucky Rifle fuckin' understands the Ba'athists. The feydayeen. You can't bullshit a grunt, sir. A grunt understands. We see these motherfuckers for real, we see the actions of the feydayeen on the street. In the desert. We know who these motherfuckers are. We understand this war, for fuckin' sure we understand it. Fuckin' Kentucky Rifle, hell yes!"

The M113s came up now, rolling hard, machine gunners in their turrets steady behind thick steel plates, scanning rooftops west and rubble east.

Big Gus and the Woodsman were back on point, sweeping the dusty shoulder with their mine detectors, Anderson and Thomson sweeping the right shoulder, sweat dripping off their faces, seagulls flocking over them and swooping south for the Euphrates.

Leclair waved to me and motioned me over, and I thanked Carter for protecting me and he gave me a thumbs-up, moving out. The Jedi Knight reached out a hand and I shook it.

"They were 155s, Mr. Tucker. This neighborhood is wrong. IED cells definitely operating here. We've pulled a lot of IEDs off this road and had many go off here. Whoever is paying the IED cells here, and throughout Fallujah, has big money and big power in this town. Fuckin' IED motherfuckers," Leclair said, wiping the sweat off his brow with an olive-green bandana, sun beating down on us as it got near eight in the morning.

We walked forward slowly, patrolling, sappers on point and Big Red One M113s providing heavy weapons fire support, machine gunners up on Alpha's trucks, Desert Yetis and Caliguire's Commandos moving south on the Dam Road toward the marshes.

Dean was pumping sweat, his face beet-red, steady on his M-4, grinning through the heat as he adjusted his handset. I asked the Jedi Knight if I could join Grimes and Hodges and he told me, "Absolutely." Radio Free Yeti shouted, "Don't step in the buffalo shit!"

Big Red One rocked on, headed toward the dam. Passing them, I saw the children still gathered by their mud hut home and greeted them in Arabic, and they jumped up and down, smiling, and returned my greeting, some of them shouting gleefully, "Amerikee!"

Up ahead, sweeping behind the sappers and patrolling southeast, Grimes and Hodges led their squads into the saw grass. A herd of water buffalo now perhaps a klick south gathered on the edge of a mudflat, the cedar trees along the Euphrates's eastern banks swaying in the mid-morning breezes. The sappers patrolled south, mine detectors out, heads bent slightly, Ultimate Gunner up on his light machine gun, flak jacket heavy with rounds and grenades.

In the saw grass, I caught up to Grimes. One of his men, Specialist Mendez, looked back toward us and fell into the mud and muck, saw grass enveloping him. Shaft laughed and walked toward him, saying, "Mendez, can you get up, wild man?"

"Fuck yes, I can get up, fuckin' mud," Mendez replied, grinning, water buffalo turning their heads, Grimes grinning with him in the marshes east of the Euphrates. Mendez stood up, boots to flak brown

Dawn, September 28, 2003. Mosque in Kurdish Mosul.

First day of new Iraqi currency, October 15, 2003, Mosul. The Iraqi woman at center of photo just moments later told our translator that she was fine, and she wondered what the new money in Iraq looked like.

One of Boggsy's Raiders on the Nimrud Raid, October 22, 2003.

Screaming Eagle sergeant pulling first feydayeen mortars out, Nimrud Raid.

Sergeant Shaun Smith—"Sgt. York"—riding back in good spirits after a dawn counter-IED patrol, Mosul. October 25, 2003.

Second Lieutenant Aaron Sherbondy, Delta Co., 3rd/502nd, with Iraqi kids in Quara-quosh, N. Iraq, October 3, 2003, early afternoon.

Raid, Fallujah. Bravo Company storms suspected feydayeen house, early morning, January 21, 2004.

Climb to Glory. Sergeant Shawn Hall, the Guerrilla Warrior, climbs cliff on patrol, November 24, 2003.

Sasquatch putting his flak jacket back on, after digging up four feydayeen 155 artillery rounds and case of 23mm rounds from enemy cache on patrol, south of Fallujah, November 24, 2003.

Holding the Corner. Fallujah. Big Red One tanker raises his M-4 where we'd taken RPGs the night before, on patrol with the 10th Mountain, December 16, 2003.

Happy kids in Fallujah, January 15, 2004.

Spartacus (Colonel Jefforey Smith), right, always led from the front in Fallujah. Here, he gets human intellignce from a Fallujah laborer (center), after we'd just been hit by RPGs and small arms. About 10:30 am, Jan. 9th 2004, Fallujah. (Interpreter's face is intentionally obscured.)

Corporal Anderson leading a raid in Fallujah with Specialist Shane Thomson on the door.

with mud, and patrolled on, gripping his light machine gun and stepping through high, golden saw grass.

"We'll patrol up to the dam, Mr. Tucker," Grimes said, keeping an eye on his squad as they moved slowly through the head-high saw grass, looking for wires used to command detonate IEDs.

The paratroopers left nothing to chance; insurgents could've dug in fighting positions in the saw grass, never been seen from the road, and ambushed the many Coalition convoys that crossed the dam bridge.

Coming out of the marsh, we hustled up a short steep rise and got to the Dam Road, tall pines on both sides. We patrolled south under the pines, Leclair running up and meeting us.

As he got close to Hodges's squad, Radio Free Yeti stumbled and did a backflip, landing scattershot in the sand. Desert Yetis guffawing as they helped him up, the Jedi Knight busting up, hands on his hips. Shaft shook his head and said, "Radio Free Yeti, he is just lacking those paratrooper motor skills. Well, we got the 155s, brother," he said, and he reached out a hand and I shook it. He pointed to Leclair's truck rolling up toward us, the convoy preparing to cross the dam. The Euphrates is perhaps fifty meters wide at the dam in Fallujah and widens north rapidly, the river brown and swift flowing and perhaps 100 to 120 meters wide just north of the concrete dam bridge. Date palms line both shores near the dam and carcasses of dead cattle and donkeys, strangely, often rot on the western shore near the dam.

"We'll secure the crossing," Grimes said. I got up in the back of the truck, Patton helping me up. The heat was intense now, and riding back to Volturno we stayed to back roads and jeep trails, Cook driving hard across the desert and shooting us across wide, rolling hardscrabble. We got in the wire just after nine, grabbed some chow at the mess hall, and cooled out at the Kingdom of the Desert Yetis, whose concrete bungalows were set on a bluff above the lake waters.

Taking our flaks off, the sweat poured; our uniforms stuck like glue to us. The warriors hung their rifles and machine guns and grenade launchers from nails on the walls and eased back on their cots, drinking MRE electrolyte drinks and water and coffee.

The Desert Yetis talked for a while of actions in September and October and remembered Staff Sergeant Paul J. Johnson, killed by a roadside bomb on October 20. He was a native of Calumet, Michigan. The Desert Yetis immensely respected "Staff Sergeant J.," as they called him, and missed him deeply. They told me he'd been a kind man, a solid NCO, a real professional.

They talked of his wife and his children stateside with real affection, Carmac saying at one point, "I wish there was some way we could tell his family that he was our brother, our comrade, and a good man. We will never forget him. He was a real professional, a solid paratrooper, and a good family man. He believed in what he was doing; he was that kind of warrior. It really tore us up when he died. Really hit Alpha hard. Our captain pulled us together and told us that Staff Sergeant J. would want us to carry on, to win this thing, to crush the feydayeen and Al Quaeda here. We'll never forget Staff Sergeant J.," Longstreet said, his voice low and steady, the men nodding to him, eyes hard. I thanked the Desert Yetis and they wished me luck. The Jedi Knight met with Shaft, Samurai, Patton, and the Sheriff to go over the counter-IED patrol.

I walked north along the lake. On the lake, there were brown-and-black feathered ducks on the shimmering blue water. I stopped by 10th Mountain and talked with First Sergeant Ernie Thrush about their counter-mortar patrol in the desert south of Fallujah, set for the late afternoon.

Thrush was big like a walking mountain, a broad-shouldered, heavily built gentleman, like a defensive tackle. I called him "Man Mountain." He carried a sidearm on his right hip.

He offered me coffee and I poured a cup, and he told me I was welcome on the counter-mortar patrol. He asked me if I had both plates for my flak jacket. I slapped the ceramic body armor plates on my flak and he grinned and said, "Good. That's a fine Kukri. Is it genuine?" I handed him my Kukri and he eyed it and said, "Damn. Outstanding." He handed back my knife and told me to be ready at four thirty in the afternoon—his company commander, Captain Scott Kirkpatrick, would be leading the counter-mortar patrol. I thanked him, walked back to my hootch, and listened to Miles Davis up on the roof of the battalion ops center, gulls flying west for the Euphrates in the late morning and into the early afternoon over far endless sands.

There was a wave of cumulus clouds, gray and white on the far western horizon over Fallujah in the early afternoon. I crashed on the roof, waking at three forty-five. I got clean, sharpened my Kukri, and pulled my gear together.

Regan offered me coffee and we talked in his hootch; he told me Attack Company had been ambushed every day in their first week in Fallujah and they held their ground, killing insurgents and keeping to the creed of 10th Mountain: Climb to Glory. The Count entered and cracked a wide grin, in the way of the Count, saying, "Well, Mark Twain here must be talking about John Steinbeck again. Are you on the counter-mortar patrol with KP and the mountaineers?" he asked, grinning.

Regan smiled and I told the Count that I was headed out with 10th Mountain.

"Not 11th Mountain, not 13th Mountain, but 10th Mountain! Now, why'd the army pick ten? Go figure. Bust for your dust. Strange old world. Shotguns, KP's guys like shotguns. Gotta' make the hit, make the hit. Good luck out there. See you at the targeting meeting," he said, grabbing a cup of coffee and heading back to the operations center.

Regan nodded to him and I shook his hand. The Count rolled out and now it was getting on to four thirty. I grabbed my flak and Kukri and thanked Mark Twain for the coffee. Captain Kirkpatrick entered the room as I was leaving.

"You good?" he asked me, waving to Mark Twain. I nodded and we got in an up-armored truck, clouds drifting gray now over Volturno, and headed out to the south gate.

Kirkpatrick was a great runner, a 9:06 two-miler, and he was lean and tough. His heroes were the great American middle-distance runner Steve Prefontaine and Thomas Paine—he quoted Paine, as we got in the truck: "If there must be trouble, let it come in my day, that my children may have peace." He asked me if I had water; I told him I had a full two-quart canteen with me, and he told me that I needed more, we had crates of bottled water in the truck. "But no cold beer, sorry 'bout that," his driver said, grinning.

Kirkpatrick carried a pistol-grip shotgun and a sidearm. I called him the "Ironman." He had a K-bar fighting knife on his flak and a smaller blade jammed in a leather sheath on his right boot.

His radioman, Specialist Smith, was from Blacksburg, Virginia, in the far southern highlands of the Shenandoah Valley in Virginia. On the thin blue line where the mountains meet the sky at dusk in the Shenandoah, the Virginians say you can see forever. *Shenandoah* is a Cherokee word and means Daughter of the Morning Star. I called Specialist Smith, "Shenandoah Warrior." He was eagle-eyed and tall, carried an M-4 and two fighting knives, and he spoke of Civil War generals from both North and South with a warrior's respect.

We rode in thirteen trucks, heavy machine guns and .50 calibers and MK 19s mounted, squad leaders carrying shotguns. Attack Company, I would discover, always rode into combat loaded for bear.

We dismounted in pure desert well south of Fallujah, gray skies flooding the western horizon. Into the desert we patrolled, 10th Mountain warriors stalking the sand and cliffs and muddy ravines like Zen Master and Sergeant York in Mosul, eyes on, clips jacked in, moving silently through the desert in the early dusk. I was damn happy; finally, we were doing what we'd talked about up north, running counter-mortar patrols, seeking out the enemy, and making it clear we would strike and kill at any and every opportunity.

The light infantrymen were tight and together, silent in the desert, scoping far lines of palm trees for snipers, solid on the long counter-mortar patrol in sands Xenophon's light infantry had stalked so long ago.

At seven in the evening we rolled back hard, wheelmen racing us back through the desert. There was no sign of mortar activity in that area: no mortar pits dug, no stakes or stones used to aim mortars left on the ground, no footprints near hasty fighting holes—no fighting holes for that matter.

The Ironman dropped me off back at Battalion TOC and I thanked him, and Shenandoah Warrior shouted, "10th Mountain. Climb to Glory!" and gave me a thumbs-up.

I woke at seven the next day and ate chow with Regan. He told me there was a big shindig that morning with the sheikhs and imams at Forward Operating Base St. Mere. I checked with Spartan Six, who confirmed the meeting and welcomed me to join him. He told me the Judge would meet us there. I rode to the meeting with Legendary Medic and Drinkwine at 9 A.M., Specialist Stephens, cool behind the wheel, his M-4 in arm's reach on the way to St. Mere. There were gulls out all along the route and a few hawks high on the eastern horizon, dark wings spread wide against the indigo sky. There were cold desert winds and blue skies and the rubble of Saddam's Iraqi Army on the sides of the potholed asphalt road to MEC, Iraqi tanks and armored personnel carriers (APCs) rusting in the desert east of Fallujah.

Colonel Jeffrey Smith, 3rd Brigade commander, 82nd Airborne Division, was right on time and shook Drinkwine's hand hard, greeting him in the bright mid-morning sun on November 20, 2003. I called Colonel Smith, "Spartacus." He had immense command presence. He was about six feet tall and sledgehammer-tough, face tanned and eyes intense, and his hair was white. With the Judge and Spartacus in the room, it was like having two heavyweight prizefighters on hand if anything got out of control.

The sheikhs and imams were late and when they finally did show, it was getting on to ten. While we waited, Legendary Medic told me that previous meetings had been held downtown, in the mayor's cell. Task Force 1Panther's convoys had been attacked with AK-47s and RPGs by Iraqi insurgents each time on their return to Volturno. I asked him if the sheikhs had left first, following the end of each previous meeting. He told me the sheikhs had left roughly ten minutes before the paratroopers, in each case.

The sheikhs and imams are targeting the Coalition at these CMO meetings, I reckoned. It was too easy; all the sheikhs and imams had to do was call in their departure to the feydayeen in Fallujah, make their getaway, and the feydayeen could drive up, set up their ambushes, and drive away. But not at St. Mere.

The sheikhs and imams waltzed in, wearing their gold sunglasses and dark robes over business suits and dishtashas. A welder named Ra'ad, who Legendary Medic told me had been handpicked by Sheikh Gazi Al Bowisa and Khamis Sirhan to be the next mayor of Fallujah, showed up. Ra'ad was about five foot six, chunky, and had salt-and-pepper hair. He wore a brown three-button suit, gray shirt, and a gold tie.

The mayor resigned twenty minutes into the meeting and Ra'ad was elected mayor by the ruling council of Fallujah, the sheikhs, and the imams gathered on the compound. Mayor Ra'ad knew his term was only temporary and intended to last only to December 15, 2003. He accepted the praise of the sheikhs and imams and sat back, smiling.

An Iraqi-orchestrated chaos ensued for the rest of the meeting, sheikhs and imams jabbing their fingers at the colonels, Legendary Medic translating in fits and starts.

At one point, a fat mustachioed sheikh stood and pointed at both colonels, jabbing his hands toward them, leaning forward, his voice rising as he ended his diatribe against the Coalition in Fallujah. "And I tell you, as Allah is my witness, you Americans have no power in Fallujah! We will show you the power we have! We control Fallujah. You will feel our fury! You will see our days of wrath!" Sheikhs and imams did nothing to stop him throughout his rant, and many of them nodded, grinning slightly, as he continued standing, glaring at the colonels. Lambert jumped up from a couch, set one hand on his sidearm, and looked directly at the ranting sheikh.

Spartacus leaned forward slightly, nodding to the assembled gathering. He glanced at Drinkwine as if to say, "I'll handle this," and Drinkwine nodded very slowly. Smith said to Legendary Medic, "Make sure you translate each word."

"Yes sir," Legendary Medic replied.

Smith sat up, ramrod straight. The ranting sheikh, still standing, started to speak but Smith shot out a hand, swift and sharp, cutting him off.

"My turn."

The sheikhs and imams looked around the table at each other. The ranting sheikh sat down. Lambert kept a hand on his sidearm.

"Know this," Spartacus said, looking around the table, crows-feet deepening about his eyes.

"I am not a policeman. I am not a police chief. My men are not policemen. My men are warriors. I am a warrior, and I command warriors."

Legendary Medic translated slowly and the sheikhs and imams looked down. The ranting sheikh was meek now, hands in his lap. Spartacus looked straightaway at the ranting sheikh.

"If you threaten me or threaten any of my men, I will kill you. And furthermore, some of you have demanded I pull Coalition forces out of Fallujah. The only way I'll pull Coalition forces out of Fallujah is if attacks on my men, and on all Coalition forces, especially convoys, cease. When the feydayeen no longer has a home in Fallujah, and attacks on my men cease, I'll be happy to pull my men out of Fallujah. That is all I have to say. Let's continue with the meeting," Spartacus said, and the Judge glanced around at the now quiet gathering of Fallujah's political elite and sat down.

That evening, back at Volturno, Legendary Medic told me that he thought Khamis Sirhan, a key insurgent leader in western Iraq, and

Sheikh Gazi Al Bowisa had "cooked the meeting," as we drank strong black coffee and tea in Captain Huston's hootch.

"Sure," he said, stirring sugar in his tea. "Sheikh Gazi and Khamis Sirhan cooked that up before anyone showed. Neither of them was there. Gazi wasn't there because that's his way of saving face and sending the unspoken—and more powerful for its silence—message that he controls the sheikhs, regardless of whether he is there or not. Khamis wasn't there because he knows we're out to capture or kill him. Khamis Sirhan is behind a helluva' lot of the feydayeen in Fallujah, and all western Iraq. All right, notice that no one wanted to dispute Ra'ad as a candidate; he's Gazi and Khamis's boy. He's a welder, man. The existing mayor is afraid of being assassinated by the feydayeen. That and he wasn't Sheikh Gazi or Khamis's boy. They couldn't control him.

"Look, a lot of people are giving feydayeen moral cover in Fallujah, not only financing them. It's the moral cover that is, in certain ways, more damaging. What does that say to the community? These men are leaders and must take a stand against the feydayeen, against Al Quaeda. They must show moral courage.

"There is a saying from the Koran: 'He who does not say the truth, when the truth is needed, is a silent devil.' Fallujah is a city of silent devils. We are in the midst of many silent devils. We were sitting with them today. There are two colleges in this town that we could build tomorrow. One of them would be the first college for women in Fallujah, ever. And a hospital: CPA has that money, too. We have the money and the sheikhs know it. We have the resources and the imams know it. But they want to keep giving moral cover and, some of them, financial backing, to the feydayeen. Silent devils."

Night and day we raided and patrolled on through November; Charlie Company raided for the very active, very dangerous, and very elusive feydayeen leader Abu Shihab deep in the night on November 25 and was fired on with RPGs. Abu Shihab escaped our warriors that night, but hell would come for Abu Shihab seven weeks later. Alpha Company nailed Abu Shihab in a daring daylight raid in Fallujah on January 15, 2004, capturing him and two other prominent feydayeen leaders at a shop in the heart of downtown Fallujah with the assistance of the U.S. Army Special Forces commandos Ghost, Phantom, and Cool Hand Luke. The

Desert Yetis, led by the Jedi Knight, were the main effort for the January 15 raid on Abu Shihab.

Four days after Charlie Company's night raid on Abu Shihab, I was out the wire with First Platoon, Attack Company, the Ironman carrying his shotgun and Shenandoah Warrior scoping the desert with his M-4. Thanksgiving was over, but we were all giving thanks to be alive in those desert autumn days in Fallujah.

November 29, 2003, was a brilliant, sunny day, with high, blue, cloudless skies all around, shepherds and goatherders waving to us as we entered desert and skirted gravel pits, rolling south of Fallujah. We dismounted near deep ravines, heading west on foot, First Lieutenant Adam Bohlen, a brother Marine infantry veteran, wiping sweat from his eyes and signaling to Kirkpatrick as we veered southwest. The men carried their weapons at the hip, spreading out some twenty meters apart in the wide-open hardscrabble desert, jumping over irrigation canals, and covering down for one another.

There was a blue-green line far on the horizon; I scoped it with my Steiner 6x30 binoculars and saw it was a beautiful line of date palms, high and green and thick. There were children racing through the date palms, long bolts of cloth streaming from their hands while they ran and chased each other under the western Iraqi sun.

I called Bohlen "Lieutenant Chesty" because he often talked of the legendary U.S. Marine infantryman and combat commander, Brigadier General Lewis B. "Chesty" Puller. Talking with him and Sergeant First Class Steve Huber, his platoon sergeant, the night before, Bohlen had said, "Chesty Puller was a warrior, one of our greatest ever, in any service. And at least three of those Navy Crosses should've been Medals of Honor. He was no friggin' politician, he kissed no backsides! You don't win wars by praising those who also stand and wait. Wait in a firefight and you're dead. You could add at least two divisions to the army, and a division to the Marines, by handing out rounds and weapons and MREs to people in the Defense Department. We shouldn't even call it the Defense Department. That's bullshit! It's the War Department, that's who we are, warriors. Long live Chesty!"

Now it was getting on to four in the afternoon and we'd humped some five klicks on patrol in the desert, Lieutenant Chesty leading the

Old School Warriors into gullys and up over berms, Huber scoping far earthen berms and lines of date palms with his M-4, signaling to the Guerrilla Warrior, Sergeant Shaun Hall, to spread his fire team out as they swept up over a berm. There was a pond glittering east of us, gulls flocking over the dark pond waters.

"Hell yes!" Kirkpatrick exclaimed, crossing the berm. He raised his shotgun high and waved us forward. The ground was steep on the other side, loose and sandy, and there were mortar pits everywhere with white-painted aiming rocks pointing east toward Volturno. The mortar pits were lined with gravel and sandbags and were scattered over some one hundred meters of undulating desert terrain.

Lieutenant Chesty's men hustled over to each pit. His platoon sergeant, Sergeant First Class Steve Huber from Hawaii, the "Old School Warrior King," talked into his I-Com and motioned to the lieutenant that there were more mortar pits near the pond, 10th Mountain light infantrymen marking the position of each mortar pit.

We patrolled on south, nearing a sandstone cliff, jeep trails curving around the southern side of the cliff. Old School Warrior King called to Guerrilla Warrior on his I-Com to climb the cliff and check it out; it looked ideal for mortar firing positions. Date palms swayed in strong winds southeast of the cliff and gulls swooped over the desert, swarming in huge flocks right over us, headed for the pond. The air was clean, scent like hemp rope and sand and dried palms burning, dry desert heat like the Mojave where I'd trained as a Marine long ago. We patrolled toward the cliff, machine gunners carrying their light machine guns from the hip, fire team leaders scoping the far sands. There was only one way up the cliff, roughly forty meters, without ropes; a steep, sharp groove cut by rain and wind and time into the cliff on its western side. Hall slipped his M.203 over his back, climbed hand-over-hand, and kneeled on the top of the cliff. I climbed up and he reached down and pulled me up as I got over the edge, and I thanked him. He covered the cliff, scoping it. There were tombstones and mounds of dirt at one end of the cliff.

I reached down and pulled up Private First Class Ainsworth, and he sorted himself out and pulled up another brother light infantryman. "It's a cemetery, brothers," Hall said, his M.203 shouldered, scoping gullies and gravel pits east of us, Kirkpatrick and Bohlen together now, patrolling north toward sloping dunes, their radiomen by their side. There were piles of feces throughout the cemetery, and we covered our faces with bandanas.

Hall's fire team joined him and he motioned for us to take a knee. Back to back, making a cross of sorts in the cemetery on top of the cliff, his men covered one another as they scoped the desert in all directions.

Route 10 ran east of us, traffic light on that late November afternoon. Hall called in our position to Huber, told him there was "nothing up here but graves and shit," and informed him that we were headed back to re-join the patrol. We were all pumping sweat now, and we moved slowly down the cliff and out north into the desert to rejoin our comrades. North of us, Kirkpatrick was kneeling on the side of a dune, his warriors securing a perimeter in all directions. He waved to us, pumping a fist, smiling. We jogged up to him, Ainsworth checking our six.

"Four 155 rounds. Fresh feydayeen cache," he said, pointing to the other side of a dune. "We'll either blow it in place or take the 155s back to Volturno. Feydayeen IED cache, four 155s, daisy-chained; that would kill at least fifteen of my men." He gripped his shotgun hard and gazed north, shaking his head slightly, squinting. Gulls were diving in the pond now and I could see flocks of small birds, perhaps starlings or sparrows, on the far side of the pond and date palms beyond, wide green palms a brighter green in the strong desert sun. The wind carried the smell of fresh burning hemp rope.

The four 155 artillery rounds were packed with Semtex and TNT. The artillery rounds had South African markings, like many in Iraq. Footprints leading down the dune ended at fresh tire tracks in a culvert. Kirkpatrick's light infantrymen were eyes on, machine gunners in the prone now, barrels flush on burlap laid over piles of sand, sun burning hot on us from the west. Staff Sergeant Steven Hassell, a wisecracking, amiable staff sergeant who was six foot five and massive like a nose tackle, came up over the dune and said, "Sir, we've got a crate of 7.62 ammu-nition." I called Hassell, "Sasquatch."

The captain grinned and waved his radioman over. Smith called Task Force 1Panther, wiping sweat from his face with a black bandana as he made the call. Staff Sergeant Jeremiah Patterson from Illinois, "Big Pat," a jovial father of three young daughters, was taking pictures of the cache and jotting down notes in a small, green, pocket-sized notebook.

"Well, we could blow it in place. I'd rather do that, myself. Hate riding back in a truck with four 155s," Big Pat said, grinning.

The order came down to secure the 155s in a truck and it was Patterson's truck that carried them. Our patrol convoy rolled up, dust drifting over us as they neared, light infantrymen shouting, "Hua! Fuckin'-a, we got a cache!" as the first truck in the convoy halted.

A dirt road ran east to west through the desert. There was a bend in the road perhaps one hundred meters south of our southern perimeter. 10th Mountain warriors dug in on staggered dunes on our southern perimeter, facing south and southwest. Our machine gunners, set in on the dunes, covered wide fields of fire on the hardscrabble desert south of Fallujah. Gulls were diving on the pond now, some rising with small fish in their beaks. I scoped palms far southwest of us and saw shepherds, men wearing gray dishtashas over jeans, moseying about near huge flocks of sheep and goats. A bulldozer was parked on the shoulder, at the bend in the dirt road. A white pickup truck stopped just in front of the bulldozer as Sasquatch and Big Pat started moving the 155 rounds, hand over hand, to the truck, walking slowly in the late afternoon heat, their rifles slung across their backs.

A man wearing a white-and-red-checked kaffiyeh and a long white dishtasha got out of the white pickup and stood, arms folded, glaring at us. I pointed him out to Kirkpatrick. The Ironman grimaced, squinting hard, shaking his head. The captain pointed out the man to Bohlen. The man was some two hundred meters from us, but no more than seventy meters from our machine gunners on the edge of our hasty perimeter. The man, watching us watch him now, reached for a chest pocket in his dishtasha, pulled out a mobile phone, and dashed behind the bulldozer.

"Sir, he's likely feydayeen, but without a weapon . . ." Lieutenant Chesty said to the Ironman, shrugging. Kirkpatrick nodded, biting his lip. The captain cradled his shotgun and his eyes narrowed in the desert east of the Euphrates and south of Fallujah.

The man came around to the front of the bulldozer now, and a second pickup raced up, dust flooding over it as it slammed to a stop. Four men in collared shirts and jeans were in the second pickup. One of them was wearing a white-and-red-checked kaffiyeh loosely around his neck. They talked with the man we'd first spotted and gestured excitedly, pointing toward us.

Our machine gunners were very alert now, up on their guns, ammo bearers scoping the men by the pickups with small binoculars. One of the men in jeans pulled out a cell phone and stepped behind the bulldozer. I unsheathed my Kukri. Ironman nodded to me.

I held the Kukri high and walked to our machine gunner closest to the men, waved the knife, and shouted, "Mala Mustafa Barzani, peshmerga, peshmerga, Kurdistan, Mala Mustafa Barzani!"

The man behind the bulldozer dashed back and his friends just looked at me, expressionless, and got in their trucks and hung a U and drove west. They sped away, dust clouding their wake, and our machine gunners cheered. Huber shouted, "Fuckin'-a, well-done, damned right!" The Old School Warriors joined him, howling in the desert, the pride of 10th Mountain. Bohlen said, slapping me on the back, "Hawk, you can join us on every mission brother, outstanding."

We returned to Volturno in the early dusk, rolling by Bravo Company, the Wild Bunch, as we made our way toward the sappers' home on the eastern edge of the huge base, flocks of seagulls dotting the blue lake water, saw grass bending golden in the twilight breezes. The Wild Bunch was checking out their trucks, doing preventive maintenance, hoods up, machine gunners working on their gun mounts. I had chow with Bohlen and Huber, celebrating the counter-mortar patrol.

Two nights later, Caliguire's Commandos raided deep in the night and captured Abu Jasim, a prominent feydayeen IED financier, bomber, and insurgent cell leader. Caliguire's Commandos again raided the following night, nailing a key Ba'athist general and feydayeen leader, Brigadier General Darhan Al Mehemdi; the Count had again planned simultaneous raids throughout all Fallujah to seize him. Three raids went down in Fallujah that night, all after Darhan. Serpico's sources on the street in Fallujah had confirmed deep feydayeen links to the Ba'athist general.

Vegas and his warriors captured him; I was with Attack Company far to the north, in a field near a schoolhouse, watching the moon high to the west at two in the morning, our raid a dry hole, when the call came down for us to leave.

Lieutenant Chesty exclaimed on the ride back, highway south a long ribbon of asphalt in the night, "Fuckin'-a, right bubba! Alpha got the Ba'athist sonofabitch. Paratroopers, baby! Hell yes, it's too damn cold, let's get back to base, Hua! 10th Mountain Climb to Glory!" The men were jubilant coming through the wire; nailing Saddam's generals really pumped us up. Fighting spirit was high, coming through the wire in the zero dark thirty cold in Fallujah, stars blazing deep in the night over date palms amber in the darkness.

In the morning, I ran flak jacket PT near noon. Finishing the run, Viburs hailed me from the Desperados' small concrete hootch. He was kicked back, taking in the sun, drinking water from a plastic bottle. He seemed to be in a good mood and I asked him why and he replied, "You're damn right! Oh yes, first time we ever had Iraqis coming up to us on the street in Fallujah and congratulating us, first time. This morning, by God and General Grant! We're out on patrol, all right. Making contacts, dropping off leaflets, doing our regular 'hit the street and meet and greet whole nine yards groove' in Fallujah. Oh yes! First time ever Iraqis of all ages coming up to us and saying, 'You got that Ba'athist general last night, you got Darhan! Thank you, thank you. He was an evil man, all Ba'athist generals, you must capture them. Good, good, tell the Americans they did good. Thank you for capturing Darhan, thank you.'"

He guzzled down some water and set the jug down on a wooden stool, seagulls flying west of us, gliding slowly in the desert sun. A dust devil kicked up some two hundred meters east of us on base and died down as quickly as it'd roared, a thin trail of dust falling away from it.

"Man, this is beautiful. In my duty here, it's dicey, you have to read the tea leaves, you know? You have to learn how to listen to the wind. When Iraqis in Fallujah, a Ba'athist stronghold, are coming up to us right on the street, in front of their neighbors and in front of the sheikhs and imams, no hesitation, and thanking us for taking down a Ba'athist general, then we know we're making a difference here. Oh hell yes, I'm in a good mood, brother. Man, what happened today never happened before. It was beautiful. Caliguire's Commandos, hell yes!"

Days to come, I was outside the wire on raids and patrols and reflecting on how we could take down Saddam, if he was in our vicinity. I remembered the Scouts up north talking about the same thing and Morales saying he would "set up long-range desert recon, near road junctions and just way the hell out there, scouts and snipers—you'll catch him on the fly, when he least expects it. Intel says he's moving, always on the move. Good. When he stops to eat or drink or piss, we come up out of the sand and nail him."

● ● ●

"The Marines got me before the 82nd," he said, reaching out a hand. "Sergeant First Class Lopez, Scouts Platoon sergeant. I call Lancaster, Texas, home. Small town south of Dallas. I'm from Waxachie, Texas, born and bred. Heard you were a Marine infantryman. Which outfit were you with?"

Thus I met "the Bear" near noon on December 5 at Volturno. Sergeant First Class Richard Lopez was a graduate of the Marine Scout/Sniper School at Quantico, Virginia, father of three, and a natural-born coffee-drinking career warrior. He was stocky and solid, built like the weightlifter that he was. It turned out we'd served in the same regiment, 3rd Marine Regiment of 3rd Marine Division, in the late 1980s in Hawaii. Now it was December 5, in the late morning at the battalion ops center. He was checking in with Mark Twain before riding back through the desert to "Forward Operating Base Factory, hell, we just call it the factory. It's a dump but it's home—across the Euphrates."

The Scouts of First Battalion-505th Parachute Infantry Regiment, paratrooper scout/snipers, were carrying out desert reconnaissance patrols deep in the sands roughly three hours southwest of Fallujah and west of the Euphrates, he told me as I poured a cup. The Count hailed us as he hustled past for the ops center, head down, grimacing, rubbing at his eyes, the guerrilla war chess grandmaster deep in thought.

"We might nail Saddam out there, if we can find his convoy late at night," the Bear said, standing under the gray-green and sand-colored camouflage netting outside the ops center and stirring sugar in his black coffee. "There are main north-south highway routes near us and junctions northwest that lead to Syria. He's slick; he may be traveling on the western side of the Euphrates. Who knows? He's in smaller convoys now, is what we've been told, running in five to eight vehicles. In September and October, the word was his convoys were never less than ten vehicles. We'll get that sonofabitch, yes indeed," he said, gulping down his coffee and pouring another cup. I poured a cup and we toasted to Chesty Puller.

"Well, I'm damned glad you're with us," Lopez said, sipping his coffee now. "Heard you were with Scouts up north. Screamin' Eagles. I was with them in the war here in ninety-one."

I told the Bear about Kentucky Rifle and the Guerrilla Fighter and the Pathfinder up north and he lit up, asking all kinds of questions about counter-IED patrols and the Payback Raid.

Lopez was a scout/sniper in the Marines from 1986 to 1990, honorably discharging in March 1990 as a corporal. That December he'd re-enlisted for the Persian Gulf War in the Screaming Eagles, swooped to Saudi Arabia, linked up with Second Battalion-327th Regiment, 101st, and air assaulted north in the ground war, nearly to the banks of the Euphrates.

He was jovial, even-tempered, and had flat, hard eyes, like the machine gunners I'd served with in Marine infantry from the Midwest and the South—Brown of Missouri, Lalor of Minnesota, and Culverhouse of Alabama. It was no surprise, really, when the Bear told me he'd carried an M-60 machine gun in the Persian Gulf War.

I asked him if I could join the Scouts for eight to ten days on long-range recon in the desert, and he checked it out with his platoon leader, First Lieutenant Swartwood, who was inside the battalion ops center. After a few minutes, the Bear came back out. "Buddy, you're qualified for long-range desert recon with paratrooper scouts and snipers, hell yes. We'll ride in five. Grab your gear."

We rode jeep trails and dirt roads for the Dam Road in the late morning, skirting the southern reaches of Fallujah, kids and teenagers waving to us and shouting, "Amerikee, Amerikee," black smoke drifting from burning rubber truck tires in the alleys. A few Iraqi men exchanged Arabic greetings with me as we rode through the dust. The sappers cleared the Dam Road, Streetfighter and New York Warrior leading their squads through the heart of the Boneyard down the potholed and hard-balled road's dirt shoulders, children running out from their houses and shouting, "Amerikee, Amerikee!," smiling and waving to us. Captain Cirino, the Headquarters Company commander from New York City—a wisecracking mustang officer and like many of the paratroopers under his command, an Afghan veteran—handed out candy to the children as they mobbed him. He was grinning, handing out the candy, shotgun in one hand and grabbing gobs of candy out from a bellows pocket with the other, the kids smiling, swarming all around him under a desert sun.

Crossing the Euphrates, I could see swans out on the water, on the western banks. There were date palms all along the western banks and thick high stands of saw grass and pussy willows. There was a scent there along the river that reminded me of the highlands of the Black Lahu and the Karen and Hmong in northern Thailand in the cool season, the scent of bougainvillea and slow-burning pine and cypress strong on the breezes off the Euphrates west of Fallujah. We rode down dirt roads west of the river past farms and fields of harvested wheat and cotton, shepherds and goatherders returning my greeting from fields and desert.

The farms were beautiful on the western side of the Euphrates, clustered with date palm groves. One of the Scouts, Specialist Daniel Zavala, an Afghan veteran from Southern California whom I called "Aztec Warrior," asked me to scope the date palms as we rode, checking for insurgent RPG positions and any insurgent snipers. Luckily, the ride was without incident and we arrived at one of Saddam Hussein's Iraqi Army artillery factories in the mid-afternoon, skies blue all ways, the desert a wide endless sea beyond the khaki-colored concrete and cinder-block walls of the factory.

There were artillery pieces everywhere, U.S. 105s and 90s and an occasional 155mm heavy gun. The barrels were rusted from the rain and exposure, but otherwise they looked functional, which disappointed me. I'd been told up north in late July that the Coalition had disarmed and destroyed all of the Iraqi Army's artillery and armor. In the compound, Forward Operating Base Factory, stood Iraqi Army munitions and artillery warehouses. Delta Company, commanded by Captain Brian Fedderler, had a sizeable element at the factory. The captain and his first sergeant stayed at their company CP just up the street from the Scouts' one-story concrete bungalow. Delta Company element was on Quick Reaction Force (QRF) missions, counter-mortar missions, traffic checkpoint missions (searching for feydayeen munitions and weapons), counter-IED missions, and heavy-guns fire-support missions.

I stowed my gear and drank coffee with Swartwood. The Scouts had been on desert reconnaissance late in the evening the night before and were cooling out in their hootches, smoking and joking and taking it light, listening to heavy metal and rap and late-fifties doo-wop. Camouflaged rifles and war gear hung from their walls, sniper rifles and live rounds and nightscopes and grenades stowed in sturdy plywood bins marked with their names and ranks. Their sniper rifles were wrapped with burlap and painted shades of green, gray, and sand. Aztec Warrior put a finger to his lips, nodding to me, as he stitched long strips of burlap to his rucksack, camouflaging it to match his sniper's Ghilly camouflage suit hanging from a nail on a wall in his hootch. Contemporary Aphrodites in various states of undress adorned the walls, no doubt providing the scouts with much-needed motivation and inspiration in the Iraqi desert.

Sheets of rain poured down as dusk fell, and we got hit with mortar fire, six rounds thudding down about seven fifteen in the evening. Sergeant First Class Ness, the Mortars platoon sergeant, rushed over in the pouring rain and asked Swartwood for a team of Scouts to support a counter-mortar patrol mounted reconnaissance.

Zavala grabbed his M-4 and a radio. We rolled out the wire at seven thirty, three mortar trucks and one scout truck. It was Friday night in the desert, and Specialist Jeremy Dunaway, a tall, broad-shouldered, tow-headed man from Akron, Ohio, and a keen sniper, said as we rolled out into the rain, "Definitely one Friday night we could do without—no booze, no women, and the fuckin' feydayeen sonsofbitches hitting us with mortars—Friday night in Iraq!"

Zavala and Private First Class Raymond Rosetta, a Pueblo Indian from Santo Domingo, New Mexico, rode with me, Rosetta on our nine o'clock. I called Rosetta, "Pueblo Warrior." Cold, hard, December rain soaked us as Specialist Dunaway drove, oceans away from his hometown, twenty-two years old in that bone-chilling cold desert storm. He was a sniper and assistant team leader to his comrade in the passenger's seat, Sergeant John Howerton. Howerton is a native of San Antonio, Texas, and an accomplished sniper. I called him, "Lone Star."

Lone Star led the Scouts 2nd Team. He was Ranger/Airborne qualified and an Afghan veteran. He was twenty-five years old in that late autumn.

There were three Mortar gun trucks up with us: a Ma Deuce on point; M240B, 7.62 heavy machine gun mounted behind us; and on trail, an MK 19. We rolled slowly, fields just barely visible in the hard-scrabble desert, pure desert beyond the fields like a sea at night in a storm, one vast endless wave of sand lost in the darkness.

Black clouds lined the southern horizon. Lurching, rolling, and rocking on slowly in the desert, the Scouts and Mortars made their reconnaissance, scoping the desert for any sign of insurgent mortar teams—mortar firing pits, tubes tossed askance, anything that might indicate where Aztec

Warrior and Pueblo Warrior whispered to me to look for fighting holes and mortar pits.

It was black like a no-moon night in Karen highlands in northeastern Burma. With the heavy storming rain, I could barely see in front of my hand. Dunaway negotiated a jeep trail in the cold storming darkness, shooting us through breaks in high earthen berms and around mud holes. Lights flickered from mud huts far to the west. "Farmers' huts," Zavala told me. He handed me a set of NODs and told me to scope west. Rolling in the darkness in the cold desert rain, I could see the country was built for war—specifically for siege and trench warfare.

Saddam's investment in Fallujah, like Mosul, was geared for death. The long, wide mounds of dirt that crisscross the desert near Fallujah are familiar sights in many open-desert areas of Iraq, especially near chemical factories, munitions factories, and military bases. The many earthern berms near Fallujah and throughout Iraq that are built up for no apparent reason provide immediate cover from machine gun fire. Also, the berms act as the first line of defense for trenches. And if you build the berm first, you've got plenty of cover to dig your trenches, of course. I handed Zavala back his NODs and told him, "No movement, no lights. Quiet out there, brother." He gave me a thumbs-up, saying, "Let's keep it that way, bro."

Near 9:30 P.M., Rosetta and Zavala grabbed their rifles and NODs and rucksacks and jumped off the back of the truck, inside the wire. The scouts cleared and checked their rifles, flashing their tac lights on their chambers, and then Dunaway scoped their rifles, making sure. We were soaked to the bone.

Specialist Cesario Machado Jr. from Sacramento, California, was singing, "Love the funky desert rain, yeah baby, gotta' love the Iraqi rain," as we walked in. Zavala replied, "Only the true desert warriors patrol in the rain, Machado, and you should learn how to sing. You need Britney Spears to give you some lessons, hell yes," Rosetta busting up and Machado shaking his head, grinning. I got clean, put on a dry set of fatigues, and drank coffee with the Desert Scout—First Lieutenant Swartwood.

Swartwood was an Afghan veteran from Clio, Michigan, twenty-seven years old, and a West Point graduate. He lined a shelf in his hootch with photos of his fiancée. He would smile broadly when he spoke of her, and his voice was low and there was real warmth in his words.

The Desert Scout commanded three teams of six scouts, each team broken into two separate sniper teams. Each sniper team had a sniper, spotter, and radioman. His snipers carried .50-caliber Barrett heavy sniper rifles, accurate on point targets out to two thousand meters in the desert; M-24, 7.62-caliber sniper rifles, accurate out to twelve hundred meters in the desert; and the Stoner system SR-25, 7.62-caliber black plastic and metal sniper rifle, basically a modified AR-18. The SR-25 is common to U.S. Special Operations Forces and a preferred sniper rifle of the U.S. Navy SEALS.

Staff Sergeant Jason Martin, from Lynchburg, Virginia, came in while the Desert Scout was discussing his teams, and together we talked about Fallujah and Al Quaeda and their mission in the desert. I called Martin, "the Virginian." He was about six foot even, brown-haired, and solid. Ranger/Airborne qualified, he was an Afghan veteran and like the Desert Scout, he was twenty-seven.

Swartwood leaned forward, forearms resting on his wooden desk, photos of his beloved to his right.

"The most significant threat in Fallujah is international terrorism. Al Quaeda and other bad actors linked to Al Quaeda. The Syrians and Iranians, who finance terrorist groups like Hamas and Hezbollah, look at Fallujah as a staging area for car bombs, suicide bombs, and the like in Iraq. We've been somewhat successful at rooting out Al Quaeda here," he said, and the Virginian nodded.

"Agreed, sir, and we really need a massive presence to clear and secure Fallujah. We talk about this all the time. Our experience in combat here tells us that you'd really need at least a brigade devoted strictly to Fallujah to isolate it and clear it. Secure it. And crush the insurgency. Perhaps even two brigades. Just for the city of Fallujah. [In November 2004, a Coalition force close to division size, led by three U.S. Marine regiments from First Marine Division, assaulted and cleared Fallujah.]

"It was a huge mistake not to hammer Fallujah and the Ba'athist strongholds last April and May. Hell, I would've gone right for Fallujah like we went for Baghdad, full-bore, and never declared major combat over. It's a full-on guerrilla war now," he said, Desert Scout squinting, grinning slightly as his comrade spoke. The Virginian leaned back, folded his arms, and continued.

"The threat, as far as Ba'athist feydayeen and other anti-Coalition forces—other than Al Quaeda in Fallujah—are people financing the IED attacks, the ambushes, paying for the IEDs and the weapons and the plastic explosives. Powerful people who have real clout in the community. It's gotta' be tough for Iraqi Arabs who are against Ba'athism to really stand for the new Iraq when they see the richest and most influential sheikhs in their communities refusing to back the Coalition, and thus implicitly giving moral refuge to the Ba'athist loyalists and those who got rich off Saddam," Martin said, finishing his coffee and pouring another cup. Swartwood tapped his desk, frowning slightly, and his eyes lit up. Martin glanced at him.

"We detained a card-carrying Al Quaeda Yemeni already in Fallujah. Alpha Company captured him," Swartwood said, Martin looking quickly at him. "And the intel we get, the ground intel, indicates Al Quaeda is very focused on building cells in Fallujah. They can only do that if they have support from prominent people in Fallujah—sheikhs and imams. Especially the imams."

Fifties doo-wop music drifted in from Specialist Wesley Robison's small portable stereo, and we heard Machado and Zavala belt out, "Robi's songs, Robi's songs, never out of style, Robi, Robi, he's a fifties guy!" Martin and Swartwood were grinning now, laughing.

Robison said, "C'mon guys, don't make fun of my tunes, I'm the doo-wop king!" And Machado boomed out, "Teen angel, teen angel, where are the flowers in the desert, oh, teen angel!" All of us laughed now, shaking our heads, and Robison popped his head in and said, grinning sheepishly, "Sir, I apologize for my comrades' tomfoolery. We'll pipe down, sorry sir," the lieutenant replying, "Forget about it Robison, go easy."

"He's a clean-cut kid, Robison. A paramedic before he enlisted. Utah. Good scout, excellent on reconnaissance," the lieutenant said, sipping from his coffee.

"Roger that, sir," Martin said, and Swartwood nodded to him as if to say, "Go on, brother."

"On IEDs, a huge threat in Fallujah; we're on a main resupply route out here, 1st AD [1st Armored Division] has their main supply base right smack-dab an hour and change east of here. Their convoys run to Baghdad. We've pulled over forty IEDs out of the road between here and the ASP. The feydayeen cells we've nailed in Fallujah, under interrogation, sometimes even voluntarily, prisoners have said they get paid anywhere from $20 to $50 an IED to plant it and set the charge. That means to plant those forty IEDs, which we discovered and disabled, only cost the feydayeen $2,000 U.S. You've gotta' kill the IED financiers," the Virginian said.

I told him about Einstein of Special Ops up north and his agreement with the Virginian, and the warriors peppered me with questions about First Sergeant Fulks. They clearly respected his insights and his many years of special operations service.

"I'm with Staff Sergeant Martin and can only add we need to do two things right away on IEDs. Understand the majority of the IEDs are Iraqi Army artillery rounds, like the ones you all found on the counter-mortar patrol in that cache. We've gotta' take down the guys who are planning and financing IED attacks—we've definitely had some successes there. Also—and this is very important—deny the feydayeen their IED supply. There's a plethora of old Iraqi Army artillery rounds at ammunition supply points throughout Iraq. [Author's note: Much of this ammunition came from the United States, along with many artillery cannons, shipped to Saddam during the Reagan administration, during the Iran-Iraq War (1980-88).] But we are not dedicating the resources to destroy those ammunition warehouses; we aren't dedicating the manpower to do that. And we're constantly finding small caches, also left over from the Iraqi Army.

"It's an overlooked issue, obscure in terms of the media coverage of the war, but it is crucial: We must destroy the former Iraqi Army's artillery rounds and all the old ammunition just sitting, waiting for feydayeen to creep up in the darkness and steal."

[In late October 2004, echoing Swartwood's remarks of December 2003, it was determined that massive amounts of plastic explosives and artillery shells had been stolen since early April 2004 from an Iraqi Army cache, including detonators for nuclear explosives. Colonel Joe Anderson had been ordered to bivouac at the site as he led 2nd Brigade of the 101st on its advance to Baghdad in April 2003. No one ordered him to secure the site, and his orders to advance on Baghdad were clear and firm. No one, however, has determined why the Coalition did not immediately mark and secure the site with other U.S. Army units; it is possible, of course, that there were no units available. I recommended on several occasions that at any large Iraqi Army cache, neighboring villages be evacuated so all plastic explosives and other munitions could be marked, photographed by satellites, and precision-bombed. If the U.S. Air Force dedicated itself to that mission, within thirty days all Iraqi Army caches would be destroyed. Insurgents would have nothing, at that point, to steal. Infantry companies could also get back in the fight instead of holding down guard posts in the desert.]

The lieutenant looked at his watch and smiled.

"Gents, I've gotta' call my princess. Christmas is coming. Gotta' keep my princess happy. Hawk, many thanks," he said, rising up from his desk. We shook hands and the Virginian and I talked about Stonewall Jackson's battles in the Shenandoah Valley in 1862. Confederate General Jackson, of General Robert E. Lee's army of Northern Virginia, had shrewdly and boldly used his light infantry to stunning effect, striking deep across the mountains and shocking Union Army commanders, left and right.

"Remember, General Stonewall Jackson: 'When you unsheathe the sword—'"

"—throw away the scabbard," I said, finishing it for him. "Even a Grant man knows that's right." He grinned.

"Buddy, I'll forgive you for being a Grant man! Recon patrol going out tomorrow night. You'll be on it with Sergeant McGuire. He'll carry the SR-25. SEALS like that sniper rifle. I'm fond of the old M-14, scoped out, the customized sniper version of that fine rifle, myself. Go easy, brother," he said.

Sergeant Patrick McGuire was a shaved-head, gregarious, mammoth of a sniper from Venicia, California, near San Francisco. Twenty-one, he was an Afghan veteran. Ranger/Airborne qualified and well schooled in all sniper systems—Barrett, M-24, SR-25, and scoped-out custom M-14— he was the Virginian's assistant team leader. I called him, "The Panther."

He carried his SR-25 combat-slung across his chest in the way of SAS snipers on reconnaissance, stalking the desert in the moonlit night. The ground was still damp from the storm the night before. You could see tracks of wild dogs and foxes in the wet sand. A sidearm was strapped to McGuire's right thigh. He was thirty meters ahead of me, Ghilly suit draped over him like a burlap sack, eyes on rolling desert northwest of us. Wild dogs loped and howled some one thousand meters to the west of us, loud like foghorns on a sea at night. Zavala and Private First Class Daniel Rulin were with us on the reconnaissance.

We carried out the desert recon to the north in the early dark on December 6, 2003, patrolling steadily, scouts scanning all ways, silent on the reconnaissance, patrolling for a low rise of hills at seven in the evening, highway lit up five klicks east. There was a steel gateway set over the highway, just before a T-intersection. The gateway stood over the eastern approaches to the highway. Earlier the Panther had told me that the intersection was "all wrong, that's a bad place, a lot of insurgents come up that road, pass the gate, and head north or south on the highway. We'll have a QRF, two gun trucks, down in a ravine about five hundred meters from the junction."

Sergeant McGuire took a knee and we did likewise; he looked back quickly at Zavala and Rulin behind me, waved a fist, and we rallied to him, setting up a quick 360 security in the desert, back to back in all points of the compass. I was scoping west, looking for any signs of movement. I could see far out, at least one thousand meters in the moonlight, acacia trees covering a small hill on the western horizon in the night. There was nothing around the trees for miles.

Rulin shouldered his M-4 and aimed at the highway, eyeing the spotlighted T-intersection, a taxi rolling by slowly on the hardball. Rulin was born in Moscow in 1983, and he'd lived in Utah since he was fourteen. "Stalingrad Hero" was about five foot seven and lean, with close-cropped blonde hair. Like many warriors in elite units, he had a hard-nosed, no-bullshit attitude.

McGuire snapped out the bipods on his SR-25 and got in the prone in the desert. We all got down on our bellies, Panther and Stalingrad Hero and Aztec Warrior digging in their elbows in the sand. McGuire scoped desert south of us, near the highway.

I could see a couple of wild dogs far to the west, near the acacia trees, leaping, nipping each other, and there was a long wild howl from the north, near the low rise of hills. Rulin called in our position to our reconnaissance patrol base, whispering low on the radio. Sergeant Joe LeBleu, at our recon patrol base, confirmed our position. LeBleu was from Brooklyn. His wife was in North Carolina and he spoke of her with deep affection—she was his sun and his moon. LeBleu, "Long Rifle," had been a Ranger, was qualified on all sniper systems, and had re-enlisted after September 11, 2001. He was in Manhattan when the World Trade Center was attacked and remembered "feeling godawful that this happened, and I knew I had to get in the fight; I'd only been out six months, I was still a Ranger in my blood, you know."

Like Einstein of Special Ops, the Guerrilla Fighter, Spartan Six, and the Jedi Knight, Long Rifle had served in 75th Ranger Regiment. "It's all close-quarter battle now, in this war and in Afghanistan, CQB and special ops," he'd observed earlier, over a coffee in mid-afternoon sun outside the Scouts' hootch, gulls skying east for the Euphrates over the factory's rusted warehouse roofs. "The Commando's right on reconnaissance. It's essential, you've gotta' have eyes-on human intel, but the street fight here, the war here, it's all close-quarter battle—CQB. You really have to know your rifle, your knife, and your sidearm, that's what this war comes down to," LeBleu had said, eyes hard under the desert sun as he sipped his coffee.

"We're good. Move out," McGuire whispered in the night, and we rose and moved on. The night passed quietly, the Panther guiding us far and deep on the desert reconnaissance, linking up with Long Rifle on the low rise of hills and returning to our extraction point near a jeep trail around midnight, five hours of desert reconnaissance solid under our belts. It was damn cold in the late December moonlight; Aztec Warrior's teeth chattered in the cold. The Bear met us back at the hootch with hot chow and the Scouts went over the night's desert reconnaissance, McGillivary talking with LeBleu and McGuire.

In the morning, Private First Class Penny cooked up the best Sunday brunch this side of the Euphrates. He cooked over open wood fires in a sandpit, grunts on KP duty tossing in chunks of wood. Beside the fire roaring in the desert sun in Iraq, "the Motown Magician" was dedicated to his duty. There were thick slices of French toast with hot butter and syrup, fresh steaming biscuits, western omelets, massive slices of beef bacon and Canadian bacon, ice-cold orange juice, heaps of Washington state red apples, and a table full of urns of piping hot, strong black coffee. The Motown Magician definitely laid out a spread for Scouts and Mortars, and the men appreciated his culinary skills, joking kindly with him as we filed in line to grab our chow.

It was Pearl Harbor Day and the Desert Scout reflected on WWII, saying, "We need that kind of unity stateside to win the War on Terror; we need committed, unified belief in victory over Al Quaeda. Unity is central to victory; without unity in your people, without commitment to victory, you'll fail. You will lose.

"Looking at WWII, our people believed in our cause. Our people sacrificed for our cause. We had passionate leadership, engaged leadership, and our people came together. Unity."

I was talking with him when Lopez came in, carrying mail and more tins of Christmas cookies. They had reconnaissance patrols to plan and I went outside and talked with Rulin, who was sipping a Pepsi. His father, mother, and sister were in West Jordan, Utah. Rulin had been in the U.S. Army since September 12, 2002. Earlier he'd been with the Second Platoon of Wild Bunch, under command of "the Rifleman," Captain Matthew Mobley, company commander of Bravo Company. Like his brother scout up north, McClure, Stalingrad Hero thought the CPA law on one AK-47 per household was a great mistake in the war in Iraq: "To win a war, you must disarm your enemy. History teaches that. First of all, if we want to win here, we've got to disarm the Iraqis. No weapons per household. One weapon per household is wrong, it's self-defeating. If we take away their weapons, we'd get attacked far less."

He set the can down, folded his arms, and squinted in the late morning light. "And the rules of engagement—those work against us, too. Less strict ROE is necessary to win the war. Combat ROE."

I told him of McClure's observation up north, which was similar to his, and he nodded quickly, his face serious, fire in his eyes. "Warriors understand war. We know how to fight and we know how to win. If you send us in harm's way, don't tie our hands behind our backs. Let us fight and let us win. McClure is right. I didn't come here to lose. I didn't come here to fail, and neither did my comrades. We are far too lenient; the Iraqis use our ROE against us. Iraqis will continue to allow feydayeen to attack us, from crowds and mosques, if they see we are afraid to fight. Our commanders are locked into rules of engagement that deny us combat initiative and allow the feydayeen to attack us. We can't shoot people with AKs. Under our ROE, we can't. That's bullshit. And the feydayeen know that and use it against us. That plus the asinine one-AK-per-household rule gives the initiative away to the feydayeen."

We talked for a while of his family's struggles during WWII and the heavy losses taken by the Soviet Army and the twenty million Soviet civilians who died in it. Rulin was stoic and reflective. You could see in his eyes that the suffering endured by countless Russians and Ukrainians and peoples of the former Soviet Union had hit close to home for him; it was still a real and living presence in his life. "It was very, very tough for us in that war. The war was right there, in our homes and in our fields. We stayed in the fight. We prevailed."

We shook hands and I went inside. Lopez told me there was an operations order meeting going on. The Scouts rested throughout the afternoon, cooling out, preparing for the long desert recon patrol that evening.

At six thirty we infiltrated into the desert, beginning the reconnaissance, skies overcast and dark, a cold wind ripping down on us from out of the west. Snipers and scouts stalked the dark sands as Xenophon's scouts no doubt patrolled in that long ago, falling to the prone in the night and scoping far dunes for any signs of enemy.

Dunaway led his team out three thousand meters southwest. I joined his team, the faint blurred lights of farmers' huts dotting sands far west of us. We were alone in the desert under dark skies, and the moon was hiding somewhere high and east of us, its faint white glow shining through the clouds like a light from a shaded window.

We reached the reconnaissance base, a low rise of hills some twenty-five hundred meters from the highway, and linked up with McGillivary and Howerton and their men. McGillivary whispered, "I'm sending a team out, get with Dunaway," and I nodded and rejoined Dunaway. Dunaway held point.

Swift in the darkness, Dunaway carrying an M-24 mounted with a state-of-the-art nightscope on his long barreled rifle, we moved out, Dunaway flicking hand-and-arm signals to Rosetta and "the Hard Rocker," twenty-four-year-old Specialist Jason Bailor from Hendersonville, Tennessee, who carried an M-4 and a radio. There were scattered dunes left of us and we used them to conceal our movements, Dunaway going to the prone every hundred meters or so and us following his lead, bellies down in the sand, watching for him to rise and rising with him. The skies were clearing to the east of us, and the moon was out now and glowing full in the night. Dunaway set us in behind mounds of sand. Looking east, I could see a house some five hundred meters away, and closer, perhaps 150 meters southeast, a small cinder-block-constructed blockhouse. There were two palm trees between the north side of the house and a jeep trail, and the moon was full and high to the south.

A gunshot cracked the silence like a truck backfiring on a deserted road and Dunaway whispered, "That's a high-powered rifle." He scoped the night, scanning with his high-tech night vision gear, Bailor calling it in. McGillivary verified it, telling us he'd heard it, too. Six shots followed, the gunfire sounding closer now, Dunaway telling Rulin to ready his M.203.

Out of the night, seven cars pulled up in front of the distant house, all with their lights off, tactical. Dunaway scoped the cars, some five hundred meters away, and whispered, "Dishtashas, headgear, Iraqi Arabs. Seven cars, all tactical. Very strange." The drivers were hanging back, he told us, and people were coming in and out of the house. I asked him, in a low voice, if it could be Saddam's convoy, and he said, squinting in the night, "That's his signature. It's possible. Rule out nothing."

McGillivary signalled to us to return. We low-crawled back in the sand, taking cover behind dirt mounds and small scraggly desert bushes before rising, crouching, and running, Rulin checking our six, all of us pumping sweat as we reached our recon base. Dunaway gave a quick reconnaissance intelligence report to McGillivary. LeBleu, Howerton, Bailor, and Rulin, along with Private First Class Hunt and Private First Class Nick Gibson, both from Colorado, and Specialist Steve Eggleston, from Los Angeles, scanned the far horizons, securing the reconnaissance base. Hunt was carrying an M.203 and a field radio. Eggleston carried an M.203 and a 9mm sidearm. Gibson carried an M-4 and a radio.

"I'm taking us back there," McGillivary whispered to me in a fighting hole. "Come with us. There's something very wrong about that house. Seven cars all at once roll up. Lights off, tactical. Very strange. Clandestine meeting of some kind, likely feydayeen. We'll get closer," he said, grabbing his M-24 sniper rifle, a sidearm on his right hip. Howerton nodded to him and grabbed the Barrett .50 caliber and Hunt followed their lead, his M.203 shouldered for quick action, radio on his back.

Four together, we moved out, Boss Sniper on point. We moved fast in the darkness through the desert, falling when Boss Sniper fell to his belly and rising with him, taking cover where we could find it. We headed east for a goatherd's cinder-block-walled corral perhaps two hundred meters from the house, and now I could see more cars parked every which way in front of it. Lone Star grabbed his sidearm from a hip holster and cleared the corners, checking around the walls of the corral, making sure. Boss Sniper did the same on the western side of the corral, and Hunt called in our position to Long Rifle at the recon base.

McGillivary and Howerton nodded to us. Howerton holstered his sidearm and scaled the wall. McGillivary handed over the Barrett .50 caliber to him and, slinging his sniper rifle over his back, he scaled the wall. I followed and Hunt popped over behind me, swift and agile like a leopard.

You could just see over the northern cinder-block walls of the corral. The walls were freshly mortared, the mortar still pebbled hard. Lone Star scoped the house and called Boss Sniper over.

"I've got thirteen vehicles and seven people outside," Lone Star whispered to Boss Sniper. "All men. All in dishtashas and headgear. Undetermined number inside."

The staff sergeant nodded, his eyes intense, sweat beading on his forehead.

"Feydayeen meeting; likely IED cell. Planning or financing IED attacks. We are very close to main supply routes, loads of IED attacks out here. Possibly Saddam's convoy. Possibly. We've got QRF. I want illum," he said, meaning illumination rounds over the house. He glanced at Hunt.

"I've got no illum grenades, Sergeant."

McGillivary shook his head and Howerton kept eyes on the house, scoping it, nodding slowly.

"No white star grenades, no flares?"

Hunt shook his head and said, "I'm sorry, all I've got is HE [high explosive]."

McGillivary bit his lip. He shrugged and said, "Call for illum. Call battalion. They can send an illum mission."

Hunt called it in and frowned, listening to battalion's reply.

"Battalion claims it's our guys, ODA, can't fire the mission, check fire, check fire, they want to know how sure are we that this is feydayeen," he said, eyebrows raised. ODA means Operational Detatchment A Team, U.S. Special Forces, which often operates clandestinely behind enemy lines. Howerton kept eyes on the house and said, "Got two, no three more cars. Tactical, lights off. More movement, more people going inside. Carrying satchels."

McGillivary folded his arms.

"How sure are we? Ask them why they think it's ODA."

Hunt relayed his message and frowned again, holding the handset.

"They claim it's Special Forces or CIA, or both."

Howerton raised a hand, gesturing quickly, eyes on the house, and said, "Got nineteen cars now. Jesus, there must be fifty people in that house."

"Are they fuckin' for real?" Boss Sniper whispered. "Why the fuck would at least four Special Forces A teams and CIA show up here, and all in dishtashas and headgear? No fuckin' way. What do you think, Hawk?"

"These are Iraqis," I whispered, the men nodding. "No way this is SF, they don't make stupid moves, and the CIA isn't that slick. Wherever you are in this world, you'll find CIA in blue jeans in the field, or maybe khakis. Never that native. Send the rounds. If they are feydayeen, some will swoop once the first round lights up the sky; they will run. And you'll know they're feydayeen."

Boss Sniper gave me a thumbs-up and Lone Star kept eyes on the house, saying, "Twenty-one cars now. Exactly what I think, Mac, send the rounds."

Hunt called it in. It was now ten minutes since the first call for illum.

"Sergeant Mac, battalion wants to know if you want illum." McGillivary grimaced. Wild dogs howled maybe two hundred meters dead east, and a fire sparked far to the south in the desert, flame bright in the far sands deep in the night.

"What the fuck is going on at battalion? Send the fuckin' illum for Chrissakes," he whispered.

Hunt called it in and frowned.

"Battalion wants to know, are you absolutely sure they're not ODA?"

McGillivary glared and Howerton whispered back, over his shoulder, "Tell them we are fuckin' sure. We are fuckin' sure. Send the goddamn rounds."

Hunt called it in and said, "Wait one."

"Battalion says ODA is lost on their way to FOB Factory and may be meeting at the house, to coordinate travel."

McGillivary grinned, shaking his head. I could see men moving in and out of the house, grabbing bags out of the vehicles, and heading back into the house.

"You mean there are vehicles from Special Forces—none of them SUVs by the way, and ODA nearly always rides in SUVs—and maybe CIA, lost less than ten klicks from the factory, on the only north-south highway that leads to the factory? Approximately fifty friendlies less than ten klicks from a known friendly base with only one road to it, and they're lost? And now, they're suddenly driving up tactically to decide how to get there, because—let me think—none of them have satellite phones? If they were ODA, they would've called FOB Factory already on the satellite phone. Bullshit. These are Iraqis and it's not a club social. Tell battalion to send the fuckin' illum. Send the fuckin' rounds, now."

Hunt called it in and said, "Battalion's getting approval."

Howerton kept eyes on and said slowly and very quietly, "This is how you lose a war." It was now seventeen minutes since the first call for illumination rounds. I could see the fire easy now, flames bright in the desert like a lighthouse beaming on a sea at night.

McGillivary whispered, "Tell them I said fuck it all illum. Battalion is turning this into a goatfuck." Howerton whispered, "I've got nine outside now, nine men going in and out of the vehicles. Still twenty-one vehicles. All makes, all colors."

"Battalion says OK, illum is out," Hunt said, and Boss Sniper turned toward the house, looking over the corral wall. We could hear the round but never saw it and Boss Sniper shook his head and said softly, "Dud. Dud round." Two more dud rounds followed. It was now twenty-two minutes since the first call for illum and a fourth round blazed on impact, like a huge firecracker in the night, white light, perhaps seventy-five meters from the house.

Light splashed high over the house and I could see a parachute floating above the light, a small white parachute, and Hunt said, "Goddamn it's about fuckin' time." It was the fifth round, and the house lit up now like it was under a spotlight, roof tiles crimson in the light of the illumination round, white smoke trails falling through the desert night sky like petals from a flower.

Three men clad in white dishtashas and headgear ran out of the house, dashed over to two old black Toyota four-wheelers, and hightailed it out. One man got in one truck, and two men got in the second truck. You could see the rust above the wheel wells on the second truck in the illuminated night; the gears grinded as the driver shifted madly.

The nine men outside ran toward the house, jamming up around each other near the door as they tried to get through, wild dogs barking and howling now. Howerton said, "We'll maintain surveillance. Where's QRF?" looking at McGillivary. Normally, the QRF force, set in just five hundred meters away from the steel gateway over the highway, would've been ordered to reinforce us. Hunt glanced quickly at Howerton.

"Wait one." Hunt called in Lone Star's query on the QRF and shook his head.

"Hawk 7 says Delta 6 refused to order QRF." Hawk 7 was the Bear and Delta 6 was Captain Fedderler.

McGillivary glared and muttered, "For Chrissakes!" Lone Star kept eyes on and whispered, "Goddamnit our QRF is a stone's throw away and they can't move. Bullshit."

I gestured to McGillivary and he glanced at me, nodding.

"Ask battalion if ODA's called in our illum."

Boss Sniper grinned and whispered, "Damn right. If they were ODA, they would've called it in; if they didn't, you know for a fact it's feydayeen." Lone Star nodded, looking through the scope of his sniper's rifle, and said, "No shit, if they'd been ODA—"

"—then we'd know by now," McGillivary whispered. "I can't believe Delta 6 didn't send our QRF."

Hunt nodded, saying, "You realize it took over twenty minutes just to send those rounds?"

Howerton whispered, "How the fuck do we know that's not Saddam? It's his signature; the convoy is the same size."

Hunt called in the message on ODA and battalion told us that ODA had seen no illumination rounds. It was not an ODA meeting, McGillivary was sure of that now. In truth, he'd been sure of that from jump street. Howerton, McGillivary, and Hunt were certain from Dunaway's field intel, his hasty recon patrol report, that everything about that house was wrong. Without the gun trucks and fire support from Delta Company, however, we were out of moves. There was no way Boss Sniper could take down fifty feydayeen all by his lonesome with just two sniper rifles, a .203, and a Kukri. We had no idea what kind of weapons, and how many, the fifty or so men inside that house might have.

We scaled the wall and hustled back through the sandy ravines and gullies and hardscrabble sand to our recon base and set in, waiting for an hour before making the long patrol back across the desert. The flaks weighed heavy on us deep in the night in the desert, moon over the Euphrates and Orion high to the west a welcome presence over the far endless sea of sand.

In the morning, Ness from Mortars Platoon told Swartwood that Iraqi Arab sources had confirmed that the strange activity and meeting we'd discovered was indeed a feydayeen meeting of Fallujah black market gasoline dealers doling out the cut to the feydayeen.

I rode back to Volturno on December 14 with Lopez, Rulin, and Private First Class Chris Knouse from Sarasota, Florida, a young reconnaissance warrior, twenty years old, who carried an M-4 on the long ride to Volturno. Gray skies blanketed the eastern horizon as we rode through desert and fields on jeep trails and hardscrabble dirt roads. I remember thinking how strange it was that Iraqis of all ages were waving to us and children were ecstatic. We talked about it on the ride in, and none of us could make heads or tails of it.

At the battalion ops center on Volturno we halted. As I grabbed my gear, someone said, "Did you hear, did you hear? We got Saddam!" It was Cothern and we'd caught him by chance as he was rushing out of the ops center, grinning. Cothern was a big dude, lean and tall, and the Bear raised a hand and asked, "Are you sure? Did we really nail the sonofabitch?"

Cothern grinned like he'd won a jackpot at Vegas and shouted, "Fuck yes! Fourth ID. Tikrit. Fourth ID and Special Ops. Right on! We got the sonofabitch," and he shook Lopez's hand, and we waved to him as he headed toward the lake.

"Damn, I'd like some vodka tonight, brothers," Stalingrad Hero said, and Knouse and I laughed. Lopez grinned and said, "Watch out now, the next two weeks all the Saddam diehards will flood out; it'll get hot. Fantastic good news though, fantastic. About damn time we captured him."

Knouse grinned and a musing look came over his face. He nodded his head, M-4 between his knees, rucksack at his feet. Paratroopers waved and shouted to us as we headed for St. Mere; the Bear wanted to get the men to the PX.

Coming in the wire at St. Mere, we saw buses of Iraqi workers heading home. The workers were clapping their hands and smiling at us and waving joyfully. Riding through St. Mere to the PX, paratroopers and soldiers of all ranks waved to us—everyone got well that day at St. Mere.

⦿ ⦿ ⦿

Still in good spirits following Saddam's capture, I ran the base in my flak jacket and boots, the guards shouting, "We got the bastard!" at the south gate, raising their shotguns high in the morning sun of December 15, 2003.

Skies grayed west in the early afternoon. I grabbed some chow and coffee under the camouflage net behind the ops center. The ops center was busy as ever, the Count and Major Cool conferring with Spartan Six on upcoming raids and patrols, Legendary Medic talking with Scout of the Far Afghan Hills and Captain Love.

Captain Dave Eaton, the hard-charging and clever Charlie Company commander, whom I'd nicknamed "Wyatt Earp," was set to run a reconnaissance patrol that night at nine o'clock throughout downtown Fallujah and the northern reaches beyond the train station. Gordon and Private First Class Meismer were headed outside when Cothern frowned, listening to the batallion net.

Meismer turned and held the handset to his ear. He glanced at Gordon and said, "Get the colonel. Mayor's cell." Moments later, Drinkwine, poker-faced, listened in, handset at his ear, lines in his forehead deepening. "I'll get hold of Mayor Ra'ad. Thanks. Roger, over." Legendary Medic was at the colonel's side now. The colonel pointed to the phone on Legendary Medic's war belt.

"Call Mayor Ra'ad. And call the imams. There's a riot going down. Crowd of maybe two hundred people, some armed with AKs, headed for the mayor's cell. Call around town, find out who's behind this. Apparently there are people going around putting up broadsides saying that Saddam was not actually captured, it's all a hoax, rabble-rousers. If we can get the imams on their loudspeakers, denouncing the rioters, maybe we can defuse it. The mayor's at the cell."

"Roger that, sir. Commanders' meeting still on?"

"Absolutely. As soon as you get the imams, let me know. I want to talk with them," the colonel said, heading into the operations center.

"Yes sir," Legendary Medic replied, punching out a number on his secure satellite phone, rolling his eyes, shaking his head slightly. "Last thing we fuckin' need today, Mr. Tucker, is a riot. Saddam loyalists, my gut tells me. Ba'athists, who can't deal with the fact we nailed their hero. Well, they better fuckin' well deal with it. Saddam is in a jail cell."

I nodded to him and headed back to my hootch. I sharpened my Kukri, checked the plates in my flak jacket, and listened to Miles Davis. As for the riot, I felt that Sheikh Gazi was behind it—previous rioters, once detained, claimed that they had been paid to incite riots in Fallujah. Paying people at the drop of a hat to incite a riot two days after your former confidante and Ba'athist good buddy had been nailed was no accident, I thought. Sheikh Gazi had motive, opportunity, and money; plus, fundamental in Arab Bedouin culture, he was the tribal chieftain for Fallujah. I was certain that nothing of this size moving against the Coalition could go down in Fallujah without his approval.

At four fifteen I returned to the battalion ops center. There were now scattered reports of Ba'athist feydayeen riding in open-bed pickup trucks, waving AK-47s and RPGs, the trucks stacked with loaded magazines, assault rifles, machine guns, and RPG grenades. Legendary Medic jotted down notes furiously, talking Arabic and English seemingly at once, translating, Major Cool and the Count off to his side, trying to make sense of it.

Legendary Medic had two phones working and Mayor Ra'ad came up on one of them. The mayor was loud, frightened, and speaking Arabic in a hurried, anxious tone. I asked the Count if the imams had denounced the rioters as Drinkwine had asked. He said that some imams had indeed denounced the rioters but, "at this point, the Ba'athists are bat-shit crazy down there, they're not going to listen to anybody. They think Saddam is still free; it's as much a celebration of their illusion, that Saddam's free, as it is a riot against us. Strange friggin' country, brother," he said, shrugging his shoulders, Watson nodding in agreement.

The colonel came over, his hands on his hips. The majors nodded to him and he folded his arms, poker-faced. Legendary Medic put one finger to his left ear, a mobile phone hard against his right ear, and listened closely. It was four fifteen. Legendary Medic said "*Nam, nam,*" Arabic for yes, and set the phone down by a map of Fallujah.

"Sir, the mayor reports over two hundred people moving toward him on foot and in pickup trucks. There are still reports coming in from northern and western Fallujah of feydayeen in pickups. Trucks are loaded with RPGs, AKs, machine guns, and grenades."

Drinkwine frowned, breathing out slowly. "Keep him on the line; how many IPs does he have?"

Legendary Medic nodded and got on the horn again, staccato bursts of Arabic punctuated by long silences. Watson shrugged and stepped back into the operations center, shaking his head slightly.

Eaton stepped in the battalion TOC as Legendary Medic continued speaking. The captain had his flak jacket on. He kept his sidearm behind a hip and up against the small of his back, in a small leather rig. He took off his helmet and set it under his arm and nodded to the colonel. Drinkwine gave him a thumbs-up.

"Thirty, sir. He says he's got thirty. The mayor sounds very nervous."

"I'd be nervous, too, if I had to rely on Fallujah police for security," I said, Meismer and Gordon busting up laughing, the colonel and Legendary Medic grinning in the late afternoon.

Eaton smiled and hung his helmet on a hook on a wall.

"Mike, the words *security* and *Fallujah police* should never be mentioned in the same sentence."

All of us laughed now, radio operators and artillerymen and paratroopers guffawing, Legendary Medic saying to Wyatt Earp, "that should be engraved over the mayor's cell," the captain smiling. Legendary Medic nodded quickly and glanced at the colonel, spoke a burst of Arabic, and said, "Sir, the crowd is still building. The mayor is asking for support, sir."

"Has anyone fired on the mayor's cell?" the colonel asked.

Legendary Medic spoke quickly and listened in and then said, "*Masallahmah,*" the Arabic farewell.

"No fire on the mayor's compound, sir."

"All right. Tell him to get the imams again. Broadcast denouncements from the mosque loudspeakers. Iraqi police at the mayor's cell with AKs. We gave a hundred rounds each to those guys ten days ago. Tell them to hold."

Legendary Medic relayed the colonel's message in Arabic, steady and calm now. Listening to Drinkwine, I remembered that the Fallujah police had received two hundred rounds each since early November. With the additional one hundred rounds, that made three hundred rounds of 7.62-caliber ammunition per policeman.

Major Cool came back, talking with the Count and Wyatt Earp. The mayor answered that he'd try again to reach the imams.

"Well, tell him he'd damn sure better try real hard; that crowd has a lot of try in it," the colonel said, turning back into the ops center, commanders following him. Steinmeyer, frowning and his face flushed slightly, began pre-plotting artillery to counter an attack on the mayor's cell. I could find no fault with Spartan Six's decision: the mayor's cell was Iraqi police turf to defend, and it was time for them to take their stand. Ultimately, the Iraqis have to police themselves.

Legendary Medic was sipping tea and looking pensive.

Arabic screamed from his phone. He motioned to Meismer and waved toward the ops center. Meismer leaped up as if his chair was on fire and got Drinkwine and Eaton. They rushed over to Legendary Medic's side. It was getting on to five thirty now.

"It's the mayor, Colonel. The compound's been overrun. He's with IPs, heading to his house, sir."

"Keep him on the line."

"Roger, sir."

Eaton grabbed my shoulder, and said in a low voice, "Grab your gear. We're likely headed downtown. We'll go to my CP first."

I nodded, gave a thumbs-up to the paratroopers in the battalion TOC, and rushed out, grabbing my flak and Kukri. I couldn't find my helmet, so I went without it. Eaton was already out the door, and I slung my gear and followed him. Early dark was coming on, a gray winter horizon like you see in the American West deep in the winter, a long line of gray clouds forming over Fallujah. Eaton, calm behind the wheel, drove around the lake. He asked me if I shot photos at night and I told him no, because flash gives away position. He nodded and said, "Good, good. That's the right answer. Just do two things: stay out of the way of my men, and keep up with them. Never get out in front of my men. Never. You don't want to be in the line of fire, if anything goes down."

There was a light rain falling now as Eaton stopped the truck beside two captured Iraqi 82mm mortar tubes in front of the Gunfighters' command post. I called his men, Charlie Company, "The Gunfighters." His men had seized the mortar tubes on a counter-mortar patrol in October. Eaton was an agile man, and he leaped out of the truck and headed for his company office. Inside, his men glanced up at him and he nodded to them as if to say, "Go easy." "Are you good on gear?" Eaton asked, taking off his flak. I told him I was solid and he nodded, wincing as he took his 9mm rig off the back of his war belt. "Good. You'll go with Lieutenant Pullen's men. Sergeant First Class La Hoda is his platoon sergeant.

You'll be on main assault element to retake the mayor's cell." I regretted not having a helmet, but I had been on missions before without flak and helmet—and besides, there was no time.

I shook his hand and he entered his CP, a whirlwind of radio chatter as paratroopers manned their communications stations in the Gunfighters' command post. The captain, who'd fought in the Persian Gulf War in the same battalion as an enlisted man, told me to make myself at home. I poured a coffee and read *The Gambler, the Nun, and the Radio*, a fine short story Ernest Hemingway wrote during the Great Depression in 1933.

First Lieutenant Pullen came in and introduced himself. First Lieutenant Williams, the Gunfighters' executive officer, also stepped in, talked with us briefly, and turned his attention to the radio operators. At six fifteen Wyatt Earp stepped out of his hootch, his sidearm reset on the small of his back, lieutenants folding their arms, looking at him. I stashed Hemingway's short story in a Ziploc bag and stuffed it in a bellows pocket.

The captain shook his lieutenants' hands, looking each platoon leader in the eye. He spoke quickly, ordering them to gear up for the assault on the mayor's cell. The Gunfighters' mission was to assault and capture the mayor's cell. Hand on one hip, gesturing to a wall-sized satellite photo of Fallujah glued and taped to the concrete ceiling, he grabbed a broomstick and jabbed at the mayor's cell in the heart of Fallujah.

"We will seize and hold. Keep your powder dry and your head down. Do not slow down. Tell your men, absolutely, do not slow down. Assault and drive on. Here, we'll attack," he said, pointing to a side entrance of the mayor's cell, near the south side, facing Highway One, the entrance some seventy-five meters west of the Stoplight from Hell.

A radioman raised his hand and Eaton got quiet and looked straight at him.

"Tell it."

"Sir, we have one tank and two Bradleys. Big Red One."

You could feel the joy in the room—everyone grinning, Williams nodding to Eaton, the lieutenants glancing at each other, First Lieutenant Garcia giving me a thumbs up. I'd been on patrols with Garcia before and nicknamed him, "Doc Holliday." Pullen tapped my shoulder and said, "Abrams and two Bradleys, great, that's good stuff. Solid fire support, heavy guns. Good stuff," and I nodded to him.

The heavy metal was definitely welcome. Having a tank in support, with two Bradleys, on a combat assault in urban warfare is very good news. It was a dark, cold night in Fallujah, and we made to raid.

Up on the trucks near the south gate at six thirty, the men checked and rechecked ammunition and gear, pounding each other's body-armor plates, working the action of their rifles, and sharpening fighting knives. As a light rain began to fall, you could hear a low metallic rumble near the gate, and the Gunfighters cheered.

An M1A2 Abrams rolled in with two Bradley fighting vehicles behind it, swung down into the gravel-lined ravine, and turned around. Specialist Franklin, a lean and quiet machine gunner, was at our twelve o'clock up on his heavy machine gun. Specialist Kawakale, "the Hawaiian Soul Brother," Franklin called him, carried a .203 and was opposite me in the truck. The rain became a cold misting rain. A voice boomed at us, from the back of the truck, from out of the darkness. I could still see the palm trees amber in the darkness in the fields on Volturno. Wild dogs howled to the east.

Sergeant First Class La Hoda hollered, "Listen up! The mayor's cell has been overrun. Rebels control it. There is an RKM machine gun firing from the roof. Shoot anyone in the compound carrying a weapon. Do not hesitate. Clear?" He was just barely visible in the night as he stood at the back of our truck, all eyes on him.

"Hell yes!" Franklin shouted, and around us the Gunfighters were shouting, "Clear, all the way, Hua, Airborne!," slapping backs in the misting cold darkness, engines roaring on and the convoy jumping to life, tac lights making a long red-and-green line of the Gunfighters' assault convoy. As misting rain slowly soaked us that night, I realized the rules of engagement were straight combat.

A translator jumped on our truck, falling over as he got in, helmet askew on his head. Specialist Johnson and Specialist Torres, a rifleman and a light machine gunner, helped him up. He was a bit groggy from the fall. Franklin glanced back at him as we rolled out the gate, Big Red One tank on point for the convoy. We were two trucks back of the tank, and Fallujah was a glimmer of white and yellow light west in the misting darkness. Gunfighters were wiping their scopes dry with small rags, cursing the mist and the cold drizzling rain.

"Hell, it's Peshi," Franklin exclaimed, and turned his eyes back on the road. Nearing the overpass the rain and mist ceased, and Peshi introduced himself. He was the captain's interpreter, a Kurd, and he'd fallen asleep when the assault convoy had assembled.

There was a crescent moon high over Fallujah on the western horizon, and Peshi asked if this was the captain's truck. I told him it wasn't, but we could get him to the captain once the assault started. He rubbed his eyes, adjusted his chinstrap, and said, "Oh my, I am not with my captain! I must be with my captain!" La Hoda called the captain and told him we had Peshi.

"These are bad men we must capture. They have done a bad thing tonight. Why do the Iraqis love Saddam? I hate Saddam! Oh Saddam is the devil. He is Satan! I am glad, so glad the Americans captured him! These are bad, bad men we must capture," Peshi said, tugging at his thick black mustache as we sped up, heading down the main drag now.

He was frowning, looking worried, so I told him to stay with me, that I'd lead him to Captain Eaton. He squinted, smiled slightly, and said, "Thank you, yes, I must help my captain!" From the TC seat, La Hoda boomed again, "Tracers all over, men. Tracers all over. There are cars circling the mayor's cell. Take out the RKM [Russian-make machine gun]. I say again, take out the RKM—.203 gunners, check your rounds."

A minaret broke the darkness northwest, whitish-yellow in the misting night, and a man bobbed up from a roof northwest of us, his silhouette clearly visible some eighty meters away. I called out, "Rooftop, two o'clock, one man," and Torres swung his light machine gun up and the man disappeared.

We rolled on, Bradleys checking our six, green flashes of light swarming from atop the mayor's cell. Green tracers from the RKM. We were near the Stoplight from Hell now, and we could see the green tracers everywhere, gunfire cracking in the night. Cars roared away west down the main drag and we broke hard near the mosque. Trucks jolted to a stop ahead of us. Gunfighters jumped off the back and sides of the trucks and sprinted toward the Stoplight from Hell. Smoke from trash fires in alleys near the mosque drifted gray and black over us. We hustled, Franklin carrying his machine gun like he would take down all Al Quaeda himself, all by his lonesome, if need be.

Peshi followed me, saying "My captain, oh where is my Captain?" and I told him to hang on to my shoulder. He looked out of sorts, his eyes big. He grabbed my right shoulder and hung on. AK fire cracked in the night and sergeants were shouting, "Move, move, move, keep moving, move it up," as we ran toward the mayor's cell. I assured Peshi that we'd find the captain, and he said, pounding my shoulder, "Are you sure, are you sure?"

"Hell yes, I'm sure! He's Wyatt Earp. He's our captain. And you will see him again. Very soon," I said, hustling up behind Torres and Johnson, the Hawaiian on point up ahead, Franklin just behind the Hawaiian, smoke acrid in the air, thick smoke now as we passed Hazelit barriers in front of the mayor's cell. Peshi hung on to my shoulder, holding a bandana to his mouth against the smoke.

Torres looked back, light machine gun strapped over his shoulder, and shouted, "Peshi still there, Mr. Tucker?" There was distant gunfire now, scattered single shots; it sounded at least two hundred meters northwest of us.

"Roger that."

"Good, because the captain's just ahead."

Wyatt Earp was hunched down near an opening in the concrete wall to the mayor's cell, Hazelit barrier giving him good cover from the west, his radioman on one knee. The tank was some fifty meters west of us, its turret swinging, machine gunner up in the turret, scanning rooftops and alley corners in the night.

"Captain," I said, and he looked up and I nodded back at Peshi.

"Well-done. Peshi, how good to see you. Glad you could join us," Eaton said, standing up now, a grin on his face, his eyes narrowing. Smoke drifted over him and his radioman scanned rooftops west.

"My captain!" Peshi exclaimed, raising his arms. "Oh my captain, I am here now." Eaton shook his head, hands on his hips. I ran inside, Johnson ahead of me. With Franklin on point, we ran through the muddy compound, black and gray smoke drifting all around us in the night.

Smoke and fire and darkness, the shattered remains of the mayor's cell. Fires cast shadows on the walls as the Gunfighters shouted, moving fast and hard, securing doorways and stairwells. Scorched walls lined rooms where Huston and Zawachewsky had once sipped tea with sheikhs and various ministers. Smoldering fires glowed in that cold December night in Fallujah.

Pullen was already on the roof when we got there, conferring with La Hoda, paratroopers up on their guns holding the rooftop. Franklin set his heavy machine gun on the northeast corner facing the firehouse, where the Wild Bunch and Caliguire's Commandos had taken fire in the Halloween Siege. Torres set his light machine gun on the northwest corner, AK fire erupting west of us, and Torres said he thought it was at least a hundred meters away. There were tracers mixed in the distant fire, long green lines arcing in the night.

The damp cold was bone deep. Paratroopers tugged at their gloves and their neck gaiters. Johnson faced west with his .203, scanning the night, eyes on. The tracers ceased. A squad leader went from man to man, checking rounds, verifying fields of fire, talking low and quick to the Gunfighters on the O.K. Corral rooftop. Big Red One Bradleys were in a half-crescent south of us, just in front of the O.K. Corral, their turrets moving like clockwork. I remember thinking, thank God for Big Red One. The warriors famed for their actions in North Africa, Sicily, Italy, and Europe in WWII were definitely coming through for us in Fallujah. Our tank was still just west, on the main drag, securing the southern and western approaches to the O.K. Corral. The acrid scent of cordite still hung in the air. Smoke drifted black in the night. There were minarets lit up north of us, and they were strangely beautiful through the smoking fires in the mayor's compound, their blue and green tiles glittering in the electric light.

La Hoda hustled up to me and said, "We're moving. Headed downtown. Some kind of meeting. You OK?"

I assured him that I was fine and told him I'd get with Franklin, who was coming off the roof.

"Outstanding," he said, as he turned toward his squad leaders and waved his squads off the rooftop. Pullen headed down the steep concrete stairwell. The Gunfighters peeled off the roof expertly, checking each other's six, moving quickly in the night, Franklin the last one to lift his weapon and scan the night and swoop down the stairs, saying back over his shoulder, "Follow me, Mr. Tucker."

I stepped into darkness, the stairwell black like a bamboo grove in a Burmese jungle on a moonless night. A single shot cracked north of us, the distinct coughing-crack of an AK-47. There was smoke and darkness and fire on the ground floor as we came out of the stairwell. Franklin held his heavy machine gun at the hip and said, "Clear, friendlies coming out, clear, friendlies coming out." "Stay with me," he said as we jogged across the compound, paratroopers checking our six. We rushed through a gate and Eaton nodded to us. Franklin hustled on for our truck, paratroopers covering us, steady on their guns in the cold dark night.

Franklin bounded up on the truck in one swift, sure leap and the Hawaiian stretched out a hand and pulled me up. The Bradleys rumbled in the night and the Hawaiian smiled and asked, "You OK?"

I assured him I was fine. There was smoke still drifting black over the O.K. Corral, and the crescent moon hung in the west like a far white fire in the night. The skies were clearing now, and trucks were revving in the darkness.

The Hawaiian grinned and looked up at Franklin, who was mounting his machine gun, scanning the night, turret of the tank swinging slow and clockwise roughly one hundred meters ahead of us.

"Good. You good, bro?" the Hawaiian said to Franklin, and Franklin slapped the barrel guards of his heavy machine gun, live rounds laid in his feed tray, and said, "I'm straight."

We rolled downtown past two men sitting cross-legged in the dirt and sipping tea near RPG alley, fire flaming to their left, black smoke boiling off burning truck tires. I waved to them and they waved back. Iraqi men walked west toward the Euphrates on cracked pavement, twirling prayer beads and abacuses in their hands, their robes wet from the earlier rain. Near a mosque just west of the mayor's compound, flames shot out of the top of a telephone pole, and black electrical lines fell burning and smoking on the sidewalk in Fallujah.

The Gunfighters were eyes on, heading downtown, and Franklin shouted, "Watch the intersection, we're slowing down, get ready," as we neared a four-way intersection, less than five minutes from the mayor's cell.

"Right here, unass the truck, follow me!" La Hoda shouted. The truck jolted to a stop. Paratroopers leaped out, securing the intersection, Big Red One checking our six with the Abrams, the tank lying back in the shadows under cypress trees on the side of the road.

One of our Bradleys was due west, on point for our convoy and securing the western approaches. The road west led directly to the old green steel bridge that spanned the Euphrates. Beyond that bridge was Al Bowisa tribal territory. Every chopper shot down over Fallujah was shot down on Al Bowisa land, I remember thinking, as Kiowa Warrior helicopters swooped low over the rooftops west. The choppers were on reconnaissance for us and in armed support of our mission. The Kiowa Warriors looped back north and south, peeling in opposite directions as we set in on alley corners. Paratroopers went guns up behind concrete walls and in doorways to small shops, machine gunners keeping to the shadows. Torres and Johnson held their corner. I took a knee just right of Johnson.

Torres was in the prone on his light machine gun, eyeing balconies some 150 meters southeast. The tank was a welcome presence just fifty meters north of us, its turret turning slowly in the night. Our second Bradley commanded a fork in the road south of us and edged up slowly, machine gunner scoping the night. Torres wiped his forehead with a green bandana and said, "Johnson, be ready brother," and Johnson said softly, "Roger that, brother."

North of us, on the opposite side of the tank, Iraqi men stood in front of what appeared to be a government building, a three-story khaki-colored concrete structure with long balconies on its second and third floors. There were some Iraqi men hanging out on the balconies, smoking and talking loudly. They were wearing black leather jackets of the kind favored by both feydayeen and Iraqi police in Fallujah.

La Hoda came up, checking his men. "Mr. Tucker, there's some kind of meeting going on down the street. Colonel and the police chief. Hang a right at the corner. Captain's headed that way."

I told Torres and Johnson I was going to check things out. They said, "Roger that, stay safe," and I thanked them and ran across the street, the Judge slapping me on my back as I passed him and headed on, looking for Captain Eaton. The Gunfighters were everywhere, scoping rooftops and alley corners, talking on their I-Coms, holding down the intersection.

North the road was wide and wet, potholes puddled over, para-troopers pointing three hundred meters north to a tall, six-story concrete building, Eaton running with his radioman toward the building. I caught up to him and he told me that Drinkwine was meeting with the police chief and that the mayor was safe and well in his house. Peshi was with us, grinning now, his hand grabbing at the helmet as it bounced around on his head.

"Get ready Peshi. Time to earn your keep," Eaton said, punching Peshi on a shoulder as we neared the building, paratroopers nodding to us.

"Captain, I must translate. Ah, very good, very good," Peshi said as he headed up a short flight of wet concrete steps into the building.

On the third floor, Eaton entered a room at the end of a hall, then turned back and said to me and Peshi, "You guys will have to wait; it's classified inside." Peshi said to me as the captain shut the door, "Very good, yes. My captain will return?" he asked, raising his eyebrows. I assured him that Wyatt Earp would indeed return, and that seemed to comfort Peshi.

Three Iraqi policemen came out of another room and they approached us, grinning, AK-47s hanging off their wrists. I greeted them in Arabic and they returned my greeting; I asked Peshi to translate for me. One of the IPs stepped forward, getting up in my face. I set a hand on my Kukri, and Peshi told him in Arabic to back off.

He backed off and I asked Peshi to tell him the IPs were cowards for abandoning their positions.

Peshi translated and all three IPs scowled at me.

The one who'd tried to get up in my face looked down, scratched at his unkempt beard, and spat out a stream of Arabic.

"He says they are not cowards, but the Americans do not give them enough ammunition."

"Tell him I know that each policeman has received three hundred rounds in the last month. On three separate occasions, each policeman at that mayor's cell received exactly one hundred rounds."

Peshi translated and all three IPs smiled. The one closest to me spoke again in Arabic, smiling broadly now.

"He says they cannot remember exactly how many bullets the Americans have given them, but each man only has three bullets, tonight. It is impossible to fight against the feydayeen with only three bullets," Peshi said.

"Tell him I know that he sold ninety-seven bullets, each time, at the weapons market. Ask him if he thinks the weapons market will stay open forever."

Peshi spoke to him and the policeman laughed and nodded his head, as did his mates. He spoke to Peshi and Peshi frowned, shaking his head.

"He says you understand the police well, perhaps too well. And he says that as long as the Euphrates River has water, there will be a weapons market downtown in Fallujah, and nothing the Americans do will change that."

"Tell him I look forward to meeting him in the weapons market. Many American warriors will be with me. There will be water in the Euphrates. And we will decide on that day if he is feydayeen or police. Or perhaps, he will decide."

Peshi translated and the IP lost his grin. He looked at his mates and they looked away. As they walked down the hall, I said to them, in farewell, "Mala Mustafa Barzani, Kurdistani, peshmerga!" "You are for Mala Mustafa and our brave peshmerga?" Peshi asked, lighting up a smoke in the hallway.

"Hell yes," I told him, and Peshi smiled and shook my hand. Eaton came out, setting his helmet back on and gesturing down the hallway. His radioman followed him, and Peshi and I walked with them out of the building. Back on the street, headed south now toward the main intersection, Wyatt Earp moved out, his radioman checking his handset, paratroopers hailing us as we double-timed past them.

There was a misting rain now, the very faint mist the French call *crachin*. Tablas and ouds and keyboards rocked from rooftops, the Arabic music percussive over the stone and cinder-block rooftops in Fallujah, and I could see minarets, faint and unlit, perhaps a hundred meters west. I reminded Peshi to stay with the captain and told the captain I was going back to the corner, near the tank. He nodded and I jogged on up the street, scattered gunfire echoing from near the Euphrates. On the corner, Torres lay in the prone on his SAW, eyes on balconies beyond the Bradley, Johnson covering his nine o'clock and steady on his .203.

"Lights coming on, Johnson," Torres said, scoping the balconies. There were lights flashing on beyond the Bradley south of us. North of us, the men on the balconies looked directly at the tank and began taking out their mobile phones. Another paratrooper came up from behind me and took a knee.

An Iraqi man, blind to the tank, walked out some thirty meters behind it. I pointed him out to Johnson, who said, "Roger, I've got him." Johnson scoped the man with his .203 and said, "He's pulling out a cell phone." A second Iraqi man joined him from out of the darkness, likewise pulling out a cell phone. Both men watched the tank as they punched out phone numbers, raised their cell phones, and began talking.

Some eighty meters west of us, near our other Bradley, Wyatt Earp was under a steel canopy with his radioman and Doc Holliday.

Torres called out to his squad leader, "Sergeant, these two dudes are surveilling us. Idiot Number One is calling on his cell phone. Idiot Number Two just put his cell phone away. In back of the tank."

"Roger that," his squad leader shouted back. "I'll send it up."

Johnson hailed the machine gunner in the turret of Big Red One's steel lion and shouted, "Two motherfuckers behind you, they're surveilling us," and as the tanker turned his machine gun on them, they bolted, running into the government building. The tanker gave a big thumbs-up to Johnson. Stars were sparkling between drifting clouds in the eastern skies, Orion ablaze to the southeast.

"RPGs, RPGs!" I heard a paratrooper screaming behind us, and Johnson turned and said, "Motherfuckin' RPGs!"

There was red flame and a trail of fire and a blast. Thank God, the first RPG missed us, I remember thinking. And then a second whirring sharp blast roared past us, a smashing roaring sound. We slammed against the wall, tank cannon elevating, paratroopers shouting, "RPGs, RPGs, get against the wall!" Torres swung his light machine gun south, holding the corner. Johnson scoped the Iraqis who'd earlier surveilled us beyond the tank.

I turned and looked west and saw three more RPGs floating toward us, red trails of fire snaking through the darkness. I glanced east and the two men were now down behind a parked car, one of them pulling out his cell phone. I heard a blast, and to the left of us, perhaps twenty feet away, sparks flew up from a blaze of fire—an RPG exploding. We turned toward the wall, covering ourselves down against the wall. Paratroopers were shouting and taking cover behind our parked trucks. A machine gunner next to me yelled, "Fuck, the motherfuckers hit me, feydayeen motherfuckers!" His left boot was smoldering slightly and I checked his boot.

There was no blood. A hunk of RPG metal lay up against the thick, high curb where it had lodged after exploding in the street. The machine gunner stomped his foot, cursing, and La Hoda sprinted up, shouting, "Stay against the wall, stay against the wall! Torres, watch for ambush! Feydayeen may be coming for this corner, drawing us down the street with RPGs! Hold the corner, brothers!"

Three more RPGs sailed toward the tank and flew over it. The two Iraqi men raced into the government building, and the Iraqis on the balconies ran back into the rooms. The tank lurched forward slightly, the machine gunner up in the turret gripping the triggers of his M240B, 7.62-caliber heavy machine gun.

And the tank shot forward like a panther coming out of a crouch; it slammed forward, jumping the median, engine racing in the night. A blur of cannon and treads and machine guns as it headed into the fire— the Big Red One. Someone shouted from down the street, "Stay on your corners, hold, hold!"

Gunfire erupted from the west, due west beyond the Bradley on our western security, and Torres shouted, "That's a Bradley, fuck yeah!" I told Johnson I was headed west and he nodded, keeping eyes on the government building. Torres and Johnson and the light machine gunner were now the far southeastern security for all the Gunfighters.

I moved west along the wall to an alley and stepped in, joining the paratroopers who held it. They affirmed that seven RPGs had been fired at us and the Bradleys were engaging now, squad leaders on their I-Coms, machine gunners holding down the alley corners. I could see First Lieutenant Fernando Garcia about thirty meters away, north of us. It was good to see Doc Holliday with his men. He was a cool hand under fire. Eaton stood near him, talking into his handset, his radioman scoping rooftops south of us. I told a squad leader I was headed across the street to Doc Holliday and Wyatt Earp. He informed his fire team leaders and said to me, "All right, it's clear, keep your head down."

"Good to see you. What's going on, brother?" Doc Holliday said, scoping west down the street, Big Red One's tank headed west for the Bradleys as I jogged up to him. Garcia's machine gunners were in the prone, facing west, cement blocks and concrete rubble shielding them from any fire. Streetlights flickered on and off in the night. A cat roamed out on the street and then dashed back into an alley. The high, fierce rattle of a Bradley 25mm gun west of us pierced the dark winter air like thunder in Fallujah.

Garcia gazed south and motioned to the paratroopers I'd just left holding down the alley corners, and they gave him a thumbs-up. "We'll hold here, for now," he said. "Bradleys and Abrams are taking care of business." I told him about the machine gunner, whose boot had been hit by the RPG shrapnel. The lieutenant winced and nodded his head east up the street, toward Torres and Johnson.

"Is he OK? He's not bleeding, is he?" he asked.

"He's good, no bleeding. Four aspirin and a Hail Mary and he'll get well soon," I told him. He nodded, eyes lighting up.

"Thank God. You all were damned lucky. That RPG shrapnel, most of it, must've hit the curb. Mercy. Stay with us. We may move out down the street."

Gunfire rocked, sporadic and intense, from the Bradleys. The Gunfighters held there for perhaps fifteen minutes more before Eaton, whipping a hand about in the night, signaled to all his paratroopers that we were moving out. The Bradleys and Abrams started back, trucks kicking on and paratroopers leaping up on the trucks, scoping the night, eyes on, the convoy racing back to Volturno in the darkness.

At the south gate, 10th Mountain light infantrymen were standing guard, shotguns at the ready, and they gave us a thumbs-up and shouted "Hua!" as we came in through the wire, men clearing weapons once inside. The air was clear and cold now, the *crachin* rain gone to bed after midnight in Fallujah. The Gunfighters were slapping each other on their helmets and flak jackets as we rolled back toward their lakeside quarters, rifles either between their knees or on their laps. Franklin rested one arm on his machine gun. The wind was cold on our faces, but I wasn't feeling the cold anymore.

Back at the Gunfighters' CP, I dismounted and walked with Garcia to a gathering circle of paratroopers. Eaton stood in the center of the circle, helmet under one arm, his dark brown hair plastered to his head with sweat, his face red and his eyes intense.

"Men, I'm damned proud of you," the captain said slowly, his eyes scanning the darkness. "It's an honor to lead you. You were solid downtown, you were professionals. Thank God we had the Bradleys and Abrams with us. Big Red One, are you out there?" he said, and from somewhere in that circle of warriors came a shout, "Hell yes, Airborne, we're right here with you!" and the Gunfighters shouted by the lake, "Hua, Hua!"

The captain smiled and gazed at his warriors and all his attachments circled around him, Orion west of us now that it was about midnight in Fallujah. He wished us all well and told us, "Get some rest, and be ready in the morning."

Regan was still up when I got back to the battalion ops center, and there was fresh coffee in his hootch. He was leaning back behind his computer with arms folded and talking about *The Grapes of Wrath* and the Depression and Steinbeck's other great novel of the Depression, *In Dubious Battle*. He talked about Steinbeck with real respect and admiration. "He knew those folks well, he had true empathy for them," he said, "the migrants from Oklahoma, Missouri, the Dust Bowl. Folks the Depression hit so very hard. They went to California in those old jalopies and any which way they could, looking for that pot of gold at the end of the rainbow. Hard times, they found. No gold or pots to hold it in.

"That's the World War II generation, you know. Those men who were teenagers in the Depression. And hell, younger—you figure if you were just a boy in 1933, maybe nine or ten years old, well, ten years later you were in North Africa with Colonel Darby or on a beach in the Pacific with Chesty Puller under fire. Staying in the fight. You've gotta' stay in the fight to win the fight. You've gotta' fight the war to win it. Those were Steinbeck's folks, and Hemingway's and Faulkner's. The best we had. I look at the young men in this war and I realize their grandsons are doing it, now. Maybe even their great-grandsons, some of them. Fighting the good fight. That's why we'll prevail. We'll win here and in Afghanistan because our men understand there is no turning back. They know what's at stake here. They know what kind of tyranny ruled here. And what happened on September 11 must never happen again. We have struck at Al Quaeda, right here in Fallujah. And we need to crush Al Quaeda. I think our people, stateside, understand that, too. I damned sure do."

I shook his hand and thanked him for the coffee and he told me, "Anytime, brother." It was always good talking with Mark Twain after a mission. You knew he had a listening heart. I was still wired from the assault, so I wrapped a blanket around me and went up on the roof. I drank brandy from my steel canteen and listened to Miles Davis. The skies were clear all ways now, stars glimmering far over the desert south and over the distant lights of Fallujah west. The crescent moon went down around three in the morning. I took eight hundred milligrams of Motrin and went down, too.

● ● ●

"The feydayeen are firing on the mayor's cell," I heard, a whisper in the darkness in my hootch. It was Meismer and he was shaking my shoulder. "Sir, you told us to wake you if the feydayeen attacked us anywhere. Tenth Mountain is headed out in about twenty mikes. Feydayeen are trying to retake the mayor's cell again, sir."

It was eleven in the morning, and I asked Meismer, the slim and tough paratrooper who would drive us on December 16, if there was coffee. He said it was black and strong. I got clean and gulped down two cups of coffee, filled a canteen with coffee, and grabbed my gear. The Ironman and Shenandoah Warrior were waiting for me at the battalion ops center, and the Ironman said, "You sure you've got your helmet this morning," and I held it up for him to examine.

"Well-done last night. Charlie assaulted strong. Big Red One came through shining," he said as we hustled over to his command truck in the convoy. Attack Company warriors lined up by the south gate. "Big Red One is with us. Abrams and two Bradleys. We're going heavy, but there's room with Captain Love," he said.

"Everyone's loaded for bear," Love said, hailing me from a nearby truck. "Roll with us. On patrol you're free to attach to 10th Mountain. Everyone's carrying beaucoup rounds. Friggin' rain is coming on," he said, glancing northwest at the gray storm clouds rolling in hard over Fallujah. He carried an M.203 and a sidearm strapped to his right thigh, 40mm grenades filling the front of his flak jacket. I got up in the truck, Quinones and a Syrian translator already in the truck. We rode under gray skies in a solid convoy, heading for the mayor's cell, Attack Company gun trucks and Delta Company gun trucks in support. The Count was with us in a command truck, four antennas jutting up from his truck. He carried an M-4 and a sidearm.

Iraqi police were milling about outside the mayor's cell when we arrived. Lieutenant Chesty's Old School Warriors leaped from their trucks, secured the rooftops, and held down the gates and corners. There were scattered shots west of us, at least three hundred meters west. "Feydayeen just fuckin' with us way out there, Hawk," said Huber, scoping RPG Alley under gray skies, First Lieutenant Adam Bohlen nodding nearby and talking quietly with Patterson up on the roof. We damned sure weren't there long before Bohlen shouted, "We're rolling, Big Red One, hell yes!" pointing to our tank, now some one hundred meters west of the mayor's cell, treads grinding on the pavement.

Huber nodded and listened to his I-Com and shouted, "Old School Warriors, we rock! Let's roll, get back to the trucks, we're headed downtown, fuckin'-a Old School Warriors!" I followed him out through the mud, Patterson on a .203 and "the Wildman" Marston—who feared no feydayeen and rocked hard and rode free—on a heavy machine gun coming up behind me. Iraqi police looked down as we ran out for our trucks. Love raised his rifle toward me and shouted, "Right here, Mr. Tucker."

There were Iraqis at a market across the street, men and women of all ages in front of stands of apples and eggplant and carrots; I waved to them and they waved back, the children grinning. Heaps of trash smoldered near them, the lingering remains of trash fires in Fallujah.

With Big Red One on point, we rode to the same intersection we'd taken seven RPGs at the night before. There was a single shot, fairly close—Love thought it was maybe a hundred meters—and the Attack Company warriors rushed to alley corners and crumbling cinder-block walls, a light rain falling now, Kirkpatrick checking his perimeter, shotgun in his right hand, his sidearm holstered. The sergeants set their men in on street corners and alley corners.

Old School Warrior King and "Cool Papa," Staff Sergeant Rodney Pittman from New Jersey, both took a knee behind a busted-up concrete pillar, making sure their men's fields of fires overlapped on a deserted lot. Cool Papa was all eyes, listening to his brother warrior in the cold drizzling rain on that winter day in Fallujah, both of them carrying thirteen clips plus one jacked in their M-4s. They were 10th Mountain sergeants and their men were set in solid; I pitied anyone who would be foolish enough to tango with Kirkpatrick's warriors. A dark wave of clouds covered the northeastern horizon, minarets stark against the far black skyline.

Our Bradleys checked our six. The Count held a meeting with one of Fallujah's witless, gutless city fathers, and we got word there was a fire at the train station. An undetermined number of anti-Coalition elements with undetermined weapons had attacked a Coalition Forces supply train. One thing had most definitely been determined; we were now riding to counter-attack and secure the train.

Ironman's Warriors hustled back to our trucks and Big Red One's steel lion held point and led us east down the main drag, Bradleys on our six. We hung a hard left onto the wide road that led north, directly for the train station. Love scoped rooftops and alley corners, and the rain tapered to a fine mist. Kids came out on the street as we rode north, waving and smiling and shouting "Amerikee, Amerikee!"

Now everyone was up on their gun, eyes on, and Love said, "Keep your head down and your powder dry, Mr. Tucker. Stay low and look alive, a train's on fire, we don't know what hit it, and beaucoup feydayeen are out there. Brother, I am a long friggin' way from Columbus, oh yes, there must be snow on the ground now in Ohio, sweet Jesus."

Riding through the heart of Fallujah, north for the train station, we swooped under an overpass and there were children everywhere, some carrying cans of Pepsi and others carrying brand-new notebooks and pens. A plume of black smoke was roiling up through gray sky as we came upon the immobile train, its cars in all colors halted on the tracks. The train, carrying a full load of Coalition PX supplies—sodas, potato chips, notebooks, pens, and a few very sensitive items for the U.S. Air Force—sat like a wheeled steel dinosaur on rails that ran west into endless desert toward Syria and east toward Baghdad. The burning car, only two back from the lead engineer's car, was across a muddy field about a thousand meters from us. The skies were gray now. Black smoke jetted up from the gutted, burning car, red and gold flames boiling out of it.

As we halted, looters bolted from the train, grabbing at torn-open boxes in the mud as they ran toward cars and pickups about fifteen hundred meters west of us. One man stopped, looked back, and grabbed a case of sodas; he stared at us and then ran on.

A Big Red One machine gunner was up on his 7.62 on a Bradley, turret swiveling toward the train, a great field of grass and mud west of us. You could smell the smoke now; warriors were dismounting and getting behind trees and boulders, Big Red One Bradleys securing our flanks.

Kids rushed out from stone and glass apartment buildings behind us, waving and giggling. There was a fence between us, and the kids grabbed onto the wire. Bohlen was taking a knee near our tank and I hustled up to him.

"We're heading into the field. Come with us. Ironman wants me to check out the train," he said, pointing to the thick black smoke.

There were concrete houses—two and three stories some of them, others fairly well-built farmers' huts—northwest of us beyond an irrigation canal on the north side of the field. Outside one house, a family stood gazing at us, a farmer holding his wife around her shoulders and four kids at their feet, the smallest child sucking her thumb, silver bracelets with silver beads on her wrists.

Lieutenant Chesty pointed to the houses and said, "Old School Warrior King thinks we might take fire from those houses, heading across the field. We've got plenty fire support, but keep your head down and your powder dry, brother. Someone hit that train and hit it hard. And they're likely still around. Trying to sucker us into an ambush. Unsheathe the Kukri," he said, reaching out a hand.

I shook his hand and he led us into the field, Kirkpatrick nodding to us, Old School Warriors spreading wide behind us as we moved out on patrol, mud covering our boots. I unsheathed my Kukri.

Guerrilla Warrior led the point fire team, Private First Class Sanovich carrying his light machine gun on point, held from the hip, and scanning the horizon. Specialist Patrick Lybert from Ladysmith, Wisconsin, Bohlen's radioman, carried his M-4 in his left hand and kept his right hand free, patrolling across the muddy field, skies darkening all ways now. Lybert's nickname was "Radio Free Wisconsin."

I waved to the Iraqi family and they waved back, children joyous, beaming, the father grinning. The field was now clear of looters. Passing the farmers' huts and houses, we leaped over an irrigation canal and Huber gestured to his squad leaders—Pittman, Patterson, and Hassell.

As the platoon sergeant made his hand-and-arm signals to his squad leaders, the lieutenant scoped north, checking a slow-moving, rusted, red pickup truck, and he spoke quickly to Lybert. Scoping the truck, I could see four men in it, all wearing red-and-white-checked kaffiyehs in the feydayeen style, wrapped around the head and face, only their eyes visible.

Radio Free Wisconsin called in to Ironman, "Attack 6, this is 1 Romeo. One Actual has suspicious activity, possibly feydayeen. Red pickup truck moving toward your position, four possible feydayeen. Over."

There was a burst of static, and then Kirkpatrick's hard gravelly voice was calm over the radio as we patrolled on, stepping over boxes and crates and bags of beef jerky and cases of sodas cast asunder in the huge muddy field.

"Solid copy, 1 Romeo. We've got it. Attack 6, over."

The lieutenant nodded and gave Lybert a thumbs-up, and he grinned slightly to his lieutenant, sweat beading on his forehead.

"Roger that, Attack 6. One Romeo Out."

I scoped the pickup again and it halted. Bohlen, seeing it stop, raised a fist quickly and his warriors got down in the mud, in the prone on wide-open ground, some of them dropping behind small mounds of dirt. The Wildman aimed his machine gun right at the pickup and it reversed quickly, mud kicking up behind its rear tires as it spun around and drove west. Old School Warrior King hollered, "Don't fuck with the Old School Warriors, feydayeen motherfuckers!" and the Old School Warriors cheered him and Lieutenant Chesty grinned and said, "Radio Free Wisconsin, remember this day."

Lybert smiled and said, "Lieutenant Chesty, it's Fallujah. Give it a minute and it'll change, feydayeen crossroads." The lieutenant grinned and replied, "The road to wisdom is full of many blind curves, Midwestern grasshopper, friend of dairy farms and cold beer," and Lybert shook his head, laughing. The scent of burning chemicals and plastic was thick on the air now, and black smoke still poured from the fire, mixing with green smoke pluming up from a mauled red rail car.

A blast shattered the calm and men dropped around us, in the prone now as Bohlen and I kept walking, someone shouting behind us, "Not an RPG, not an RPG. That came from the train!" The Old School Warriors got up from the mud, covering each other, Lybert saying, "Something must have exploded in that fire, sir," to Bohlen. The lieutenant nodded to him and turned back, looking over his squads, and waved to Old School Warrior King. Grinning wildly, Huber waved back, mud covering his flak now.

Muddy and hungry and flaks heavy on us, we headed south for the tracks, Cool Papa's squad checking our six, Old School Warrior King pointing to an underpass below the railway, about three hundred meters south as we patrolled through the middle of the field.

Bohlen checked out the underpass and it was a cesspool of water buffalo manure and human dung, the stench unimaginable. Big Pat's squad secured the underpass, men wrapping bandanas around their faces, a gray chill damp cold settling in on Fallujah. Two Kiowas swooped over us, one on each side of the tracks, zooming west and then peeling off in opposite directions, no more than two hundred feet off the deck.

Gray waves of clouds flooded the western horizon in the early afternoon. Bohlen pointed up toward the train. "I'm taking Sasquatch and his warriors. Find out what stopped this train. Old School Warrior King is coming," he said. He talked to Hassell on the I-Com, Sasquatch's men rushing up through the mud, machine gunners climbing the steep hill to the tracks, riflemen scoping far in the distance in all directions.

We got up to the fire and it was intense, thick high flames like those in a blast furnace lit up the destroyed container car on the northern side of the tracks. Bohlen held point and led us around to the southern side, his M-4 shouldered as he moved slowly around the engineer's car. A fire team came up from behind him and set in on the southern side, machine gunners shouting out fields of fire, seas of saw grass and high wild grass bending in a light breeze southwest of us. There were mud-hut neighborhoods clustered on the northern reaches of Fallujah some six hundred meters to our nine o'clock.

"RPG," the lieutenant said calmly, looking at a hole in the engineer's car. You could smell gasoline everywhere. Gas was dripping from cut fuel lines hanging now from the undergirding of the engineer's car. Specialist Purvis, carrying an M-4, got inside the engineer's car and Bohlen followed him with Lybert. There were two small bullet holes in the glass windows.

"Feydayeen fucked this train up, sir," Purvis said. "Busted up the gauges. Man there's glass everywhere. AK fire."

"Roger that. Radio Free Wisconsin, call it in," and he did as they stepped out of the car, back on the southern side of the tracks now, Huber on his I-Com with his squad leaders. There was an impact crater dug into gravel near the second car, and green smoke poured out of the breached red steel of the second container car. I asked Lybert if he thought another RPG had been fired and had come up short, impacting in the gravel, and he nodded, saying, "Most affirm. RPGs are everywhere in this town."

We took a knee and Lieutenant Chesty scanned the rooftops in the distance southeast of us. Crowds were beginning to gather on the edges of soccer fields. Kirkpatrick ordered Bohlen to secure the southern side of the tracks, and all the Old School Warriors rushed over, bellies in the mud behind earthern berms, to secure the small wooden bridges over the irrigation canals. Two machine gun teams took to the tracks, one covering west and the other north; two .203 gunners near the engineer's car scoped north across the field we'd crossed earlier.

Our Kiowas swooped west again, swerving over us, and a fire truck rolled up through the mud, Iraqi firemen unsmiling. The fire truck stopped, and the driver got off and looked at the green smoke flooding out now from the red container car. He talked to the other firemen for a few minutes and they drank tea from thermoses. Then they shrugged and got back on the fire truck.

Smoke belched from the fire truck's exhaust and the tires splashed mud everywhere. It was stuck now, and the firemen, cursing in Arabic, ran around a culvert, looking for scrap wood to jam under the tires and get them out of their fix. Bohlen, shaking his head and laughing, called it in, and Kirkpatrick got Big Red One to lend a Bradley, the machine gunner on the Bradley shaking his head and grinning as he linked up chain to the fire truck. The Bradley pulled it out. Then the fire truck moved slowly uphill, stopped about thirty meters from the train, and began hosing down the fire, green smoke still flooding from the second car, Old School Warriors steady on their guns. Black smoke kept roaring out of the train fire and mixing with the green chemical smoke from the red car, which was drifting north over distant minarets.

A taxi came up. The driver and an Iraqi man asked if they could get their Pepsis. The men were clean-cut, in white dishtashas and leather sandals, mud streaking their dishtashas.

Lieutenant Chesty laughed, eyes going wide, and said, "Are you kidding me? Only in Fallujah, looters return to the scene! Sure, we'll keep the Pepsi and we'll keep them, too. Chalk up two detainees, Radio Free Wisconsin," and Lybert called it in, choking back his laughter, rolling his eyes. It was near two thirty now, and a faint misting rain drifted over us. The crowds on the edge of the soccer fields were doubled, about fifty or sixty people scattered about, Bohlen told me as he called Kirkpatrick to inform him about the detainees.

The Ironman ran over, shotgun in one hand, sweat beading slightly on his forehead. Shenandoah Warrior was with him, a translator from Baghdad doggedly keeping up with them.

The translator talked for a few minutes with the men, who were now flex-cuffed in the misting rain, and shook his head.

"They thought they should come back for the Pepsi. They want to put the Pepsi in the trunk and go home. They said everything is free in Fallujah today, because the feydayeen made the train stop."

The captain grimaced, shaking his head, glancing away. "A Coalition train gets shot up with RPGs and AK fire and they say, 'the feydayeen made the train stop.' Tell them it was a mistake to come back. They stole. Thieves steal. I detain thieves," he said in a flat, hard voice, nodding to Smith, his radioman. Smith called the Count and told him we had two detainees. The Kiowas buzzed through the sky, swooping low over the crowds south of us, and some of the young men in the crowds ran for mud huts, grabbing at their dishtashas.

Bohlen talked briefly with Kirkpatrick and Smith, Lybert checking our six, skies clearing west of us now. With Smith, a translator, and the detainees, Kirkpatrick headed back to the northern side of the trucks, passing a rusted orange-and-white taxi marooned in the mud. The firemen were pouring water garden-hose style up on the tracks, just barely splashing water on the burning car.

"Merry Christmas. We'll cross back, Hawk. Ironman wants us back on the northern side. Second Platoon and Captain McKeen are taking over this side. Let's go," Lieutenant Chesty said quickly, Radio Free Wisconsin nodding to him, his trousers and flak brown with mud, assault ruck loaded with rounds and his radio heavy on his back.

We set in on the irrigation canal, Big Red One still holding our northern security on the road across from the apartment buildings. I could see Iraqi teenage boys on the rooftops of the buildings, arms folded, kaffiyehs wrapped around their heads, gesturing toward Captain McKeen and Lieutenant Delille and 2nd Platoon as they crossed the tracks and secured the southern side.

Four Iraqi policemen approached us with an Iraqi man, who was dressed in a black shirt and gray trousers and no shoes. Mud covered his feet. A little boy tagged along. The policemen wore black leather jackets and were expressionless. They stood on the other side of the canal; Old School Warrior King said, "Watch their hands, eyes on." I spoke to them in Arabic and one Iraqi policeman, who was carrying a 9mm on a hip holster, replied in broken English, "My friend lost his shoes in field. Over there, near boxes. Shoes over there," he said, pointing into the wide muddy field scattered with Coalition PX goods.

"Are you kidding me?" Bohlen said, leaning forward slightly, eyes bugging out, an incredulous grin on his freckled face.

The IP looked poker-faced and folded his arms. His friend shrugged and then held his arms up to the sky. He looked toward the field, a pleading look on his face, and gestured toward the sky again.

"No. He wants his shoes. Not kidding. He wants his shoes."

The lieutenant laughed, shaking his head, smiling broadly now.

"Sure. He'll get his shoes. Tell him to wait a few minutes, OK?" and he waved toward Hassell, behind me, who was busting up laughing. The IP relayed the message and the man smiled.

"Lieutenant Chesty," Hassell said, the lieutenant grinning at him, "only in Iraq does two shoes equal a night in detention."

Bohlen smiled and told Lybert, "Call Ironman—we need an interpreter." As he made the call, Sasquatch and Old School Warrior King talked with the IPs, assuring them that their friend would be able to enter the field and retrieve his shoes.

An interpreter hustled up, out of breath. Bohlen told him to take five and I handed him my canteen. He took a couple of big gulps and thanked me and said, "What's up?" Ravens swooped toward date palms far to the west, gray skies lightening on the western horizon.

"Well, we've got a guy here," Bohlen said, pointing to the shoeless man, "who lost his shoes in the field," and he waved an arm wide over the field. There were gulls west swooping high over the tracks leading to Syria and ravens north, gliding through gray skies. Cool Papa and Big Pat were taking a knee behind a berm, scanning a small cluster of date palms east of us near a few mud huts.

The interpreter laughed, shaking his head. "He's a looter and he came back for his shoes. This is appropriate, a crazy man on a crazy day," he said, shoving his hands in his trouser pockets. The Kiowas swept back over us, flying north to south now, peeling east right over the tracks, lead chopper making an S over the mud huts and concrete houses on the southern side of the tracks.

The lieutenant grinned. "All right, let's get the man his shoes," he said loudly, gesturing to the four IPs, the little boy staying on the other side of the canal, slapping at his cheeks and grinning, just a kid hanging out in the late afternoon. Lybert came up alongside Bohlen, and Hassell walked with the man, stepping over busted up boxes marked "CJTF-7

Baghdad." A machine gun team from 2nd Platoon was up on the tracks now, the heavy machine gun facing west about eight hundred meters from us, smoke drifting black and gray over the tracks.

It was getting on to three now and the man threw his hands up in the air and said, "*Oh, Enshallah!*" and reached down in the mud and picked up two black, tasseled loafers crusted with mud. He put his shoes on, grinning. The lieutenant said, "Cuff him, Sasquatch."

Hassell grabbed his shoulders and told him in Arabic to be still, and the man looked at the IPs and the IPs glared at Bohlen. One of the IPs shouted something in Arabic, then spat at Bohlen's feet, and Huber shouldered his M-4.

The translator got between Bohlen and the IPs, the looter flex-cuffed now. Hassell walked him over next to Huber and sat him down in the mud. The IPs began shouting more, and Bohlen said, "If this guy is a friend of theirs, tell them, tough shit! He looted, and he's going to jail." The translator spoke quickly in Arabic to the IPs, gesturing furiously as he spoke, the IPs scowling and glaring at us. I sheathed my Kukri.

"The cop says the man is a relative. They're all from the same tribe. And he says the man knows where the RPG shooter is, feydayeen who shot at the train," the translator said, shrugging.

Bohlen grinned, shaking his head, and Huber said, sarcastically, "Oh my, now that the motherfucker is flex-cuffed, he just has all kinds of good scoop on the feydayeen, oh yes, lying ass sonofabitch. Let's get outta' here, Lieutenant Chesty." Bohlen nodded to him, the lieutenant's eyes hard.

"We're detaining this guy. He looted. Tell the IPs to get in their truck and go home. They fucked up. Radio Free Wisconsin, tell Ironman I've got a detainee. Let's go Sasquatch," he said. Hassell lifted up the detainee, the man shouting in Arabic to the Fallujah policemen from his tribe and his relatives shouting back at him. Huber kept his M-4 shouldered, checking our six as we walked back through the mud to the irrigation canal, Cool Papa and Big Pat grinning, the Wildman shouting, "Old School Warriors rock, AC/DC, don't fuck with Attack Company!" One of the policemen kept staring at me, and I stared back at him and set a hand on my Kukri. He walked on.

The Fallujah policemen crossed a small wooden bridge over the irrigation canal and got in a white IP pickup truck and rode out of the field. The little boy ran back to a farmer's mud hut, waving at us and grinning.

Hassell sat the man down behind a berm and two blasts rocked, echoing fire, like bombs going off. The tank turned south, everyone taking cover. The lieutenant yelled, "RPGs, definitely RPGs, get Ironman on the horn," and looked at Lybert. The radioman was already solid, handset at his ear, calling the captain. Marston shifted his machine gun north against a possible ambush. Pittman calmly talked with his men, going from man to man among his squad, Patterson giving Huber a thumbs-up as skies cleared west.

The Kiowas swooped right over us, less than a hundred feet off the deck, crossed the field, and popped up over the burning train. They descended swiftly, peeling off east and west, Lybert saying to Bohlen, "Two RPGs fired at 2nd Platoon. One Bradley over there, did not engage. Guess he didn't see the shooter, sir. Captain McKeen said he saw the shooter run into a crowd."

The lieutenant grimaced. "Feydayeen. Using the crowd for cover." He called Huber over and the stocky, quick, intense Hawaiian warrior sprinted over and took a knee.

"Sir."

"Old School Warrior King, check rounds. I want .203 gunners to be ready. Redistribute .40 mike-mike, if need be. I want our machine gunners ready to throw down. Old School Warriors rock. Tell the men to be ready to move out," he said, reaching a fist out to the Hawaiian career soldier, and Huber tapped his fist and said, "Roger that, sir." [Author's note: "40 mike-mike" means 40mm grenades].

Bohlen said to me, "The feydayeen know what they're doing. We can't cover every contingency. This is where the stuff is," gesturing toward the stolen goods in the field, gray smoke and green smoke drifting east from the burning train, Kiowas swooping east to west now and peeling in tandem south across the tracks.

"The looters will come back. Myself, I wouldn't leave here tonight. Fine, let them come back. We should pull back, set in, and deny the enemy this terrain. This is key terrain. Take the high ground. High ground along those tracks commands lines of sight three thousand meters in every direction. Key supply line to Baghdad, this railway. I'd pull back and set in tonight and wait for the bastards to return. Let them come to us. Fight them on our terms, not theirs. Hold, kill the enemy, and send a message to Fallujah: 'If you shoot up a train with RPGs and AKs, we will kill you.'

"We didn't really learn much from Vietnam. You study Vietnam and you see we were always seizing ground in battle, securing ground, and then giving away that same ground. Ground men had died for. Our brothers. And our commanders-in-chief, Johnson and Nixon, just gave it back. Screaming Eagles took 25 percent casualties at Hamburger Hill in May sixty-nine. They took the hill, seized key terrain. Lost a helluva' lot of good infantry, to win that battle. And then we just fuckin' gave it away. Mindless, gutless leadership. On a small scale, we've done that throughout Iraq. Only, in many cases," he said, glancing at his warriors along the berm, machine gunners on their bellies in the mud, smoke drifting gray over us, "we didn't even secure ground. We never secured Fallujah, in the first place. When you go to war, you've got to fuckin' slay the dragon. You don't walk up to the mouth of the cave and just walk away. Slay the fuckin' dragon. Saddam was a stone cold evil dictator, for sure, but we didn't clear and hold and secure, we walked away from the mouth of the cave. All the Ba'athist strongholds, for that matter. What the hell were we thinking? We had the Ba'athists on the ropes, hammered them, and we walked away.

"It's an undeclared war here, which really troubles me. The feydayeen is at war with us, but we are not, *officially*, at war with them. That's stupid. I mean, you've been with us in the thick of it. We can't fire unless we're attacked first. You've seen that. That's an equation designed for one thing, historically: defeat. The hearts-and-minds slogan is bullshit. History says you can't win hearts and minds if you haven't won the war first. And history trumps guerrilla war theory hands-down, brother. I take history and you take theory, I guarantee you I'll have you at checkmate, real quick. And we haven't won here, this is still major combat and it ain't ended. It ain't ended because our politically correct culture and our political leadership stateside, part and parcel of our politically correct culture, didn't give our men in the field the declaration of war, first, and have spent every fuckin' day since May 1st sitting on their hands, denying us victory." His eyes were hard as he gazed west, and Radio Free Wisconsin gestured to him.

He grabbed the handset and listened in, frowning. He handed it back to Lybert and said, "Keep monitoring it."

I asked him what was going on and he said, "Bradley gunner asked for permission to engage the RPG shooter. Said he had him in his sights.

McKeen denied the shot. RPG shooter is running through a crowd. I got a feeling we're moving out." An A-10 U.S. Air Force anti-tank jet soared some three thousand feet over us, clouds thickening gray on the southern horizons.

Hassell and Patterson hustled over, a map in their hands. Patterson pointed to a road on the map running north from the railway, Bohlen saying, "What's up Big Pat?"

"Lieutenant Chesty, Sasquatch and I thought—"

Huber stood nearby, grinning, and said, "My God, Sasquatch and Big Pat put their thinking caps on, let's celebrate!" and we all laughed in the mud, a faint mist falling on us now, Lybert scoping west with his M-4. Lybert smiled.

Hassell grinned and said, "Old School Warrior King, have no fear, exfil magic is here." He pointed out to the lieutenant the road north, noting that our planned route of departure took us through the heart of Fallujah, while the northern road cut through fields and desert until it reached highway, a much safer route to roll on back to Volturno.

Bohlen nodded and said, "Damn right, but it's up to Ironman," and he called it in himself, saying, "Wait one," as Kirkpatrick got approval from battalion. Huber smiled and said, "Bradley's coming back, sir, both Bradleys on northern side of tracks now."

I could see 2nd Platoon hustling back toward our trucks near the apartment buildings, men shouldering their weapons, assault rucks sagging off their backs as they ran hard. Machine gunners on tail-end Charlie turned back, doing a swift turnabout and surveillance of anything behind them, machine guns at the hip, moving, moving, always moving. There was gray smoke filtering from both train fires, a faint gray smoke drifting over the RPG-mauled cars.

The lieutenant grinned and said, "Approved, we'll exfil on your route, Sasquatch. Good job, Big Pat." He flipped the handset back to Lybert, and the Kiowas swooped low again over the train. Young Iraqi men were warily coming down the tracks from the west, wearing jeans and dishtashas and leather jackets, kaffiyehs draped around their necks and shoulders.

"Sir, Ironman says return to the trucks, we're moving out in ten mikes, sir," Lybert said, and Lieutenant Chesty stood up.

"Old School Warriors, move out! We're on the exfil!" he shouted, and his men shouted, "Hua, fuckin'-a!" With Wildman on tail-end charlie,

checking our six with his heavy machine gun, we jumped the canal and patrolled back through the mud, muddy and hungry and grinning. Looters
ran up to the train now; the A-10 dropping flares and the Kiowas firing
warning shots at the looters. Lybert shouted, "Major Bottiliegere says get
on the trucks, get on the trucks, we are making the exfil." The looters
swarmed over the train now as we hustled up for the trucks.

I thanked Lieutenant Chesty and Old School Warrior King and
waved to the Ironman. He waved back, his eyes burning, shotgun in his
right hand. Attack Company soldiers were up in their trucks now, and
Delta Company gunners were steady on their weapons. I could hear the
tank's engines rumbling like the low growl of a lion before it roars.

Love reached out a hand and helped me up and Meismer shouted,
"Troopstrap up." Love buckled the troopstrap and said, "We're good,
Meismer." The convoy headed north toward blue skies, just after five in
the afternoon now. Bradley on our six and a second Bradley up near the
tank, we rode past junkyards cluttered with busted-up Iraqi tanks and armored personnel carriers stripped and gutted and rusting in Fallujah, children waving and smiling to us. There were donkeys and horses in a field
under date palms and men and women digging in rows of plowed dirt, as
we neared an overpass north of Fallujah. We swung down the other side
and rolled hard east, headed for Volturno in the late afternoon.

"Hold on," Meismer shouted and we grabbed at the wooden side
rails as he broke, veering off the road, as all the convoy broke, trucks and
Bradleys peeling off on both sides of a two-lane hardball road, hardscrabble desert east of us. Love leaped off the truck and jogged up to the
Count's truck. He returned a few minutes later, frowning.

"Reports of feydayeen headed to the train station, we're rolling, guns
up, men, guns up," he said, and he checked the clips in his flak jacket.

Our trail Bradley held point now, the convoy hanging a U, and we
slammed down the highway for the train station in the heart of Fallujah.
Iraqi children on sidewalks waved to us as we rolled hard and fast off the
highway. We passed the soccer field, the train station on a distant mound
west as we swept past the soccer field we'd passed a million times on patrols and raids. Now Big Red One was on point, Bradley turret swiveling as it rocked hard down the potholed hardball past houses and
mosques and huts, Iraqi men on the sidewalks stopping and staring,
women walking on.

Skies cleared in the west, sun in our eyes as Big Red One rolled right at the T-intersection we'd rode by earlier. Serpico was steady on his M.203, sidearm in a shoulder holster, scoping a two-story house on the southwest corner, a concrete blockhouse up on its rooftop. Love said, "Meeting with IPs here, I think the chief of police," as the point Bradley rolled off the entrance road to the train station and secured our southern flanks. Our convoy rolled up fast and gun trucks set in on overwatch in all points of the compass.

Our Abrams roared about, dust swirling as it dug in, and commanded views of the rooftops south of us in the heart of Fallujah. We could see wide, empty fields and a huge mosque some two thousand meters west along the road.

There were Iraqi policemen in black leather jackets and blue shirts and dark trousers at the train station; the Count rushed up to meet them.

Tenth Mountain warriors hustled into firing positions, getting in the prone, taking cover behind mounds of dirt and broken-up concrete.

Love glanced back at me. He gave me a thumbs-up, and then a wall of fire hit us. Someone shouted, "Holy shit goddamn fuckin' mother-fuckin' RPGs!"

It was a red-gold cracking wall of fire, fire and flame and thunder, RPGs soaring over us, AK fire was ripping between us and above us, men taking cover, readying their weapons, and rising quickly to pour counter-fire back at the feydayeen, RPGs still sailing over us. Lieutenant Chesty was on one knee as three-round bursts flamed from his M-4, and massive counter-fire roared from the Old School Warriors.

Old School Warrior King was in the prone on concrete and he screamed, "One o'clock, one o'clock, kill the motherfucker, kill the motherfucker!"

Wildman blasted at the rooftop with his heavy machine gun. Big Pat and Cool Papa and Sasquatch shouted to their men. Alley corners and rooftops lit up, RPGs flying high over us now, at least ten meters above our heads. Iraqi Arabs were running toward a mosque some fifteen hundred meters west up a long road bordering a field of sand and trash and rubble.

Love rose, zeroed in, and fired, steady on his rifle, left elbow tucked in his side, shooting off-hand. Meismer was right with him, RPGs still flying over us. Iraqi policeman crawled into corners behind concrete barriers, AK-47s lying on the sidewalks where they'd thrown them down.

There was a man in the middle of the T-intersection, kaffiyeh wrapped ninja-style about his face and head. He was setting up an RPG on his shoulder, and then he disappeared, his body exploding under a hail of fire. The Bradley and Abrams pumped rounds, 10th Mountain warriors shouting, "Feydayeen you die today, die motherfuckers, die!"

Bohlen pumped an arm to his gunner on an MK 19 and 40mm grenades blazed *thump thump thump thump thump*, hammering the concrete blockhouse on the rooftop, Big Red One Bradleys fully engaged. Abrams machine guns pumped out rounds and men shouted, Love and Meismer leaning forward now, squinting, elbows on the hood of the truck, sighting in and firing, precise and accurate fire, the Count about twenty meters from us and steady on his M-4.

Scattered AK fire still came at us, black smoke boiling up from the rooftop, the Fallujah policemen tugging their knees up to their chins now, all dog-piled in corners.

The Guerrilla Warrior was on one knee, aiming carefully and firing three-round bursts. He swung west and laid down fire on an alley corner, and Iraqis ran up sidewalks west. I scoped the huge mosque west, and there was a crowd of at least five hundred Iraqis gathered now along the sidewalks and in the road near the mosque.

"Cease fire, Cease fire!" shouted the Count, slashing across his chest with his right hand, and his warriors passed on the order, giving the hand-and-arm signal, silent now. Blue-gray smoke drifted from the men's barrels, Bradley gunners and tank gunners up on their machine guns, all eyes. Fallujah policemen were still in the fetal position, AKs still lying askance on the sidewalks behind me.

I told Love I was headed over to the Old School Warriors and he said, "No problem, get with us on the exfil," and the Count pumped a fist to me and I gave him a thumbs-up. Serpico and Meismer still scanned the rooftops with their rifles.

"Great to see you!" Guerrilla Warrior shouted as I ran up to him, and we shook hands, Old School Warrior King smiling. Lieutenant Chesty shouted, "The bastards threw down on the wrong honchos, baby. Hua, Old School Warriors rock, we killed the feydayeen sonsofbitches!"

We were all behind his MK 19 truck now. Old School Warrior King ran over to Wildman and told him to adjust his field of fire, to shift west toward where the crowd was swarming back and forth in front of the mosque. I remember thinking that the Old School Warrior King was keen, anticipating fire from the mosque. Kiowas swooped low and raced through the sky, Bradley gunners steady on their heavy guns.

"Fuckin'-a, Big Red One!" someone shouted from Bohlen's men, and Bohlen answered, "Big Red One!" and all of us answered him, "Big Red One, Hua!"

Bohlen grinned and eyed the heavy black smoke boiling out of the concrete blockhouse on the rooftop.

"RPGs came from there," Bohlen said, pointing to the rooftop, "and from the street corners. Bastards are still out there, be careful. What happened to the IPs?" he asked me, and I told him they'd thrown down their weapons and curled up in the corners of walls, inside the train station. He shook his head. "God hates cowards and He loves 10th Mountain. Sergeant Guiza," he said, pointing to the sergeant. Guiza was talking with a .50-caliber gunner, verifying fields of fire, telling the gunner to make sure the center of his field of fire was locked on the T-intersection.

"Sir," Guiza said, his face flushed and sweat pouring down it.

"How are you doin' sergeant?" the lieutenant asked, taking cover behind the wheel of a truck, and we took cover with him.

"Good sir. Men are good. Adjusted to nine o'clock on the Ma Deuce. Gunner is fine. Jesus, the MK 19 put down rounds, Lieutenant Chesty."

The streets were empty all around the T-intersection, no one on the sidewalks. To the west, the massive crowd once surging and receding outside the mosque was now completely inside it.

I lifted my binoculars, scoped the rooftops, and saw houseplants and cinder-block walls and sheets and blankets riddled with holes. Some Iraqi police rolled up near the intersection in a white pickup, and a crowd began to swarm out of an alley. Black columns of smoke poured from the blockhouse.

The policemen spoke to the crowd and the crowd held, unmoving now, one policeman drawing a sidearm and entering the house with the rooftop blockhouse.

"Damn right. MK 19, brother. That's what it's for," Bohlen said, and Radio Free Wisconsin slapped a hand on his shoulder.

"Sir, Ironman says two mikes, exfil. Two mikes." I ran back to Captain Love's truck. Attack Company hustled up on their trucks, machine gunners standing tall on the guns like Franklin had the night before. Big

Red One held point, a Bradley leading us out slowly, turret swiveling as the Bradley rolled south and swung a hard left east for Volturno. An Abrams checked our six.

Children swarmed on the streets as we rode east, waving and leaping, shouting at us, "Amerikee, Amerikee, Amerikee." We all waved back, keeping eyes on rooftops and alley corners, kids giving us thumbs-up as we neared the soccer field. All the players stopped and waved, and I shouted *"Assallamm Ah Laekkum,"* and for the first time in Fallujah, all of them shouted back, *"Wa Laekkum Assallamm."*

The skies were clearing east of us now, as Big Red One on point and tail-end charlie headed back to Volturno in the early dusk of December 16.

On December 18, "Sumo Warrior," the platoon sergeant for Leclair, insisted that I shoot three hundred rounds of reflexive fire "just in case we need you to back us up in a firefight, Hawk." His real name was Sergeant First Class William Kopti. I called him Sumo Warrior because he was an aficionado of Japanese culture and knew his haiku from his kendo. He was a great fan of Kurosawa's classic film, *Seven Samurai.* Sumo Warrior had a rough deployment, returning home on emergency leave twice for the funerals of his father and brother.

He and Jedi Knight and the Desert Yetis schooled me on reflexive fire on the range, an hour and a half of steady movement and fire—shoot and move, move and shoot—in the sunny and dry desert heat. You jack in a clip and walk slowly and turn, either left or right, and put rounds downrange; you also walk forward, stopping every ten meters or so to fire straight ahead.

The Jedi Knight said as I jacked in my last clip on an M-4, "Reflexive fire is the closest you can get to actual close-quarter combat. If you can shoot well at reflexive fire, it's a very good indication you'll shoot well in combat. You've gotta' shoot and move, you know, just like in CQB [close quarter battle]." Kopti grinned, checking my target, saying, "I guess you really were a Marine, after all," all of us laughing with him, Bozzelli slapping Kopti on the back and Leclair shaking my hand.

When we weren't raiding and on the range, we were thinking through the Slay the Dragon raid planned for early January. The special operations commandos Phantom, Ghost, and Cool Hand Luke—U.S. Army Special Forces commandos who were in the field night and day on raids and patrols with Task Force 1Panther—huddled over maps under the camouflaged netting near the ops center in the late afternoons. Lambert and Regan would talk with Caliguire and Kirkpatrick about infiltrating the weapons market area on the eastern banks of the Euphrates, working out different routes. And in the Kingdom of the Desert Yetis, within the Jedi Knight's castle, Leclair and Kopti would sketch assaults on whiteboards in their hootch—squad leaders eyeing the assault sketches with them and tossing in their two cents.

And we'd roll out the wire and raid and roll back and grab chow and guzzle down coffee and listen to an op order and link up again for another raid, the men, as ever, checking clips and grenades and sniper rifles and machine guns and .203s. Machine gunners lit up smokes in that late December in Fallujah and talked of their women and their dreams.

In that time, Americans from other government agencies raided with Charlie Company. They were quiet and calm and brave, and the paratroopers of Charlie Company, the Gunfighters under Wyatt Earp's command, respected them. They nailed $270,000 of Al Quaeda's funds in Fallujah, seized key documents, and as one of the special agents said, "We lost a lot of good people on September 11, and it only took roughly five hundred grand for Al Quaeda to launch their attacks. The 270 grand we seized tonight was vital to the War on Terror, gentlemen. It's been an honor and a privilege."

Before the New Year came, we raided Al Quaeda again in Fallujah. Bravo Company, the Wild Bunch, led by Captain Matthew Mobley, raided Al Quaeda on December 30th, a night we launched three simultaneous raids for the following Al Quaeda terrorists: Mohammad Abid Diya, Salam Fiyad Ahmed, Abdel Salaam Mohammad, Salam Mohammad Audiuu, and Faras Hassan Mohammad.

I was with Attack Company that night, but our raid came up empty, a dry hole. With Cool Hand Luke and the Ghost supporting us, we'd raided three houses on the south side of Fallujah, but no dice. Rolling back on the exfil, no casualties, the word came up on the horn, Lieutenant Chesty shouting from the TC seat in the darkness in Fallujah, "We got Al Quaeda, we got Al Quaeda! Captain Mobley got all those sonsofbitches, all five of them at the same house. Bravo Company hell yes! Fuckin'-a nailed Al Quaeda terrorist motherfuckers. Remember September 11th! Remember September 11th!"

We all cheered and shouted as we rolled down dead-empty streets through the heart of Fallujah—two o'clock in the morning on December 30, and five Al Quaeda terrorists captured by the Wild Bunch in one swift, sure, solid raid. It was damned cold that night, and riding back, Lybert said, "Lieutenant Chesty, it's fuckin' freezing back here, sir, goddamn!"

Bohlen glanced back, grinning.

"Radio Free Wisconsin, you're a fuckin' ice fisherman, bubba! You are the King of Winter Wonderland. This is Lybert weather, this is Ladysmith, Wisconsin, weather, land of the Great Lakes, go Packers, Brett Favre on the money, touchdown! Get hard, Wisconsin! Snow and ice and many dairy products, Green Bay, Green Bay, Lombardi rocks! Gut it out, Radio Free Wisconsin!" We busted up laughing, Hall and Huber slapping palms in the night and Lybert shaking his head, eyes bright, laughing with us in the darkness.

Back at the hootch, we drank hot chocolate and celebrated nailing Al Quaeda as we listened to AC/DC and Judas Priest and Metallica and Sade, Pittman hipping us to Sade's beautiful ballads. Huber teased Hall, "What's up, Guerrilla Warrior, you can't dig the heavy metal sounds, what's wrong with you," and Hall laughing, exclaimed, "German techno-disco is the rave, Old School Warrior King, you gotta' love disco, German disco rocks!" Lieutenant Chesty was ebullient, in his element with his brother warriors. Big Pat, subdued and quiet, a green wool scarf wrapped around his neck, sat on his cot drinking hot chocolate and reading Christmas cards from his wife and daughters. I was grateful that we had all got back in the wire alive and damned happy that Mobley's Wild Bunch had struck hard at Al Quaeda in Fallujah in late December 2003.

There was a cold dawn and a blue sky with the Wild Bunch on January 2, 2004, in Fallujah. "Hope you like your coffee black and strong, Mr. Tucker, because that's all we've got," Sergeant First Class Coy, "the Veteran," said to me as he handed me a mug full of piping-hot longshoreman's coffee. We walked outside near the lake with his platoon leader, First Lieutenant Rory O'Brien, "the Missouri Scout." The Veteran and the Missouri Scout were both Ranger/Airborne qualified, like their company commander, the Rifleman, Captain Mobley.

Coy was about five foot ten and lean and spoke in a gruff, low tone. I thanked him for the coffee and he nodded and said, "You're riding in my truck. Specialist Perry's up on the machine gun. Stay low and stay alert, really tight alleys and streets down there. It's all Indian country, the weapons market." Private First Class Sphrae and Private Webb shouted "Hua, Airborne!" as Coy neared our truck, and he shook his head, grinning slightly, and said, "Happy New Year, Mr. Tucker," paratroopers laughing up on the truck. Sergeant Walburn was our wheelman, all business, an M-4 by his side. Sphrae carried a light machine gun and Webb carried an M-4.

Perry was mounting his heavy machine gun as I jumped up on Coy's truck. I called him "the Point Man," because he had that combination of fearlessness and combat savvy you find among all outstanding point men, a natural calm that gave you confidence going into combat with him. He was about five foot ten, broad-shouldered, and lean, like a natural middleweight.

Perry wore dark shades against the blinding desert morning sun. Wild Bunch paratroopers were working the action on their rifles, sharpening fighting knives, and loading up assault rucks with 5.56 and 7.62 live rounds as seagulls flocked on the lake waters. The wind was strong on that winter dawn, and the coffee tasted especially good. The Point Man pointed to my knife and gave me a thumbs-up.

"Dig that Kukri," he said, and I unsheathed it and handed it to him. He hefted it, checking it out, and said, "Genuine Kukri. Excellent fighting knife. Hey Sergeant, why don't we get issued Kukris," he said, grinning, as our truck revved and we began rolling toward the south gate. Coy replied in a low gravelly voice, "Perry, we've got enough knives, son, steady on your machine gun." The skies were high, blue, and cloudless all ways, Kiowas swooping low over our convoy as we rolled out the wire.

There was thick traffic north on Route 10 as we followed the Count and Spartan Six's battle plan, an ingenious, excellent example of deception and stealth. Shepherds with scarves wrapped thick around their necks waved to us and I waved back, Wild Bunch steady on their guns and scoping groves of date palms and clusters of acacia trees.

The Gunfighters were across the Euphrates and set in near a bridge. Caliguire's Commandos were rolling at a set time, far from the weapons market near the river Euphrates, as if they were on a reconnaissance patrol.

Ironman's Warriors were in the roving groove, ready to strike and secure the southwestern perimeter of the weapons market.

And the Wild Bunch was the main element on the raid, led by Phantom, Ghost, and Cool Hand Luke. First Lieutenant Cook and his 2nd Platoon paratroopers were rolling in big white bread trucks, the kind you see making deliveries all over Iraq.

The night before, over a coffee at battalion ops center, Scout of the Far Afghan Hills had told me, "Every unit in Fallujah has planned a major operation to crush the weapons market, planned it to op order stage, then backed off."

Zawachewsky pointed to the weapons market on the map, near the Euphrates in the northwestern edges of Fallujah.

"We know the weapons market is a key link between the feydayeen and Al Quaeda and all anti-Coalition forces in Fallujah," he said. "We know the IED makers are in there. Be friggin' careful out there tomorrow, be very careful. The weapons market is officially designated by the U.S. Army as 'extremely hostile.' There are feydayeen lookouts everywhere," he said, his voice hard now.

"If we get the drop on them, infiltrate clean, we'll shock the hell out of them and seal off their exit routes. The key is the initial assault; Phantom, Ghost, and Cool Hand Luke are on point with Lieutenant Cook and his men. It's a complex mission, on the one hand, but it really all comes down to one thing—deception. Charlie Company will set off a line charge and roll to it, make the feydayeen think they are reacting to an IED. That sets off the raid. We all roll toward the IED, once that line charge goes off. Diversion. Alpha Company will be rolling on what would appear to be a company-sized reconnaissance—we've done that frequently before, for real. Again, diversion. Deception. Attack Company is roving south of town; they've rolled out there many times on counter-mortar patrols and reconnaissance—again, deception. And Bravo Company—you're on main element with Bravo—will head north, way the hell north, then shoot into town and just do a meet and greet, seemingly psy ops mission. So if you're feydayeen, on mobile phones throughout Fallujah, you see four different companies in four different parts of town, none of them near the weapons market."

We slowed as we neared the railroad tracks, entering Fallujah, and hung a short sharp left into the apartment buildings' complex. Children raced out to greet us, and young men in leather jackets and jeans on rooftops pulled out mobile phones as we rolled in. Iraqi men, ranging from their late teens to early fifties, I reckoned, gathered in twos and threes in the small lanes of the complex; they, too, pulled out mobile phones.

The Fallujah Scouts, led by the Virginian, handed out candy to the kids. Eggleston and Zavala and McGuire played rocks, scissors, paper with the laughing Iraqi children. We talked to the kids, and some of the paratroopers broke out small digital cameras and took pictures of them. We cooled out, drinking tea and smokin' and jokin', teenaged girls giggling and hanging back in the shadows.

"Saddle up," Coy shouted as word came around to mount up, and Webb looked at Sphrae and said, "We're going to fuck their shit up today; feydayeen have no idea we're raiding the weapons market." Sphrae nodded and, glancing up, asked, "Eyes in the sky?" We were rolling now, and kids were grinning and waving goodbye as Perry answered Sphrae. "Roger that. Eyes in the sky, Kiowa Warriors. Snipers on rooftops. Take the high ground," Perry said.

Barreling west down a long stretch of potholed hardball, the Point Man reminded me to scope rooftops and alley corners, and I nodded and raised my binoculars.

Sphrae covered our three o'clock, light machine gun shouldered, and shouted, "Damn right. Use those scopes, Mr. Tucker. Give us the lowdown on everything two to three hundred meters ahead," and I did, scoping minarets and rooftops downrange. Walburn shot us down the back alleys and rubble-strewn, empty streets of Fallujah. To the west I could see date palms and saw grass rushing in high gold stands along the Euphrates. Webb nodded and said, "Right, listen for the blast."

The Veteran had his M-4 outboard and he raised it, sighting in, and shouted, "Two minutes, men!" A Kiowa Warrior swooped no more than one hundred feet off the deck. It roared over the rooftops, and we swung a hard left out of an alley. Iraqis walked along on that Friday morning, staring at us, and I smiled and waved to them.

The blast of Charlie Company's line charge rocked us, the echo of the blast booming now from across the Euphrates, and Walburn shouted, "Fuckin-a' that was a helluva' line charge!" A gray-and-black cloud rose on the western banks beyond the approaches to the old green steel bridge.

Ahead, Wild Bunch trucks were halting and paratroopers were leaping out. O'Brien was already out and pumping a fist, his radioman with him as they hustled down a narrow street toward the weapons market.

Iraqis ran into small shops and alleys as we made the raid. I scoped the minarets and rooftops of a mosque some fifty meters south of us and it was clear, and I jumped off, following the Point Man, who was carrying his heavy machine gun like it was a toothpick as he rushed south for the weapons market.

Wild Bunch sergeants were pumping fists and shouting, "Move move move, goddamnit move, fuckin'-a!" Webb and Sphrae were up ahead of both me and Perry, and gunfire cracked in the distance somewhere east of us in the city, the deep, coughing, cracking, distinct signature of AK-47 fire.

Paratroopers were rushing east now, down alleys and narrow potholed streets, pumping sweat in the rising heat.

Coy glanced back, eyes hard, and nodded and gestured east. We sprinted for a corner and ran into the heart of the weapons market.

Iraqi men carrying wooden stocks for AK-47s and pistol holsters were huddled up against the walls. Cook's paratroopers were already confiscating AK-47s and RKM machine guns, and paratroopers were shouting, "This lane sealed, this lane sealed."

I glanced up and saw the scout/sniper Eggleston from southern California who loved his girlfriend in Los Angeles. "She's kept me going, here and in Afghanistan, night and day. I don't know how I'd make it without her." He was getting in the prone now, scanning east and south from a rooftop with his M-24 sniper rifle.

Staff Sergeant Martin was in the prone beside him, raising high-powered binoculars while bursts of AK fire perhaps fifty meters east of us cracked in the mid-morning heat. I called Eggleston "L.A. SWAT," because he'd told me he was thinking of joining the LAPD as a SWAT police officer after Iraq. "It's my second combat tour, Iraq, and I'm not a career army guy. I've done my time, brother, and I miss my woman very much. She means the world to me."

Now we turned a corner into an alley and sappers were cutting open steel doors. Ghost shouted "Get some!" and the "Commando Sapper," Corporal Anderson from Fayetteville, North Carolina, slammed his combat Skilsaw into a lock, white flame whirling on the door, sparks rocketing off the lock.

Commando Sapper busted it open and paratroopers rushed in shouting, "Clear, clear, motherfuckin' AK motherlode!" and I rushed in behind them into a shop loaded with AK-47s hanging off the walls, broken down machine guns with spare barrels piled in a corner, and crates full of RPG grenades.

Commando Sapper and his buddy, Private First Class Brown from Pasco, Washington, "the Woodsman," a great hunter who always had delicious elk and beef jerky in his hootch, came up into the room as the paratroopers piled up AK-47s and counted the RPG grenades. Corporal Anderson carried an M-4 slung off his flak jacket and a sidearm holstered on his right hip. Brown carried an M-4 and a battering ram. Their faces were flushed and red, sweat pouring off them. I shook their hands and wished them well, and Corporal Anderson said, grinning, "Brother, we got the drop on these feydayeen sonsofbitches. Nailing beaucoup weapons and rounds today, fuckin'-a, slay the fuckin' dragon."

AK fire snapped in the distance, easily two hundred meters east, single shots, and then a burst of fire. Stinking green chemical smoke drifted up the alley, a terrible, acrid, vile smell. Warriors wrapped bandanas around their faces and shouldered their weapons, squinting.

I hustled back to a main road running east to west through the weapons market. Cool Hand Luke was in the shadows, just behind a cinder-block wall, speaking into a mouthpiece, leaning over slightly, a massive Heckler Koch USP .45 ACP automatic pistol on his right hip, twenty-four clips snug in khaki nylon pouches covering his custom flak jacket, each clip holding twelve rounds.

Cool Hand Luke nodded to me. I glanced up an alley, sappers busting up illegal weapons dealers left and right, and gave him a thumbs-up, and he grinned. Coy jogged up to me and I told him I was headed north up the alley, and he slapped me on my back and said, "We got the drop on the rat bastards, Mr. Tucker." He kept on moving, shouting to his paratroopers, the Missouri Scout in the shadows on the radio. The radio handset stretched to his radioman, who stood back-to-back with the lieutenant. His radioman scoped an alley with his M-4, checking our six.

Streams of fire flashed from sappers' combat Skilsaws in an alley north, and O'Brien ran ahead of me, gesturing left and right and guiding squad leaders down dark alleys. A shout came up from behind us, "Oh yes, money in the bank, baby!"

The sapper specialist Shane Thomson, a witty, funny warrior much like Kentucky Rifle up north—I called Thomson, "the Jester"—stood next to a paratrooper sergeant, the trunk of a taxi open before them. I hustled up to them and the Jester shouted, "Take a look, Santa's still around, baby!"

Four AK-47s and heaps of magazines filled with live rounds lay scattered over gray blankets in the trunk of the orange-and-white taxi. The driver was up against a wall on his haunches, glaring at us. I shouted, "Mala Mustafa Barzani, peshmerga!" and the taxi driver flinched and looked down.

I slapped the Jester on his shoulders and scanned the streets. I could see paratroopers at every alley corner and machine gunners in the prone behind crumbling cinder-block walls and slabs of concrete. Paratroopers carrying shotguns were rushing down alleys and slamming open doors and shouting, "More here, goddamn, all kinds of AKs over here!" The chemical stench was gone now and a breeze rushed off the Euphrates, the scent of saw grass and date palms fresh in the streets.

Sappers raced with the Ghost and Phantom down alleys west of me, battle-axing their way into shops and slamming their Hooligan tools into locks and metal doors, shouting, "7.62, all kinds of 7.62," and carrying out heaps of 7.62 metal-jacketed live rounds. Two fire teams rushed past me and headed for Mosque Armory #1, a real problem mosque in the past for our warriors in Fallujah, and one reported to have ample AK-47 caches and God only knows what else.

I raised my scopes and checked rooftops east, and a sergeant shouted to me from out of the shadows of an alley, "You see anything strange, anything, let me know, bro," and I gave him a thumbs-up, paratroopers racing past us.

Warriors of all ranks were shouting, "Get out, get the fuck out now!" to Iraqis in clothing and tea shops, near the main east-west road in the weapons market. The paratroopers herded men and boys to the north side of the street, alongside parked cars and taxis and pickup trucks, as sappers went among the Iraqis and pointed to locks on the vehicle doors and trunks, asking for keys. A translator came up and again asked for keys. The Iraqis went quiet.

The translator pointed to a gray pickup and shouts of "*La, la,*" the Arabic for no, erupted from the men as they sat back on their haunches along a wall, hands on their heads. A sapper pulled out his Hooligan, slipping it off his back, and a Wild Bunch sergeant nodded and said, "No keys, so be it. We're searching all vehicles. Fuck it up, fuck it up!"

Glass flew everywhere as the sapper battle-axed the window. He leaned in and opened the door and searched the vehicle, shouting, "Fuckin' blasting caps, feydayeen motherfuckers! Got blasting caps for IEDs." Machine gunners watched the Iraqis who were looking down now as the sapper pulled out strings of blasting caps from beneath plastic rice bags and burlap bags, nodding grimly as he held the blasting caps up for all to see.

"IEDs. Straight up, these are for IEDs," he said, the Wild Bunch sergeant checking them out. Coy jogged up to us and talked with the sapper and the sergeant, spoke briefly to the translator, and then grabbed his own set of keys out of a bellows pocket. He turned toward the Iraqis along the wall and shouted, "Keys, keys?" shaking his keys and waving them about.

"*Nam, nam,*" the Iraqis shouted now, Arabic for yes. Paratroopers hustled up to them and escorted them to their vehicles. Two Kiowa Warriors swooped low over us, flying in straight runs less than one hundred feet off the deck, trail chopper roughly fifty meters behind the lead chopper, covering its right flank and headed west across the Euphrates. It was near eleven and the sun was hot now. I could hear the sappers buzz-sawing down the alley north of us, and I told SFC Coy I was headed up the alley. He nodded and gave me a thumbs-up.

"Friendly coming up!" I shouted, moving up the alley past tailor shops and tea shops with tables full of half-empty, small, hourglass-shaped glasses, teaspoons all lined up in clean, shining order on a small white table, flies buzzing over an open bag of sugar.

The alley was perhaps three meters wide, no more, a jagged winding way over broken concrete and uneven bricks. There was a dogleg left and I shouted, "Friendly coming up, friendly coming up!" as I turned the corner. The sappers were pumping sweat, flame shooting off their combat Skilsaws, paratroopers securing the breach, checking their six with shotguns and machine guns.

"This one's a stone bitch," said Sergeant Robert Merritt of Rochester, New York, a hard-eyed, laconic, twenty-seven-year-old Afghan vet with four years in the U.S. Army, as Specialist David Lane, a twenty-five-year-old Afghan vet from Dexter, New York, who grew up on Lake Ontario in upstate New York, slammed his combat Skilsaw into a heavy iron lock at the base of a metal door. Lane was breathing heavily, sweating fiercely in the shadow and light of the tight alley.

A Wild Bunch sergeant tapped the barrel of his .203 about chest-high against the sliding metal door. "Breach here. Cut across, we'll peel it." Lane rose up and sliced open the thin metal, sparks dancing off his saw as he angled it across horizontally and then jagged down hard, making a long, deep vertical cut all the way down.

The burly paratrooper sergeant kicked it in and rushed forward into a small room filled with rifles of all makes and ages, shotguns, Bren guns, and a Lewis gun, a machine gun that predates WWII. Merritt and Lane entered and I followed behind them, Merritt eyeing the room and saying, "Gunsmith, gents, and he was working on this one," pointing to a Lee Enfield .303 of WWII vintage. "Modifying rifles to fire automatic," said the paratrooper sergeant, and Merritt and Lane nodded to him, pointing to Lee Enfields hanging from the walls, AK-47s piled up in one corner, rifle stocks and barrels scattered all over a stone floor, one old bolt-action rifle still in a vise.

Ghost, Phantom, and Cool Hand Luke entered the illegal gunsmith's shop. The Ghost, cradling his HK MP5 submachine gun, whistled long and low. "Motherlode, baby," he said, and Phantom and Cool Hand Luke squinted as they scanned the room.

Directly across the alley, paratroopers and sappers were in another illegal weapons shop stuffed to the gills with AK-47s and 7.62 linked, live rounds. I talked briefly with Cool Hand Luke and headed north up the alley, shafts of sunlight bursting through breaks in a flimsy thatched roof above. A paratrooper carried a light machine gun at the end of the alley.

A Kiowa Warrior swooped very low, maybe sixty feet off the deck, heading west for the Euphrates and the Al Bowisa tribal land beyond, and it was getting on to noon. From out of nowhere, Spartacus and Command Sergeant Major Burgos, his brigade sergeant major, rushed up the alley. We talked briefly. Spartacus always made you feel that you would raid and win in Fallujah. I told them about the motherlode up the alley and they smiled and wished me a Happy New Year, and I moved on, reaching the machine gunner at alley's end.

There were .50-caliber gun trucks some thirty meters west of him on a narrow street facing the alley, and paratroopers were securing all street and alley corners. The sappers were ripping open metal doors and locks left and right, sweating furiously in the noon heat, shouts of "AKs here, RPGs here," coming from down the street.

There was a specialist up the street with an I-Com, and the machine gunner told me he could relay my position to battalion. I thanked the gunner and hustled up to the specialist, who was taking a knee behind a low concrete wall. He called in my position to O'Brien, who relayed it to the Rifleman and to battalion. He stayed on his I-Com and frowned, wincing and shaking his head slightly, his face red.

"Hawk, Captain Hampton's dead. Her Kiowa was shot down, brother. Across the Euphrates. Co-pilot's banged up but they think he'll make it. She was an Afghan vet, sir."

The young warrior stayed on his gun, and I told him I was very sorry to hear we'd lost her. I remembered seeing her the night before at the chow hall, talking with some of the officers, her sandy blonde hair plaited up. She looked at ease, cheerful, and her eyes were bright. Leclair told me later that night before the raid that Captain Kimberly Hampton from Easley, South Carolina, was deeply respected by the paratroopers, who knew that she'd volunteered for combat in Afghanistan prior to her tour of duty in Iraq. She was one of ours, a warrior going in harm's way in Iraq, and like every other casualty of war we'd taken from helicopters being shot down in Fallujah, she was shot down on Al Bowisa turf. Sheikh Gazi Al Bowisa's turf.

The specialist told me Alpha Company was up the street and around a corner, "Hang a left at the .203 gunner, head north about fifty meters, they're right there, stay low, brother." I thanked him and moved up the street, shouting "Friendly coming up!" The .203 gunner turned and nodded to me.

Around the corner, I could see Vegas and his paratroopers farther up the street. Vegas waved a hand to me and I hustled up to him, the Samurai pumping a fist and gesturing to his squad behind his captain. "You're with Bravo, aren't you," the captain said, eyebrows raised, as his radioman checked his six sappers ripped into sliding metal doors about twenty meters behind us.

I told him I was but I'd heard Alpha was on the case, too, and wanted to see if they'd nailed any weapons caches. He nodded, his face hard, eyes intense.

"Seven IEDs, already. Beaucoup live rounds, Alpha Company is on the scene. My boys are doing fine," he said, gesturing to his paratroopers. I asked him if he knew that Hampton had died, and he nodded, his face grave. "She was a brave lady, Hawk. No doubt she kept us safe today. Having the Kiowas on overwatch is essential, this mission. Very sad. You knew she was an Afghan vet?" he asked, and I told him I knew.

Around us, his men were piling up RPGs and cases of 7.62 linked, live rounds; I wished him luck and told him I was headed back to Bravo. Back through the maze of narrow streets and alleys, I hustled for the main east-west road, paratroopers and sappers loading up AKs and RPGs. Warriors were soaked with sweat and still raiding hard and smart, machine guns at the hip, shotguns shouldered, alley to corner to street to door, sparks flaming from sappers combat Skilsaws in the heat of the day in Fallujah.

There was water boiling in a big steel kettle over a low blue flame in a tea shop on the main east-west road. Corporal Mullin on a .203 and Specialist Lane on a light machine gun stood near the kettle.

They were facing up an alley and it was getting on to two in the afternoon now, L.A. SWAT still in the prone high above us, holding the high ground for all of us. The Virginian was spotting for him, scoping the rooftops and alley corners with high-powered binoculars.

I talked to Mullin and Lane and they told me they were fine but getting "pretty damn hungry, Hawk, it's been a helluva' raid," Lane said. The Veteran came up and said, "Gents, we busted IED factories One and Two, take a look. Mullin and Lane, hold the alley."

I walked over with Coy; there were paratroopers at the entrance to a fabric shop, a long shotgun-style low-ceilinged shop with a blue sheet draped over a steel pole about twenty feet back from the entrance.

Cool Hand Luke threw open the sheet from the other side and said, "Ten IEDs inside, set to blow. Two different shops within this shop; this is IED central, for Fallujah. All set to blow, blasting caps in place." I nodded and told him I'd take no pictures and he thanked me.

Phantom and the Ghost were checking out the IEDs. Coy talked briefly with them and departed; outside, I could see there were maybe five feet from shop entrance to a curb.

If you set lookouts around the shop and warned people away with armed feydayeen, you could carry all ten of those IEDs—which were nothing but plastic explosives jammed down into palm-oil cans—to a pickup truck with the engine running and be on Highway One, the main drag in Fallujah, within five minutes. There were at least five kilos of plastic explosive inside each IED. Later, Ghost would tell me that there were metal shavings, "bolts, razor blades, and every piece of metal you can think of that would fit inside a palm-oil can, all stuffed inside those IEDs."

We'd now seized seventeen IEDs, huge ones, and taken down three IED factories. Shadows angled out onto the narrow streets and alleys of the weapons market, and I fixed tea for me, Mullin, and Lane.

Mullin grinned as he sipped his tea, keeping one hand on his .203. Strange gray-green smoke drifted from the southern end of the alley, and a crowd came through the smoke, perhaps one hundred meters away from us. We set our tea down and I raised my scopes.

The crowd slowly approached us. The wooden-stock of an AK-47 gripped by the barrel guards was raised through the smoke. It sank back into the crowd, like an oar settling in lake water.

"There's an AK," I said, and Mullin asked, "In the crowd, you saw an AK?" and he shouldered his .203, eyes on his scope.

I kept eyes on the crowd and told him I'd seen an AK raised.

"Keep eyes on. Lane, be ready on your SAW, brother."

"Roger that," Lane said, taking a knee, the barrel of his light machine gun resting over three concrete blocks stacked in front of him. The crowd halted now and then moved quickly forward. All I could see was heads and shoulders through the smoke, men in their late teens, I reckoned, and older, many of them in black leather jackets with kaffiyehs wrapped around their necks. Some five ranks back from the first wave of the surging crowd, a second AK popped up, and near the front of the crowd, an AK was lifted up again through the smoke.

"Two AKs. At least two AKs in that crowd," I said, and Coy heard me.

Coy looked at me and I said, "Let me go up the alley with Mullin and Lane. Use my Arabic. That crowd is coming from the mosque. If we back them up into the mosque, we can keep them from using those AKs." Mullin nodded and Lane, keeping eyes on the crowd, steady on his light machine gun, said, "Roger that."

Coy nodded to us and we moved up the alley, Mullin and Lane in front of me, hustling up the sides of the alley, using concrete stanchions for cover as we bounded up. The crowd surged back now, running back toward the mosque, bright-green smoke drifting in the alley. We ran through the smoke, Mullin turning right at the end of the alley and shouldering his .203, eyes on the mosque.

A gate of the mosque was packed with men in black leather jackets and kaffiyehs, sweat beading on their faces. Mullin said to Lane, "Hold east, I've got the mosque, 10th Mountain's on the west end." I looked west and there was a fire team from Attack Company. They were First Lieutenant Chad Jenkins's men, and they shouted "Hua!" and I pumped a fist to them.

A man clad in a collared white shirt, dark blue pants, and leather sandals came out of a tailor shop opposite us. I could see a door to the back of his shop; his shop adjoined the mosque. I greeted him in Arabic and he responded. Lane held his machine gun on the alley east, shadows dark on the broken concrete in the alley.

"Is there a problem here?" the man asked me in perfect English.

"Tell these men that if they are feydayeen, we will kill them. The choice is theirs. There are at least two AK-47s in that mosque," I said, pointing to the mosque. He translated for me and a man with salt-and-pepper hair, wearing a black leather jacket and wiping sweat from his jowls, answered, glaring at me.

"This man says there are no weapons in the mosque, it is a holy place. There are no feydayeen here. It is sacred. Iraqis would never put weapons of war in a mosque."

"Ask him if he is a wise man."

The ad hoc translator frowned, shrugging his shoulders.

"Whatever do you mean?"

"Like I said, ask him if he is a wise man."

The translator spoke and the man on the edge of the crowd at the mosque folded his arms, looked at me, and replied slowly.

"He says that he is as wise as the desert is hot."

"Good. We are Americans and we are here to kill feydayeen and Al Quaeda. That is why we are in Iraq. There are warriors at every corner ready to kill feydayeen right now. Stay inside the mosque, if you are truly wise."

The translator spoke and the man glared and said nothing. I set a hand on my Kukri. The man turned and said something behind him, and the crowd fell back from the gate; he took a few steps back, folding his arms, looking down.

Mullin said, "Mr. Tucker, let's head back, brother," and he waved a hand toward Jenkins's men holding the western end of the alley and they gestured back to him, two light machine gunners scoping the front of the mosque.

I fell back and Lane covered me and we bounded back with Mullin to the tea stand, Coy and Sergeant First Class Marengo, the 3rd Platoon sergeant for the Wild Bunch, talking with us on our return. O'Brien called in our report on the two AKs in the crowd, and I asked Coy if I could move up the next alley, which was secured at every corner, to Jenkins's platoon. He told me to go right ahead, and I hustled past flex-cuffed detainees, Wild Bunch paratroopers gesturing to me to halt when I'd get up near them and telling me, "Go, move now," as they'd check both ways down their corners.

"Climb to glory!" I shouted to Jenkins's light machine gunners and they shouted back, "Hua, fuckin'-a, 10th Mountain baby! Braveheart's Warriors, Hua!" We talked briefly as they kept eyes on the crowd. A couple of men walked out of the mosque and turned east, looking back at us. One of them pulled out a mobile phone. I took a knee and a fire team leader came up. Staff Sergeant Craig Jackson, "the Titan," from Frederick, Maryland, joined us, scoping the entrance to the mosque with his M-4. Sergeant First Class Vernon Pollard from Hobbs, New Mexico, a broad-shouldered, lean Westerner, kept his M-4 at the ready, quick-action from the shoulder. He was Jenkins's platoon sergeant and a quiet, self-contained man.

"You saw AKs in that crowd, brother?" the Titan asked me on that hot, late afternoon day in January in the Fallujah weapons market as he wiped the sweat off his neck with a small green towel. Jackson was solid like a defensive tackle, a barrel-chested, easygoing, clever warrior who was well respected by his comrades in 3rd Platoon, Attack Company. I told him I had, and the Westerner got on his I-Com, calling Jenkins, whom I'd nicknamed "Braveheart."

Jenkins hustled up, sidearm on his hip, carrying a scoped-out M-4. Jenkins was a West Pointer who'd quarterbacked its football team. He'd graduated in 2002 from the school well known to American fighting generals such as Grant and Lee and Ridgeway. A native of Dublin, Ohio, Jenkins was Ranger/Airborne qualified. He hailed me, sprinting up to us in the alley, sidearm holstered on his right hip and M-4 slung off his flak jacket. As Pollard and Jackson talked with their 10th Mountain comrades in the deepening shadows in the alley, their rifles on the mosque, crowd still inside the mosque, alley in front of the mosque dead-empty now, the lieutenant went over my sighting of two AKs.

"You told them we'd kill them, if they are feydayeen! Damned straight. Well-said, brother. We'll keep eyes on. You got them back inside the mosque. That was good. Right, we need to keep all crowds out of these alleys. Not entirely surprised, about the AKs—you know, we get human intel all the time from Sergeant Quinones that the mosques are storing weapons. Man it's hot," Braveheart said, green bandana around his neck dark with sweat.

I asked him what his toughest game was, when he quarterbacked West Point, and he laughed, keeping eyes on the alley, one hand on his M-4. Jackson was just behind a wall, his M-4 pointing down the alley, eyes on. The Westerner checked our six.

"Mississippi State," Jenkins answered, nodding to the Titan. "They had huge defensive lineman. Just overwhelmed us. I was on my back all day. They really stuck me. Couple of those guys are in the NFL, now. Outstanding football players."

It was good talking with Braveheart in Fallujah; he had come a long way from the banks of the Hudson on September 11, 2001, when, as he said, "The Superintendent of the Academy, General Olson, came and talked to us at eleven forty-five. He called the football team together and talked with us and told us it was our choice that day, to practice or not. He gave us a sit rep on Al Quaeda's attack, dispelled rumors, and really made us aware that we were headed to war. He sat us down and spoke to us, like men. We were all devastated, to know that so many of our people had died so horribly. It was a vicious, evil thing Al Quaeda did."

I hustled back down the alley. It was clear that Braveheart's men were keeping the crowd from surging out of the mosque again. Wild Bunch sergeants said to me, as I ran back down the alley, "We're moving out in ten mikes, get with Sergeant First Class Coy," and I thanked them as green smoke popped behind me, masking our exfiltration on foot.

Wild Bunch paratroopers started herding detainees onto the bread trucks and onto six-bys, engines rumbling in the late afternoon, gulls skying west over the Euphrates. Heaps of linked 7.62-caliber live rounds were stacked on wooden crates. The Rifleman came up around a corner and I wished him well and congratulated him. He grinned and said, "The Wild Bunch. That's right, none of my boys are tame, no question. Safe journey back, Mr. Tucker. Stay low, let's get in the wire solid," and he gave me a thumbs-up. Mobley was about six foot one, had coal-black eyes like Hero of the Kurds, and a laid-back, laconic way of talking. On raids and patrols, he was calm and bold, a great combat commander.

The Point Man ran up and shouted, "We're on the exfil, let's go," and I asked him about the Veteran and he told me, "No worries, Sergeant First Class Coy is already on the truck." Paratroopers were hustling up toward our trucks, machine guns at the hip, rifles shouldered for quick action, scoping roof tops and alley corners and leaping up on the trucks, covering down, shouting "Get the machine gun up, get the gun up," as heavy machine gunners would jump up and set their M240B, 7.62-caliber machine guns on the steel mounts under high blue cloudless skies, sun a far golden fire west across the Euphrates.

Webb and Sphrae jumped up, grinning in the heat and drenched with sweat. Walburn shouted, "Are we good?" and I locked in the troopstrap and shouted, "Troopstrap up!"

Coy said in a hard, clipped tone, "Watch the rooftops for RPGs, gents. Perry, look alive."

Wild Bunch paratroopers shouted back to him "Hua!" on the eastern banks of the Euphrates as we rolled hard, scattered gunfire north of us, riding crosstown for jeep trails stretching south of Fallujah, headed back to Volturno from the raid.

⊙ ⊙ ⊙

On January 2, 2004, in Fallujah, Task Force 1Panther, under the command of Lieutenant Colonel Brian Drinkwine, successfully executed Operation Weapons Market, a mission planned but never carried out by every previous U.S. military force in Fallujah. Drinkwine's warriors captured the following enemy weapons, ammunition, and munitions, along with sixty-two detainees:

- 17 IEDs (Plastic explosive packed with metal, blasting caps in place, set to blow. Each IED would've killed at least twenty Coalition soldiers.)
- 220 antipersonnel hand grenades
- 150 RPG-9 and RPG-7 grenades for RPG rocket launchers
- 55 heat-seeking RPG grenades for RPG rocket launchers
- 30 antipersonnel RPG grenades for RPG rocket launchers
- 50 Lee Enfield .303-caliber rifles modified for full automatic
- 300 AK-47, 7.62-caliber assault rifles
- ZU-23, 12.7-caliber, anti-aircraft gun (This AA system will easily shoot down a helicopter.)
- 20 80mm rockets
- 1,000 12.7-caliber live rounds of ammunition
- 10,000 7.62-caliber linked, live rounds

EPILOGUE: A HAWK FLIES
HIGH AND NEVER ALONE

◉ ◉ ◉

LIEUTENANT CHESTY CALLED ME IN MALAYSIA a couple days after Thanksgiving 2004. We'd each left Iraq in early September. It was morning in New York and evening in Tiluk Bahang. We were both drinking coffee and he was cheerful, talking of old and new dreams.

We talked of his wife and baby boy and the First Marines in Fallujah, who'd done what Boss Sniper had said would have to be done to take Fallujah: assault it with a division-size force, securing all major crossroads with tanks and sniper teams. He asked if I could get his 10th Mountain soldiers, the Old School Warriors, a crate of single-malt scotch and boxes of Cuban cigars for Christmas—truly, it would be a merry one. I told him if it could clear Customs, of course, and he laughed and paused, and said softly in a low, flat tone, "Light one for us, brother, and say a prayer for our comrades."

And he talked about Colonel Merritt "Red" Edson of Vermont and First Marines, at Guadalcanal in WWII. Edson had led Marine raiders in a desperate battle at Bloody Ridge in September 1942, holding the line and preventing Japanese infantry from seizing Henderson Field. He asked me where Edson is buried and I told him at Arlington Cemetery, on the southern banks of the Potomac River, below the Kennedy brothers. He told me he was headed for Special Forces. I wished him good luck and good hunting; I also wished him and his family well.

Before hanging up, he made one last request: "Don't forget Captain Hampton, Hawk. Please make sure people know we will never forget her. She was brave. My God she was brave. And she was the warrior we needed, our Eyes in the Sky in Fallujah. May she rest in peace, brother."

May Captain Kimberly Hampton and all our comrades killed in action to liberate Iraq from Saddam's regime rest in peace. Captain Hampton and her comrades came to Iraq to end a brutal regime. I joined them, believing that there is no wrong time to bring down a dictatorship.

Little I saw, south of Kurdistan, convinced me that Iraqi Arabs, however, are passionate about a democratic federal Iraq. I have since been asked, by old friends and comrades in America and around the world, "What is victory in the Iraq War?" The only answer that makes sense to me is that victory is an Iraq free from radical Islamic terror and a Kurdistan that is independent and free. The Kurds love us and have bled with us, and long before the Bush administration spoke out against Saddam's terror, the Kurds fought valiantly for their freedom. The Kurds, alone among Iraqis, don't need to be convinced that democracy is in their best interests.

Ground truth in Iraq lends little to support President Bush's repeated assertion, in the fall of 2004, that "freedom is on the march." I saw very little in nearly fourteen months in-country in Iraq to convince me that Iraqis, south of Kurdistan, are willing to stand and fight for a free Iraq. The hatred for America, moreover, is visceral, south of Kurdistan.

Freedom is not on the march in Iraq. Radical Islam is on the march, beheadings are on the march, ambushes are on the march, roadside bombs are on the march, and above all else, deep-rooted hatred of America is very much on the march. We have no allies among Iraqi Arabs, top to bottom, in Iraqi culture and society. There is neither affection nor sympathy for Americans in Iraq south of Kurdistan.

We will never be loved by Iraqi Arabs for ending the regime of Saddam Hussein because the damned sad truth is that south of Kurdistan, Iraqis either tolerated, loved, or were indifferent to the Ba'athist dictatorship of Saddam Hussein. The Shias, who endured horrific treatment from Saddam's regime, have done little since April 9, 2003, to build an Iraq free from terror and free from fear. The Sunnis, especially, adore Saddam, just as they adored him while he was murdering Shias and Kurds in the hundreds of thousands.

I have been away from Iraq for more than four months now and am writing in the immediate aftermath of the tragic tsunamis, which struck my island of Penang, Malaysia. We are recovering from the tsunamis and Malaysians, though still somewhat in a state of shock, are volunteering all over Southeast Asia to help our fellow islanders and our neighbors: Phuket and Phang Na in Thailand, Sri Lanka, India, and Sumatra, Indonesia.

And the war in Iraq—which President Bush through his ignorance of the ancient laws of war and his strange befriending of Ba'athist sheikhs and generals, has failed to win—continues to grind on without any sense of unity among Americans or sense of victory on the ground in Iraq. The sidelining of the Kurds is shameful, and it has gravely endangered American and Coalition forces in Iraq by denying field commanders the best damn ground intelligence in Iraq. The road to victory in Iraq, from my experience in combat in northern and western Iraq, leads through an independent Kurdistan. The Arabs will never love us for liberating Iraq from Saddam—and that goes for the Arab world in full. To Arab Muslims, we are the infidel.

There was a saying among American fighting men and women in Kuwait in February 2003: "The road home leads through Baghdad." The only safe, secure, and terror-free roads that exist for Americans in Iraq today are in Kurdistan, and likely, despite whatever geopolitical reality the Bush administration chooses to believe or deny, the long-term road to victory in the Iraq War will roll through Kurdistan.

The Kurds not only love us, they want us to stay. Victory in Iraq means taking a long, hard look at just what the threat in Iraq is, today, in terms of Al Quaeda and other radical Islamic terrorist groups that are allies of Al Quaeda. What is the strategic threat to U.S. interests in the Near East today, and what threat does Iraq pose in the war against radical Islamic terror?

Victory in Iraq means denying western and southern Iraq as a base for radical Islam to recruit, train, and operate from. Kurdistan will hold, and it is in U.S. interests for Kurdistan to hold, and get even stronger. Only the Kurds are combat-proven allies of the United States in the Near East. (I have no quarrel with the Israelis and respect their war-fighting skills and love of democracy; having said that, facts on the ground are that the Kurds bled with us in the Iraq War.)

Let the Iraqis decide how and what kind of government they want. Tell them bluntly and directly that if western and southern Iraq become bases for radical Islam, then they will see destruction on a scale they have never witnessed before. Furthermore, build a major U.S. Air Force base in Kurdistan, and sign a permanent security agreement with the best counter-terrorists in the Near East: the Kurds. Support, on all fronts—diplomatic, trade, political, and military—a free and independent Kurdistan, covering the eastern banks of Mosul, Kirkuk and its oil fields, all the way south to Halapja. Long live a free and independent Kurdistan, and death to Al Quaeda and all allies of Al Quaeda.

You cannot give someone something that they do not want. America should have learned that lesson in the Vietnam War. We are trying to do the same thing with Iraqi Arabs that we did with the South Vietnamese—give them something they do not want. The Vietnamese cared little about Americans fighting to bring them freedom, but they cared deeply about being Vietnamese and independent. The North Vietnamese and Viet Minh understood the allegiances of the Vietnamese people far better than did either the French or Americans. There is a saying I've heard from Burmese, Thais, Cambodians, Laotians, Vietnamese, Chinese, Malaysians, Arab Beduouin, Pakistanis, and Afghans in the ten years I've lived in Asia: Freedom is a full bowl of rice. Iraq is in southwest Asia. It is an Asian saying that cuts straight to the heart of our troubles in Iraq.

Who fills Iraqi rice bowls? Not only materially, but spiritually and culturally? Sheikhs and imams, since time immemorial. If freedom—the Western ideal of freedom—was a central tenet of Iraqi thought and practice, Saddam Hussein would never have come to power. If freedom was on the march in Iraq, Americans would not be dying in ones and twos and dozens, being maimed by roadside bombs and RPGs, and being hated by the very people that the Bush administration is spending billions of dollars on to give Iraq something that Iraqi Arabs, themselves, have done little or nothing to prove they actually want: a free, democratic, federal Iraq. We came to free Iraq from Saddam, and our thanks is that daily our fighting men and women are killed and wounded on supply convoys delivering reconstruction aid for Iraqis who hate us, hate our warriors, hate America for supporting Israel and the Kurds, and who are not worth one more American life.

End the war, now.

We ended the threat to Israel and Kuwait; the Ba'athist dictatorship of Saddam Hussein no longer exists. If the only tangible evidence of victory in the Iraqi War is a Kurdistan free from fear of Ba'athist terror and an Iraq that is not a base for Al Quaeda, so be it. That is strategically and morally a victory America can build on and win the War on Terror.

Sergeant Joe Thoman deeply understands something about Iraq that President Bush fails to see: There is no inherent love for freedom and democracy in Iraq, apart from the Kurds. This lesson is completely lost on the likes of President Bush, Secretary of State appointee Condoleeza Rice, and the inner circle of the Bush administration. Yet it is one I heard time and again from American fighting men like Sergeant Ruben Quinones and Sergeant Joe Thoman. Freedom is not on the march in Iraq; moreover, it has no boots on the ground, in Iraqi culture, to hike with. No amount of money and no ramping up or down of military actions will ever change that. Culture transcends politics and all things political, including money.

Our warriors patrolled down dark streets in Iraq and across moonlit sands with little but their faith in each other and the love of their beloved to sustain them. For their comrades killed in action in Iraq, for their families and friends, for all who knew them and loved them, may the Legend of the Hawk, a Karen hill-tribe legend I first heard on the banks of the Salween River in October 1992, be with you as it has been with the Karen for centuries of slavery, suffering, and survival deep in the highlands of northeastern Burma and northwestern Thailand.

It is a legend that Kurds deeply loved, when I told it to them in Kurdish highlands in 2003 and 2004. The Karen, whose struggle to live free and with dignity closely resembles the epic Kurdish revolution, will, I pray, one day be free from the terror of the Rangoon junta as the Kurds are now free from the terror of Saddam. From the Legend of the Hawk comes the Karen proverb, "A hawk flies high and never alone." This is the Legend of the Hawk:

The boy was an orphan. His father had died two weeks before in the jungle near the Salween River, killed by a rogue bull elephant stampeding through Karen highlands, deep in northwestern Thailand—in what is today the province of Mae Hong Son. His mother had died in childbirth and he was the only child. His village overlooked the wide brown waters of the Salween River. His people had lived there forever.

One morning, his grandfather woke him in the gray of early dawn. The boy followed his grandfather down the steps of their teak and bamboo hut. His grandfather grabbed an axe and the boy did likewise. They chopped wood for the better part of an hour before resting briefly, morning fires alive now in the village and older children tugging at hemp rope tied through the nostrils of water buffalo, leading the heavy-bodied, black, water buffalo out to verdant-green, terraced rice paddies below the village.

His grandfather handed the boy a cup of steaming hot goat milk, and the boy gulped it down and smiled his thanks to his grandfather. He nodded to the boy and sat on a boulder, overlooking the Salween River. A hawk soared over the river, wings spread black and wide in high, blue cloudless skies over the triple-canopy bush—high and alone in the brightening dawn in Karen highlands.

The boy frowned and asked, "Why does the hawk always fly alone, grandfather?"

His grandfather scratched at arms scarred by bamboo and tigers in his youth and smiled.

"A hawk flies high and never alone," he said.

The boy shook his head, uncomprehending. He scratched at the red dirt with one foot and looked down. East, he could see water buffalo moving slowly now through the paddies. Egrets beat white wings toward bamboo wild on the tree lines of the paddies below the village. He counted nine egrets. Again, he shook his head, slowly now, and looked at his grandfather.

"No, grandfather. Always I see the hawk alone above our village. Always I see the hawk alone above our mountains. Always I see the hawk alone above our rivers."

His grandfather grinned and said, "Set your axe down and come sit on this rock." The boy slammed his axe into a chunk of teak and walked over to his grandfather. He sat down, folding his arms. His grandfather pointed to the hawk, circling high above the Salween now, riding the currents of dawn.

"You are old enough now to understand," he said, looking right at his grandson. "Your mother died giving you life. Your father died trying to sustain your life, to support you and take care of you. My grandson, we are Karen. We are an ancient people who came from mountains without names. We journeyed here, to these highlands above the Salween, in a time before time. Always the hawk has been with us, and he is with us still. We are Karen and we say, 'A hawk flies high and never alone.' And this is the legend of the hawk.

"There was a hawk in these mountains, in the time before time. He soared in blue skies. The rivers guided him. The mountains were his home. The jungles sustained him. He took care of his family high on a ridgeline, where the mountains meet the sky.

"One day, the hawk returned to the shelter of his nest high on a mountain overlooking the river Salween. A storm had destroyed his nest. All his family was gone. He was alone like never before. No words could ease his grief. His suffering cut deep into his soul. Long into the night he wept.

"In the morning he saw again the mountains and river and sky and knew he must carry on. The hawk knew he was not alone. The mountains, river, and sky were still his brothers, still his friends, and he prayed there high on a mountain above the Salween. The hawk is closest to the gods of the sky, and so he prayed to the gods of the sky. He prayed all morning.

"When the sun rose directly above him, in the middle of the day, the hawk took flight. And he followed the river Salween south to these mountains of Mae Hong Son. He made a home in these mountains. He was the first hawk we saw, long ago, on our long journey from mountains without names to these highlands we call home.

"When our people saw him, they knew he could guide us to mountain water and many hills for good hunting. A spirit rose in us, bright as hope. Our hunters hailed the hawk, and we lit incense to honor him and sang joyful songs by bonfires in the night.

"As the hawk was guided by the rivers and skies and mountains, so, too, we were guided by the hawk. His flight became our own. A hawk flies high and never alone. Always he has the company of the sky to shelter him, rivers to guide him, and mountains to sustain him.

"Like the hawk, we are never alone. Always we have the company of the skies, rivers, and mountains to shelter, guide, and sustain us. Always we have the spirits of our people, our living and our dead, to comfort us and strengthen us. And always we have the flight of the hawk to inspire us. Your mother and father lived with faith for a brighter day. And hope for your future. They loved you, and their loving spirit is still with you. Like the hawk, you are never alone, my grandson. And know that the hawk is always with you, night and day. On every ridgeline and over each river. Where the jungle meets the river, the hawk is with you. Where the rivers run to the sea, the hawk is with you. Where the mountains meet the sky, the hawk is with you. A hawk flies high and never alone."

The boy was crying now and his grandfather wiped his tears away. The boy glanced west toward Burma. He could see the hawk soaring high now over coconut palms and vast hillsides studded with wild banana trees and clusters of bamboo. He stood and ran to the edge of a cliff and waved to the hawk and shouted, "Goodbye, great hawk, goodbye!"

His grandfather came up alongside him and stood with him for a spell. And he put his arm around the boy and said softly, "Never say goodbye. Only long life and blue skies, my grandson. Long life and blue skies. This is the way of our people."

The boy nodded, and he was no longer crying. He watched the hawk's flight until the hawk was no bigger than the head of a pin far over Burmese mountains, deep in Karen highlands, and he smiled watching the flight of the hawk. The hawk disappeared over a mountain and the boy said under his breath, "Long life and blue skies." He looked up at his grandfather and said, confidently, "Come, grandfather. We have wood to chop. A hawk flies high and never alone. Long life and blue skies!"

The boy grew to be a great hunter and the storyteller of his tribe. Long after the deaths of his grandparents, he sat around a fire deep in the night in his village, telling the children Karen legends. Each night, children and their families would gather around a fire, breath misting in the night. The jungle beyond the village would be alive with the deep-throated hoot owl's evening song and the far roar of a tiger and the soft caw of the black crow from thick clusters of bamboo. And he would smile and tell the stories of his tribe. He always began with the Legend of the Hawk.

Mike Tucker
Tiluk Bahang, Malaysia
January 3, 2005

BIBLIOGRAPHY

⦿ ⦿ ⦿

Basho, Matsuo. *The Narrow Road to the Deep North*. Translator: Nobuyuki Yuasa. New York: Penguin, 1966.

Beevor, Antony. *Stalingrad*. New York: Penguin, 1999.

Grant, Ulysses S. *Personal Memoirs of U.S. Grant*. Introduction and Notes by James P. McPherson. New York: Penguin, 1999.

Hemingway, Ernest. *For Whom the Bell Tolls*. New York: Charles Scribner's Sons, 1940.

Hemingway, Ernest, editor. *Men at War*. Introduction by Ernest Hemingway. New York: Crown, 1942.

Hemingway, Ernest. *The Old Man and the Sea*. New York: Charles Scribner's Sons, 1952.

Hemingway, Ernest. *The Snows of Kilimanjaro and Other Stories*. New York: Charles Scribner's Sons, 1964.

Henderson, Charles. *Marine Sniper*. New York: Berkley, 1988.

Homer. *The Iliad*. Translator: Robert Fitzgerald. New York: Farrar, Straus and Giroux, 2004.

Homer. *The Odyssey*. Translator: Robert Fitzgerald. New York: Farrar, Straus and Giroux, 1998.

Lawrence, T. E. *Seven Pillars of Wisdom*. Introduction by Agnes Calder. London: Wordsworth Editions, 1997. First published in 1935.

Lewis, Bernard. *The Assassins*. New York: Basic Books, 2003.

Machado, Antonio. *Selected Poems*. Translator: Dr. Alan S. Trueblood. Cambridge, Mass.: UP Harvard, 1982.

Maclean, Fitzroy. *Eastern Approaches*. London: Jonathan Cape Ltd., 1949.

McCarthy, Cormac. *All the Pretty Horses*. New York: Alfred A. Knopf, 1992.

Tucker, Mike. *The Long Patrol*. Bangkok: Asia Books, 2003.

Tzu, Sun. *Art of War*. Translator: Ralph D. Sawyer. Boulder, Colo.: Westview Press, 1994.

Wiesel, Elie. *Night*. New York: Hill and Wang, 1960.

Xenophon. *The Persian Expedition*. Translator: Rex Warner. London: Penguin, 1949.